WALT

THE ART OF WALT DISNEY

Disney

TO THE MAGIC KINGDOMS

For Sarah and Justin,

for Jenny and Emily, and for Felix

Library of Congress Cataloging in Publication Data

Finch, Christopher.
   The art of Walt Disney.

   Bibliography: p.
   Includes index.
   1. Disney, Walt, 1901–1966.   2. Walt Disney Produc-
tions.   I. Title.
NC1766.U52D533   1983   791.43′092′4   83–9937
ISBN 0–8109–8052–5

Printed and bound in Japan

Contents

Introduction

By the time he was thirty years old, Walt Disney had become a public figure. As the creator of Mickey Mouse, his remarks—both casual and considered—were translated into dozens of languages and his likeness could be found on the pages of countless newspapers and magazines. A trim mustache and a ready smile gave him a Clark Gable-ish charm which was shared by many other young Americans of the period (as was his taste for sporty jackets and boldly patterned sweaters). What distinguished him from the rest, and made his face memorable, was a sense of determination and purpose which was apparent even in his most relaxed poses. In later years he entered our living rooms and addressed us from the television screen. By that time his face and frame had broadened and he had begun to favor conservatively cut suits and sober neckties. The mustache and the smile remained, however, as did the evident purpose and determination.

By definition, public figures are known to everyone; yet, even after talking with some of Disney's closest associates, it is impossible to escape the conclusion that *nobody* really knew him. Always there was some aspect of his personality that was just out of reach. He was a man who believed absolutely in his own instincts and abilities, an artist who would go to any lengths to ensure that a project was carried out exactly as he had conceived it. He surrounded himself with talents of every kind, but at all times he was in complete control. The master plan was in Walt Disney's head and remained unknowable until, piece by piece, it was given concrete form and grafted onto the mythology of our century.

This book is not, in the ordinary sense, a biography of Walt Disney. He was a man who can best be understood in terms of the works he left behind, and this is primarily a study of those works. Many talented men and women contributed to the total impact he has had on our times, and every effort will be made here to give them the credit which is their due. The fact remains, however, that without Disney none of the films or other enterprises that are discussed and illustrated in this book would ever have seen the light of day. His energy was the driving force and his imagination was the controlling influence.

At the outset of his career Disney was often underestimated by his rivals. They were aware of the caliber of the talents he had surrounded himself with and assumed that if these talents could be lured away, the Disney Studio would collapse. It soon became apparent that the one man who made Walt Disney Productions uniquely successful was not available at any price.

In later years Disney has been underestimated in other ways. Since the values expressed in his movies are essentially the simple values of the cartoon and the fairy story, many people have been tempted into presenting simplistic pictures of Disney the man, and of what he stood for. Some have chosen to portray him as a naive genius, while others—dazzled by the success of his varied enterprises—prefer to see him as just another business tycoon. These versions of Disney bear little relationship to any ascertainable truth. Everyone who worked closely with him admits that money was important to Disney only insofar as it enabled him to produce better movies, improve his parks, or (in later years) plan the city of the future. He was a perfectionist and perfection did not come cheap in these fields.

The notion that Disney was a naive genius is equally misleading. In his movies, right is right and wrong is wrong, but—given his background and the audience he knew himself to be in touch with—this should not surprise anyone and, although he remained faithful to uncomplicated values, he was by no means a simple man. There was much more to his success than a blind faith in intuition. He knew that for intuition to mean anything it had to be implemented, and that this demanded a combination of stringent analysis and sheer hard work, backed up by the practical talents of the artists with whom he surrounded himself. Improving the product seems to have occupied his mind night and day. After hours and on weekends he would prowl the studio—familiarizing himself with the development of every project. He subjected each decision to intensive discussion, drawing upon every available source of expertise, and there is ample evidence to suggest that he sometimes mulled over ideas for years before they were permitted to reach this stage.

Having received relatively little formal schooling, Disney went to great lengths to educate himself and his artists (at times, the old studio on Hyperion Avenue must have seemed more like the art department of some progressive university than a productive component of the motion picture industry). Disney started in the field of animated films determined to be better than anyone else. Achieving this rather quickly, he embarked on a lifelong quest to "plus" his own accomplishments ("plus," used as a verb, is a favorite word with old hands at the Studio). Throughout the thirties and into the forties, amazing progress was made in the development of the animated film. The Disney Studio gave to the world painted characters who not only moved but seemed to think for themselves. By the time of *Pinocchio* and *Fantasia,* Disney had brought to a spectacular maturity an art form that had been in its infancy just a dozen years earlier.

Disney himself was not a great draftsman, and he never pretended to be one. He was always the first to admit that, after about 1926, he did not contribute a single drawing to any of his cartoons. His great abilities lay in the area of ideas— conceiving them, developing them, and seeing them through to a successful conclusion. Ideas were commodities that he was never short of (if he ever had a problem with ideas it was that he sometimes had too many to give them all the attention that they deserved). A superb story editor, Disney worked with his artists, phrasing and rephrasing the structure of a movie until every minute action, each last nuance of character contributed to the development of the plot. This was a skill that he acquired while making the short cartoons of the early and middle thirties, cartoons which—since they ran from just six to eight minutes each—demanded the greatest economy of action. When he turned to making feature films, the same principles were applied, so that nothing that was not essential to the telling of the story ever found its way onto the screen. It was Disney's intense involvement with plot development and character, along with his uncanny grasp of technical possibilities, that gave his best movies the tightness of structure that has enabled them to survive so well in our collective memory.

He was not, of course, infallible. He did produce mediocre films and even a few that were outright failures (usually the worst failures were the ones that did not sustain his personal interest). The point is that Disney, like any other artist, deserves to be judged by his best work and he was, at his best, one of the most vigorous and innovative film-makers in the entire history of the cinema.

This book will attempt to take a serious look at Disney's major achievements, presenting them within the general context of his work as a whole. It will also try to capture some of the creative vitality that went into the development of animated movies and, later, into the theme parks and other projects. Much of the visual material reproduced here has never been published before and it has been chosen, wherever possible, with a view to recapturing the excitement of the period.

Animated movies are difficult to illustrate adequately. They depend on movement to achieve their effect, and a single image taken from a cartoon will often seem static and lifeless. Fortunately, the final set-up that is shot by the camera is not the only art work involved in the making of an animated film. It is, in fact, the last link in an elaborate chain that includes character studies, model sheets, story continuity sketches, layouts, background paintings, animation drawings, color models, and the like. The work produced at various of these stages is often very lively. The artists who are concerned with story and layout, for example, have to sell their ideas to their director and the producer (in most instances they would be dealing with Walt Disney himself) and attempt to get into their drawings the "feel" of what will appear on screen. Thus, if Mickey should receive a shock that causes him to fall from his chair, the story artist must suggest both the shock and the fall in a single drawing (much as a book illustrator would do). The layout artist will take the same scene, provide a detailed context for the event, and diagrammatically map out the entire action. Either of these representations does, in most cases, give more of a sense of what is eventually seen on screen than does a single frame from the movie. Happily, many of these drawings have been preserved and we are able to use them here. Not only do they effectively convey the "feel" of what eventually appeared on screen; they are often very beautiful in their own right. Some appeal because of their spontaneity, others because of their attention to detail; and, beyond that, they tell us much about the way in which an animated film is conceived and executed.

Each of these drawings contains some clues to the secret of Disney's success, since every one of them was touched by his influence. Each drawing reflects his taste, for the artist was always aware that it was subject to his scrutiny (which was far from uncritical). Literally hundreds of artists figure in this story, but all of them functioned within the governing structure elaborated by Disney's imagination. In later years he may perhaps have exercised less control over some aspects of the operation—his interests became so diversified that this was unavoidable. In the productions on which his reputation rests, however, Walt Disney's involvement was complete.

I

A NEW
ART FORM

1 Early Enterprises

Walter Elias Disney was born into a modest Chicago household on December 5, 1901. His birthplace, 1249 Tripp Avenue, was a small wood-frame structure of the type that can be found in the inner suburbs of any Midwestern city. His father, Elias Disney, was Canadian born and of Anglo-Irish descent. At this time Elias was a building contractor, and we may judge the success of that operation by the fact that Walt later described how his mother sometimes went out to the building site with the men, sawing and hammering planks. Mrs. Disney was the former Flora Call, an Ohio girl whose family had moved to Kansas in 1879. There the Call and Disney families became friends. When the Calls moved to Florida in 1884, Elias followed and bought a citrus plantation. Four years later he married Flora, who was by then teaching school. At the time of Walt's birth, there were already three children in the family—Herbert, Raymond, and Roy. Walt was to develop an especially close relationship with Roy, who was nearest to him in age, a relationship that was to be of great importance to both of them. Later a daughter—Ruth—was added to the family.

In 1906, Elias Disney decided to pull up his roots once again and moved his family to a forty-eight-acre farm outside Marceline, Missouri. Small farms, then as now, did not offer an

easy route to prosperity. Herbert and Raymond, both in their teens, had developed a taste for city life and soon returned to Chicago. Walt and Roy were, of course, expected to help their parents with the farm chores. It was an extremely hard life, but one which Walt later remembered with considerable affection.

It was on the farm that he began to draw. We may be sure that this was not encouraged by his parents, but he did make the first tentative steps toward his eventual career. Meanwhile, the farm operation was in trouble. In 1910, Elias sold the farm with all its livestock and moved the family once again—this time to Kansas City, ninety-five miles southwest. There Elias bought a newspaper delivery business. Naturally, Walt and Roy were co-opted into contributing their services and found themselves getting up at 3:30 in the morning to meet the trucks of the *Kansas City Star*. Walt, then just nine years old, made his rounds every day, even in the depths of the Kansas City winter, which often brought several feet of snow. Roy, eight years his senior, would soon be in a position to escape this drudgery, but he maintained his close relationship with Walt, giving him good advice and finding ways for him to earn a little money (the work for their father was unpaid). The good advice included telling Walt that he need no longer stand for the beatings his father was in the habit of administering.

The hard work continued, but Walt's interest in drawing persisted, as did a growing taste for theatrical expression. In a rare gesture of indulgence, Elias Disney allowed Walt to enroll for Saturday morning classes at the Kansas City Art Institute (the elder Disney justified this on the grounds that the classes would be "educational"). Thus, at the age of fourteen, Walt acquired a smattering of formal art training. Just as important, in view of later developments, was Disney's relationship with one of his schoolmates, Walt Pfeiffer. Pfeiffer (in later years a Disney staffer, holding for a while the position of studio manager) shared Disney's budding interest in the performing arts. They evolved a kind of juvenile vaudeville act—"The Two Walts"—and made occasional appearances at amateur nights in local theaters, even winning a few prizes.

Pfeiffer remembers that getting to these performances was not easy because of the strictness of Disney's parents. "Walt's dad always hated anything that had to do with entertainment. A lot of times, when we were fooling around, getting on amateur nights and things like that, I'd go down and sneak Walt out the window. We'd be real quiet and I don't think his dad ever missed him not being in the room. When we'd get through, we'd shove him back in the window and I'd go home.

◄ Walt Disney's birthplace at 1249 Tripp Avenue, Chicago, built by his father, Elias Disney

Walt Disney at the age
of nine months

Roy Disney in 1913

Elias and Flora Disney in 1913

I'd always tell my folks where I was going because my dad encouraged me. He encouraged Walt too."

Pfeiffer recalls another incident that occurred when Disney
was about twelve. "We went to Benton School, where J.M.
Cottingham, the principal, ran the place like a king. One Lincoln's birthday, Walt came to school all dressed up like Lincoln.
He had a shawl that I guess he got from his dad, he made a
stovepipe hat out of cardboard and he got a beard from some
place downtown that had theatrical things to sell. He did this
all on his own. When Cottingham saw him, he said, 'Walter,
you look just like Lincoln. Why are you dressed this way?' Walt
said, 'Well, it's his birthday and I want to give the Gettysburg
Address.' He had memorized it. So he got up in front of his
class and the kids thought this was terrific. Then Cottingham
took him to each of the other classes and he repeated the
performance."

We know too that Disney was fascinated by Chaplin and
the other great silent comedians, so he must have managed to
visit the movies from time to time. This first Kansas City period
seems, for all its stringencies, to have provided the young
Disney with ample opportunities for learning and entertainment.

In 1917, Elias decided upon another move. This time he
returned to Chicago, where he purchased a part share in a small

Walt Disney at the age of twelve

"The Two Walts": Walt Pfeiffer, left, and Walt Disney
pose in costumes they devised for one of their
amateur night performances, c.1915

factory. Walt remained in Kansas City to finish out his school
year (Roy was still there, working as a bank teller); then he
spent the summer as a news butcher on the Santa Fe Railroad
(news butchers hawked newspapers, fruit, candy, and soft
drinks), a job which enabled him to see a little more of the
country while feeding his enthusiasm for trains—an enthusiasm
which would provide him with an important outlet later in life.
In the fall, he joined the family in Chicago and enrolled at
McKinley High School. Here he contributed drawings to the
school paper and managed to get some further art instruction
from a newspaper cartoonist named Leroy Gossett. World War
I was in progress and on June 22, 1917, Roy Disney enlisted
in the Navy. Walt had dreams of enlisting too, but he was
under age. He discovered that one had to be only seventeen to
become a Red Cross ambulance driver and, though still sixteen,
managed to join up (his mother, probably relieved that he would
be driving an ambulance rather than handling a rifle, allowed
him to falsify his birth date on the application). He was sent
to a staging post at Sound Beach, Connecticut, but the Armis-
tice was signed before he got any further. There was still, however, a need for drivers in Europe and he eventually found himself in France, assigned to a military canteen in Neufchateau,
where he soon established himself as the unit's unofficial artist,

Walt Disney, center right,
on an outing of Benton
School students

Walt Disney with the cartoon-decorated
ambulance he drove in France in 1919

In his barracks in Neufchateau,
Disney set up a drawing board
and continued his cartooning

earning a few extra francs with such enterprises as painting fake
medals onto leather jackets and camouflaging captured German
helmets so that they could be passed off as snipers' helmets.

Disney returned to the United States in 1919. His father
had a job waiting for him, but Walt was determined to make
a career in commercial art. He headed for Kansas City and found
work at a local studio where he made friends with another employee, Ubbe "Ub" Iwerks, a young man of Dutch descent who
was to become the most important associate of his early career.
Iwerks was a talented draftsman, and it soon occurred to them
to go into business for themselves. They acquired desk space at
the offices of a publication called *Restaurant News* and immediately achieved some modest success. But then Disney saw a
newspaper advertisement for a job with an organization called
Kansas City Slide Company (soon changed to Kansas City Film
Ad). This company made what we would now call commercials
for display in local movie theaters. They were, in fact, producing crude animated films. This new medium and the salary
offered—forty dollars a week—appealed to Disney. He applied
for the job and got it. Iwerks took over the business they had
started, but within a few months he, too, joined Kansas City
Film Ad.

Back to civilian life,
Disney soon found work in
a Kansas City commercial
art studio

The staff of Kansas City Film Ad Service, with
Disney seated on the right-hand brick post.
Ub Iwerks is standing seventh from the right

Throughout the nineteenth century, scientists and inventors intrigued the general public with a whole series of devices which could take a sequence of drawings and make them seem to move. Most of these were variants upon a simple machine which had been hit upon almost simultaneously by Dr. Joseph Antoine Plateau of the University of Ghent and Dr. Simon Ritter von Stampfer of Vienna (the inspiration for their experiments was a paper entitled "The Persistence of Vision with Regard to Moving Objects," which Peter Mark Roget presented to the British Royal Society in 1824).

The Plateau-Stampfer device consisted of two disks mounted on a single shaft. The images to be viewed—they might portray a man running or a horse jumping—were attached in chronological sequence to the rim of the inner disk. When this disk was rotated, an observer looking through one of the slits cut into the rim of the outer disk would receive an illusion of movement. This system was developed into the zoetrope, which remained a popular toy for many years.

Photography had meanwhile come to the public's attention in 1839, and its own more spectacular development paralleled that of these "wheel of life" novelties. In 1872, Eadweard Muybridge began his famous photographic studies of animals and hu-

eyes hold disregard for others? The door opened noisily—Marie stood in the bright glare of the hall lamp.

"I beg your pardon," she murmured, backing into the hall, "my friend used to rent this studio. I did not know she had moved."

The door was closing—in a moment she would be gone—

"Marie!"

The door reopened.

"Won't you please come in?"

Marie came in and upon his invitation demurely seated herself on the edge of the chair before the painting.

"Oh! You are drawing my picture, aren't you?"

Kenneth was one vast monument of suppressed emotion. Marie knew this very well, but her gaze was as innocent as a baby's when she turned. Her smile brought out dimples—two of them.

Was she playing with him? He did not care. She was at least worth another trial.

"I—I didn't wait to hear your reason for not marrying—that is not caring to marry me."

He was a very embarrassed young man.

Again she smiled.

"I haven't any reason now. You see I was afraid people would say that I married you for your money. I thought I couldn't stand that. But, do you know, I've been thinking it over and I can't see that it matters what people think. *You'll know that it isn't so*—so I think I will marry—Kenneth—Kenneth you're mussing my hair—Kenneth really—now—please—I haven't any powder with me and my nose—"

A very flushed young woman made her appearance.

"Kenneth," a pause, "by the way—I—I—haven't any friend who ever lived here. I looked you up and came on purpose to make you ask me again. Now—Ken—"

The End.

"Oh! You are drawing my picture, aren't you?"

The title frame
from a Laugh-o-Grams cartoon,
c. 1922

◀ While at McKinley High School
in Chicago, Disney contributed
numerous drawings to the
school paper and, during his
service in France, sent an
illustrated letter to his
former schoolmates

Walt Disney's letterhead,
c. 1922

mans in motion (his work was sponsored by Leland Stanford,
founder of Stanford University, and utilized equipment devised
by John D. Isaacs, an engineer on the staff of the Central Pacific
Railway). In 1887, aware of Muybridge's work, Thomas Edison
began to experiment with the idea of motion pictures (he
thought of them as a logical extension of and accompaniment
to his phonograph). By 1889 he had built the first kinetoscope,
a kind of peepshow viewer which held fifty feet of film, enough
to run for about thirteen seconds. The machine made its commercial debut on April 14, 1894, at a kinetoscope parlor at
1155 Broadway in New York City. Several of these machines
were exported to Europe, leading a number of engineers there
to explore the possibilities that were opened up by this invention. In 1895, the brothers Louis and Auguste Lumière took out
a patent on a device which successfully combined the principles
of the kinetoscope with those of the magic lantern—which is to
say that it was able to project moving pictures onto a screen.
They called their machine the *cinematographe*. By the following year, Edison films were being shown on a more sophisticated
projector built by Thomas Armat of Washington. The Armat
machine, known as the vitascope, was the direct ancestor of the
modern movie projector.

These sudden advances, from the kinetoscope onward, were
made possible by the fact that, in 1889, George Eastman of
Rochester, New York, had begun to manufacture flexible strips
of photographic film using a nitro-cellulose base. This film—far
more convenient than anything available until that time—was
designed specifically to meet the mechanical requirements of

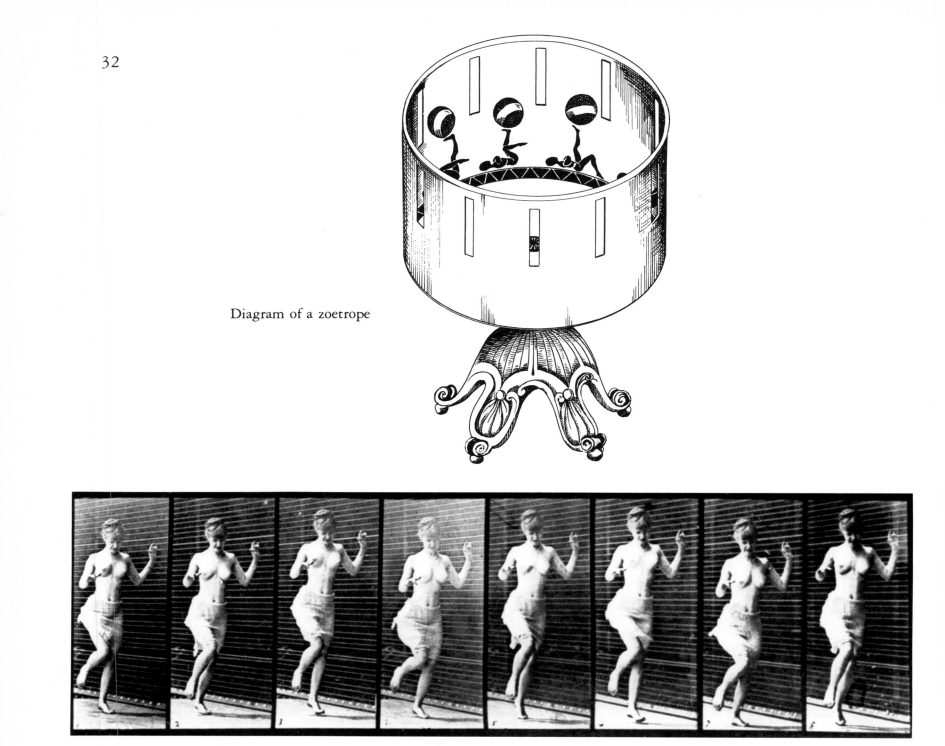

Diagram of a zoetrope

Eadweard Muybridge, *Figure Hopping,* 1887

J. Stuart Blackton's 1906 *Humorous Phases of Funny Faces,* left, was the first animated film. Winsor McCay's *Gertie the Trained Dinosaur* was the first cartoon to enjoy a popular success

"roller photography" in the Eastman Kodak camera. It was also ideally suited to the needs of the men who sired the motion picture industry, and it followed naturally that movies evolved primarily in terms of the photographic image.

It was not until 1906 that the first animated film was attempted. In that year J. Stuart Blackton, a commercial artist who later produced movies for Edison, conceived a little entertainment which he called *Humorous Phases of Funny Faces*. The level of animation achieved in this first effort was, needless to say, rudimentary. It did not capitalize so much on drawings seeming to move as on drawings seeming to complete themselves (though there was some primitive use of movement—a man might, for example, appear to wiggle his ears). The notion that one could photograph drawings and make them appear to move did, however, spark the imaginations of one or two other pioneers. In 1908, Winsor McCay put his comic strip character Little Nemo into an animated film. Later he toured the vaudeville circuit with a cartoon titled *Gertie the Trained Dinosaur*. McCay appeared on stage as the film was projected and the gimmick was that Gertie seemed to obey his commands, concluding her performance by "catching" an apple which he pretended to throw to her. McCay was a gifted draftsman and, viewed today, the animation in this movie seems surprisingly accomplished (he selected a dinosaur as his subject so that nobody could accuse him of tracing photographs). The fact that Gertie was devised to fit in with a stage act may account for the fact that the story line, such as it is, is well enough shaped so that the film can still be watched without embarrassment.

McCay's success prompted several other producers to experiment with animation. In 1913, two series were launched—*Colonel Heeza Liar,* devised by J.R. Bray, and *Old Doc Yak,* created by Sidney Smith. Bray's series was the more popular of the two (apart from anything else, he made it more comfortable to watch by using a range of grays, rather than just black and white, thus reducing screen glare), but within a couple of years he had three major competitors: Paul Terry launched *Farmer Al Falfa,* Wallace Carlson entered the market with *Dreamy Dubb,* and Earl Hurd introduced *Bobby Bump.* Hurd is a key figure in the history of animation, for he invented the idea of painting the animated figures onto celluloid. Previous to this, everything—including the static background—had to be drawn anew for each frame of the picture. Now, only the moving characters required this attention. A single background could be placed under the sequence of celluloid sheets—"cels," as they came to be known—and remain there until the scene was

The photograph at left, taken in 1922, was probably intended to promote the young Disney's image as a film-maker (the man with the gun is Walt himself). At right we see him in another role, behind the camera

Disney, left, and an assistant filming on location

Disney at work in the Laugh-o-Grams office, 1922

Top: the Laugh-o-Grams office, 1922; center: filming *Martha,* with Disney in the director's chair; bottom: Disney, at right, with friends at an artists' ball in Kansas City, 1922

changed. This system offered an enormous saving in time and money and, although other methods persisted for a while, it was the one that became generally adopted throughout the industry.

By 1917, the International Feature Syndicate was releasing animated versions of popular newspaper cartoon strips, including *Bringing Up Father, The Katzenjammer Kids, Krazy Kat,* and *Silk Hat Harry.* That same year, Max Fleischer introduced his *Out of the Inkwell* series, in which live action was combined with animation.

At that time the industry was centered in New York City. One of the several studios there was that of Raoul Barre, best known for his early work on the *Mutt and Jeff* series. Dick Huemer, later a Disney animator and story man, was, in 1916, a student at the Art Students League and living in the Bronx, where the Barre studio was located. He recalls seeing Barre's business sign on the door of a hallway at the corner of Fordham Road and Webster Avenue.

"I had done a lot of illustrating, in yearbooks and things like that. One day, out of curiosity, I just walked upstairs and there was this plump little guy sitting there—a very genial character with a French accent. I told him I'd seen his sign and would like to be a cartoonist. He said, 'All right—go into the next room, they'll put you to work.' And that's how I got into the business. Because, in those days, who knew about animated cartoons? I don't believe the name had even been coined yet."

The picture Huemer paints of the industry in those days is not one that suggests that *Snow White* was barely two decades away.

"I'm afraid that we only did our cartoons to please ourselves. There was no story—we'd say 'Let's have a picture about building, it'll add up in the end.' Each guy sat at his desk with a pile of paper and did his animation, and when it was finished he handed it over and they would put it together. Enter left, exit right—that's what it amounted to. No definite plot line. Never. We were having fun. We'd laugh at each other's stuff, but when it ran in the theater—plop! Nothing. . . . Because we hadn't considered what the impact of what we were drawing would be. What were these old cartoons, anyway? There was no reality or life in them."

In these comments, Huemer is a little too hard on himself and his fellow pioneers. The movies they made possess, if nothing else, a certain period charm. It is undeniable, however, that they were very crude both in terms of animation and of plot construction. As for character development, that we cannot even discuss, since characters were established in the most schematic

of ways. They were recognizable because one had a big nose and another flat feet. Rough exaggeration of physical characteristics served as a substitute for personality.

This, then, was the state of the art when Disney joined the staff of Kansas City Film Ad.

The animation done at Kansas City Film Ad was, in fact, even cruder than that which was coming out of New York. It consisted mainly of stop-action photography of jointed cardboard figures—a technique that precluded any serious effort toward naturalism. Nonetheless, it provided Disney, still just eighteen years old, and Iwerks with the basic training they needed. Before long, Disney borrowed a camera and tried some animation on his own. The result was a little reel of topical gags—reminiscent in character of newspaper cartoons—which he managed to sell to the Newman Theater, a local movie house. A number of short "commercials" and illustrated jokes—known collectively as the Newman Laugh-o-Grams—were made for the theater. They dealt with such topics as shorter skirts and police corruption. Technically they were very competent by the standards of the day, and, encouraged by this initial success, Disney managed to raise enough capital to leave Kansas City Film Ad and set up on his own, retaining Laugh-o-Grams as the company's name. It might be assumed that a young man just emerging from his teens would have been content to stick with familiar material, at least for a while, but Disney was ambitious and immediately started work on a series of updated fairy tales. Six of these were made: *Cinderella, The Four Musicians of Bremen, Goldie Locks and the Three Bears, Jack and the Beanstalk, Little Red Riding Hood,* and *Puss in Boots.* The Disney archives have prints of *The Four Musicians of Bremen* and *Puss in Boots,* and they provide clear evidence that Disney was not overestimating his ability when he entered production at this tender age. *Puss in Boots,* for example, is rather well animated, and the story displays a nice sense of humor (the fairy-tale atmosphere is updated so that, for instance, the King rides around in a chauffeur-driven convertible).

In the course of producing these short cartoons, Disney began to build up an able staff which soon included, besides Iwerks, Rudolf Ising, Hugh and Walker Harman, Carmen "Max" Maxwell, and Red Lyon. Unfortunately, the Laugh-o-Grams were not selling (one sale was made but the purchaser went bankrupt after making a $100 deposit), and the Disney production team was always looking for alternate sources of income. They worked on a live-action short called *Martha* and,

◀ Arriving in California,
Disney set about rebuilding his career,
using his Uncle Robert's garage to
construct an animation-camera stand

Early Alice Comedies involved a good deal of live-action filming. The original Alice, featured on this page, was Virginia Davis, whom Disney brought out from Kansas City to star in the series

Poster for an Alice Comedy ▶

Clowning on the Alice set:
Rudy Ising holds the hose;
under the umbrella are
Hugh Harman, Ub Iwerks, and
Walt Disney

A later Alice, Margie Gay, seen here
with animated friends and, at top, with
director Walt Disney

sponsored by a local dentist, even made a film on dental hygiene which combined live action and animation to get its didactic message across. Max Fleischer had been using this same combination in his *Out of the Inkwell* series, and it had the advantage that the live-action sections of the movies were relatively inexpensive to produce. At some time in 1923, Disney decided to try to save his Laugh-o-Grams venture by making just such a movie, in which a human heroine could cavort with cartoon characters. Rather than simply imitating Fleischer's technique, Disney hit on the idea of reversing the basic principle so that the live action would be introduced into the cartoon, whereas *Out of the Inkwell* specialized in adding animation to the live action. The film that resulted was *Alice's Wonderland*.

For his Alice, Disney chose a little girl named Virginia Davis, who had had some modeling experience with Kansas City Film Ad. The story begins as Alice explores the Laugh-o-Gram offices. She discovers Disney seated at his drawing board, on which a dog kennel has been sketched. Suddenly a dog emerges from the kennel and, before she knows what has happened, Alice has become a part of the cartoon and finds herself involved with a variety of animals, including a quartet of lions who eventually chase her over a cliff (the surviving print is, unfortunately, incomplete).

The effect of blending the real Alice with the cartoon characters was achieved by photographing Virginia Davis against a white background and then combining this film, in the printing process, with another strip on which the animation was shot. The technique worked well, but *Alice's Wonderland* exhausted Disney's remaining credit and he was forced to close the studio.

42

He was not, however, the type to be put off by a setback of this kind, and immediately planned to restart his career. Evidently he could not do this in Kansas City and so, with very little hesitation, he made his move. We can assume that he considered the possibility of trying New York, which was still the center of the animation industry, but he chose Hollywood. There is reason to suppose that he considered abandoning animation and trying his luck with one of the major studios, most of which were by now established in the pleasant foothills of the Santa Monica Mountains. Another important influence was the fact that his brother Roy was already in the West, recuperating in a Veteran's hospital from a bout with tuberculosis. In the summer of 1923 Walt Disney, aged twenty-one, took a train to California, carrying *Alice's Wonderland* with him as a sample.

On arriving in Los Angeles, Disney moved in with his uncle Robert Disney at 4406 Kingswell Avenue. Walt began to look for a job and, in his spare time, used his uncle's garage to build a stand for the animation camera that he had purchased (this would have been a conventional movie camera converted to shoot stop-action).

Two months after his arrival, Margaret J. Winkler, a New York distributor, agreed to contract for a series of Alice Comedies which Disney would produce. With Roy, Walt rented space in the rear of a small office occupied by Hollywood-Vermont Realty at 4651 Kingswell. They paid a rent of ten dollars per month. On October 16, 1923, they signed their first contract and were in business. The following January they increased their overhead by another ten dollars a month, renting a vacant lot on Hollywood Boulevard, about three blocks from the Studio (this lot was needed for outdoor shooting on the Alice films). By February they had outgrown their original studio space (the staff had grown to seven) and moved into the adjoining store, at 4649 Kingswell, which they rented for thirty-five dollars a month. A separate garage was rented for seven dollars a month.

The initial contract called for one Alice Comedy a month. Virginia Davis's parents had visions of her achieving Hollywood stardom, and they brought her out to California so that she could continue to play the lead. The first half dozen or so of the Alice Comedies featured a great deal of live action which involved Virginia with other children in fairly conventional comedy situations. Animation sequences were kept to a bare minimum, since they cost more and took longer to produce. It seems that Miss Winkler was not entirely satisfied with the results and wanted to cancel the contract. The Disneys were not prepared to loosen their tenuous grip on the future and per-

The series of cartoons Disney ▶ built around Oswald the Lucky Rabbit was successful enough to attract merchandising tie-ins. The model sheet on the opposite page, top right, shows that Oswald anticipated some of the physical characteristics of Mickey Mouse. The page of story continuity sketches, bottom right, illustrates how cartoon stories were worked out in this period

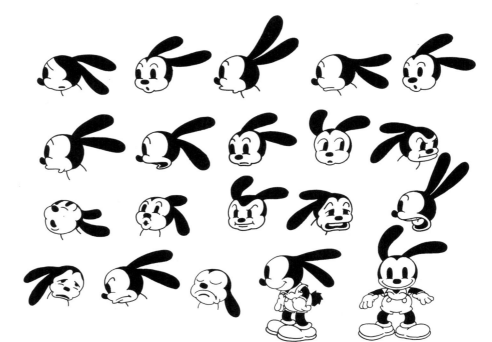

suaded Ub Iwerks to join them in California. He arrived in July (Hugh Harman and Rudolf Ising followed in June of 1925). Iwerks was just the man to streamline their productions. Soon they were able to increase the amount of animation included in each film and the series began to enjoy a modest success. Virginia Davis was replaced, briefly, by a young lady named Dawn O'Day and then by Margie Gay, who held the role for the remainder of the series. Virginia Davis had had something of a post-Victorian image—her appeal was that of a juvenile Lillian Gish—whereas Margie Gay was more the flapper type, and this updating of Alice's image may have contributed something to the increasing popularity of the series.

Further additions to the staff had to be made to accommodate Alice's success, and one new employee was an Idaho girl named Lillian Bounds. She often worked nights, and Walt would sometimes drive her home in his car. A romance blossomed and, in July, 1925, the pair were married. Roy Disney had meanwhile married Edna Francis, his Kansas City sweetheart.

Another consequence of expansion was that the Studio was once again outgrowing its accommodations. On July 6, 1925, four hundred dollars was deposited to secure a lot at 2719 Hyperion Avenue, quite close to their existing premises (Hyperion lies just to the south of Griffith Park, not far from the present-day site of Dodger Stadium). A single-story building was erected there and this formed the nucleus of the plant which was to serve as their base for the next fifteen years (it was almost constantly being expanded). By 1927, it became evident that they had to find a replacement for Alice if the Studio was to remain in a healthy economic state. They were by then approaching their sixtieth episode in the series, and evidently could not keep it going much longer. Apart from anything else, the use of live action placed severe restrictions on them and Walt was anxious to get back to full animation. They began work on a new series which was to be based on the adventures of Oswald the Lucky Rabbit.

By now Disney had completely abandoned his career as an animator to concentrate all his energies on the production side of the business. Animation could be left in the capable hands of Iwerks, Ising, and the Harman brothers, along with other draftsmen such as Ham Hamilton and Friz Freleng. Disney was also recruiting apprentice animators, young men who showed some enthusiasm for the business. One of these was Les Clark.

"I was working a part-time summer job at a lunch counter and confectionery store on Vermont and Kingswell," Clark re-

Margie Gay poses with, ▶ left to right, Ham Hamilton, Roy Disney, Hugh Harman, Walt Disney, Rudy Ising, Ub Iwerks, and Walker Harman

calls. "Walt and Roy used to come over there for lunch. While I was still in high school, I asked Walt for a job. He said, 'Bring some of your drawings in and let me see what they look like.' Well, I copied some cartoons out of *College Humor* and showed them to him. I told him I had copied them but he said I had a good line and invited me to start work the following Monday. So I graduated from high school on a Thursday and I went to work on Monday and I haven't been out of his employ since."

That was in 1927. What Clark did not know at the time was that the Studio was on the brink of a major crisis.

Most business crises are brought on by incompetence. The near catastrophe that the Disneys faced in 1927 resulted from the

very opposite. The new cartoon series turned out to be very successful, making Oswald the Lucky Rabbit a desirable property.

Oswald was a likable little creature, all soft curves and energy. He had no voice, of course—this was still the silent era—but the adventures he found himself caught up in were, to judge by surviving examples, inventive and well constructed for the time. The Disney animators were becoming very skilled, and they took full advantage of the fact that they no longer had to compete with a live Alice. With Oswald, Disney equaled—and perhaps surpassed—the best products of his competitors. *The Mechanical Cow,* for instance, is chock-full of zany invention and surrealistic humor.

There was just one snag. Disney had signed a one-year contract with Charles Mintz, who had married Margaret Winkler in 1924 (their distribution outlet now tied in with Universal Pictures). The advertising announced "Oswald the Lucky Rabbit, created by Walt Disney," but—and this proved to be the fatal flaw in the contract—Oswald's name belonged to Mintz (who had, apparently, picked it out of a hat). As the first year of the series moved to a successful conclusion, Walt Disney and his wife embarked for New York, where he expected to renegotiate the contract with provisions for a modest increase of income. He had kept in close contact with his distributor through George Winkler, Margaret's brother, who had made several visits to California, and there was no reason to suspect that anything was amiss. When Disney arrived in New York, however, the true reasons for Winkler's visits became painfully obvious.

Instead of offering an improved contract, Mintz actually proposed one which would entail a *reduction* of income for the Studio. This was clearly absurd, since Oswald had been very profitable. Obviously, Disney could not accept such a deal, and the reality of the situation became apparent. Mintz had decided to repossess Oswald. The character's name belonged to him, and his brother-in-law had persuaded several of Disney's best animators to take over production of the Oswald series. The motive was, of course, reduction of costs to the distributor. Mintz was the first of many people to underestimate Disney. He figured that if he could hire away Disney's best men, he would be getting the same product for a reduced outlay.

Disney was shocked and hurt by this revelation. He had trusted Mintz and he had trusted his employees. It is not hard to imagine the kinds of thoughts that must have run through his head as he and Lillian waited out the long, slow train ride back to California. He was disgusted but not, as the next few months would prove, discouraged. His team was depleted but

◀ Original art by Hugh Harman and Carmen Maxwell for an Oswald poster

Standing in front of their
storefront studio, Walt and Roy
Disney with, left to right,
Walt's wife Lillian, Ruth Disney,
and Roy's wife Edna

it still included his two most important associates—his brother
Roy and Ub Iwerks (who was, by then, a partner in the business). More important still, Walt Disney had faith in his own
abilities. He had reached the age of twenty-six after touching
many of the bases of hardship that had come to seem archetypal
of America in the first quarter of this century. His personal
creed must have included the notion that success does not come
easily.

2 Mickey Mouse and Silly Symphonies

It seems appropriate that the birth of Mickey Mouse—a creature of mythic stature—should be shrouded in legend. Walt Disney is said to have conceived Mickey on the train, returning to Hollywood from his angry encounter with Mintz. There is no reason to suppose that this is not essentially true, but over the years this story became so polished by repetition that it began to lose its sense of reality and to take on the character of an official myth. A further dimension was added to the legend by the fact that Disney had managed to tame a mouse in his old Kansas City studio, a mouse that he had nicknamed Mortimer. The name Mortimer now became his first choice for his new character but, before any Mouse cartoons were released, the name was changed to Mickey (it seems that Mrs. Disney thought the name Mortimer was a little pompous for a cartoon animal, but pressure from potential distributors may also have had something to do with the switch).

What we can be reasonably sure of is that the Mickey Mouse who made his debut in New York City in 1928 resulted from a collaborative effort between Disney and Ub Iwerks. It seems probable that Iwerks, easily the best animator of the day, was largely responsible for defining Mickey's physical characteristics. Mickey did bear a family resemblance to Oswald, but

Iwerks—either on his own initiative or at Disney's suggestion—made the figure more compact. He was constructed from two large circles, one for the trunk and one for the head, to which were appended two smaller circles, representing ears, and rubber-hose arms and legs which terminated in plump hands (ungloved at this early stage) and large feet which gave him stability. He was also equipped with a long, skinny tail and short pants decorated with buttons fore and aft. The circular head was made expressive by the addition of a mischievous snout, a plum-shaped nose, and button eyes. He was designed for maximum ease of animation (it had been discovered that circular forms were simpler to animate effectively) but, beyond that, Mickey's identity had a dimension which was quite new in cartoons. Certainly a character such as Felix the Cat was immediately recognizable, but he did not have a real personality. Mickey did have one, and an audience could identify with him in much the same way it would with a human performer.

The gift of personality was probably Disney's own contribution to Mickey. Iwerks made the whole thing possible through his skill as a draftsman, but it was Disney's control over the situations in which the Mouse found himself that allowed this personality to develop. Even at this early date, Disney had grasped the notion that cartoon characters should seem to think for themselves. In some ways he may even have viewed Mickey as his alter ego. Certainly he always maintained a special affection for the Mouse, a fact which suggests that he was intimately involved in every stage of its creation.

The Disney brothers had managed to save enough money to go ahead with the first Mickey Mouse cartoons even without a distributor, and work began almost at once. This was carried out in secret at first, since the Oswald contract had not yet completely expired. On October 23, 1927, a bombshell had hit the motion picture industry. Warner Brothers released *The Jazz Singer* and the sound era became a reality. Lee DeForest had developed a practical sound system at least four years earlier, but the Hollywood production chiefs had fought shy of this new development. Now they had to confront it.

As the first Mouse cartoons went into production, the industry was still in chaos. One Disney cartoon, *Plane Crazy,* had been completed, and another, *Gallopin' Gaucho,* was on the drawing boards before the decision was made—perhaps the most important decision that Disney ever made. He wanted Mickey to have real impact, and he saw that the future lay with sound. What he had in mind was a cartoon in which music, effects, and action would all be synchronized. Max and Dave Fleischer

Mickey Mouse was originally drawn by Ub Iwerks, top, who was given credit in early publicity; center: an early poster. At bottom, a girl inks Mickey onto a cel

-Main Title-

Orchestra starts playing opening
verses of ' Steamboat Bill ',
as soon as title flashes on.

The orchestration can be so
arrainged that many variations
may be included before the title
fades out.

It would be best if the music
was arrainged so that the end of
a verse would end at the end of
the title...... and a new verse
start at beginning of the first
scene.

Scene # 1.
Opening effect of black foliage
passing by in front of camera
gradually getting thinner until
full scene is revealed

Action......Old side'wheel river
steamboat paddleing down stream.
The two smoke stacks work up
and down alternately.... shooting
black chunks of smoke out as they
shoot up....smoke makes stacks
bulge out as it goes up and out.
(16 drawing cycle) 12 Ft. from
opening, the Three whistles on top
of cabin squat down before they
whistle tune ' TA--DA-DE-DA-DA---
DA-DA-'.....2 Ft. of action after
whistle and cut.

Scene # 2.
Close up of Mickey in cabin of
wheel'house, keeping time to last
two measures of verse of ' steamboat Bill '. With gesture he starts
whistleing the chorus in perfect
time to music....his body keeping
time with every other beat while
his shoulders and foot keep time
with each beat. At the end of every
two measures he twirls wheel which
makes a ratchet sound as it spins.
He takes in breath at proper time
according to music. When he finishes
last measure he reaches up and pulls
on whistle cord above his head.
(Use FIFE to imitate his whistle)

The first page of the *Steamboat Willie* continuity script.
Disney kept this souvenir of his first major breakthrough
in his office

In *Steamboat Willie*, 1928, the first cartoon to feature a fully synchronized sound track, Mickey and Minnie transform the cargo of a riverboat—including livestock—into an orchestra

Plane Crazy, 1928, was the first Mickey Mouse vehicle to go into production, but it was not released until after the success of *Steamboat Willie*

GALLOPING GAUCHO # 2

Gallopin' Gaucho was the second
Mickey Mouse cartoon to be made, but,
like *Plane Crazy,* it was produced as a silent
film and not released until a sound track
had been added

The Karnival Kid, 1929, used gags derived directly
from earlier situations devised for Oswald

An early Mickey Mouse model sheet
which shows the basic simplicity
of his design

MICKEY MOUSE   MODEL N°1

Scenes from *Mickey's Choo Choo,* 1929,
and *The Fire Fighters,* 1930

Rough story ideas were often worked
out in thumbnail sketches, as in this example
by Wilfred Jackson

had already produced a cartoon which used a Lee DeForest sound track, but the track had been unsynchronized and the experiment had had little impact on the industry. Disney's plan was for something far more radical.

Wedding sound to animated drawings was not, he realized, something that could be approached casually. Where live actors were concerned, it might be enough for the audience to hear them speak—that seemed like a miracle after the decades of silence (the fact that sound pictures were quickly labeled "talkies" indicates just where the public's interest lay)—but Disney did not have the ready-made stars to whom he could return the gift of speech. He had to come up with a more imaginative solution.

When the great French director René Clair was first exposed to talking pictures, he quickly realized that there would be an enormous difference between mere "talkies" and those that used sound creatively. Walt Disney, prompted by circumstance and encouraged by his temperament, was to become the first producer to find a genuinely creative way of using sound. Cartoon animals making noises might have offered something in the way of novelty, but novelties have a tendency to become clichés all too quickly. Evidently Disney was quite conscious of this danger—but animated creatures synchronized to a carefully structured sound track would be something quite different. He and his team began to develop a third Mickey Mouse story, this one conceived specially for sound. Cartoons had always depended on action rather than verbal jokes (in the silent era one could not afford to break up a short sequence of animated gags with title cards), so Disney decided to preserve this emphasis on action while underpinning it with carefully timed sound effects and a strongly rhythmical music track.

Not that this was the simplest of things to achieve. To start with, no one at the Studio had any real knowledge of music theory and there were also important technical problems to be solved. They had to proceed by trial and error. In their favor was the fact that Iwerks was something of a wizard with machinery and that almost everyone at the Studio knew something about practically everything within the animation field (specialization was still in the future; Walt himself had a firsthand knowledge of every aspect of the business, from cameras to inking). A young animator named Wilfred Jackson played the harmonica and, since his mother was a music teacher, was familiar with the metronome, which, he suggested, might provide a means of relating a musical beat to frames of film.

Les Clark, who was party to these early experiments, describes the system that was devised as follows:

56

In his early films Mickey often appeared as an entertainer. The examples shown here are, top to bottom, from *The Jazz Fool,* 1929; *Just Mickey,* 1930; and *Blue Rhythm,* 1931

"We worked with an exposure sheet on which every line was a single frame of action. We could break down the sound effects so that every eight frames we'd have an accent, or every sixteen frames, or every twelve frames.[Sound film runs through the projector at twenty-four frames a second.] And on that twelfth drawing, say, we'd accent whatever was happening—a hit on the head or a footstep or whatever it would be, to synchronize to the sound effect or the music."

By setting a metronome to correspond with the accents thus established in the action, a rough sound accompaniment could be improvised to the animation. One legendary evening, Disney and his co-workers presented a short sequence from *Steamboat Willie*—such was the title of the new cartoon—to an audience of wives and girlfriends. Roy Disney projected the film from outside a window (to eliminate motor noise), while his brother, along with Iwerks, Jackson, Clark, and a few others, improvised their sound accompaniment, live, in another room—all of them working carefully to the beat of the metronome. Jackson played his harmonica (the tune was probably "Steamboat Bill") while the others provided sound effects with cowbells, slide whistles, tin pans, and the like. This accompaniment was transmitted to the audience by way of a crude loudspeaker system set up by Iwerks. The wives and girlfriends were only mildly impressed, but the performers were convinced that they had now found the answer.

By September, 1928, a complete score had been committed to paper and Disney set out for New York to have it recorded. At that time, most recording devices were controlled by patents belonging to RCA and Western Electric, so it was necessary, first of all, to locate someone with "outlaw" sound equipment. Eventually Disney came to terms with a man named Pat Powers, who operated a renegade sound system that gloried in the name Powers Cinephone. Walt wrote to Roy and Ub that Powers was a very much respected personage in the film business. "He is very shrewd and capable. He is careful and cautious." He might have added, had he known, that Powers was also somewhat notorious for his efforts to outflank producers in the sometimes informal business atmosphere that had prevailed earlier in the history of the film industry.

Disney hired Carl Edouwards, who had led the pit orchestra at the Broadway Strand and worked for the Roxy chain, to provide a band and conduct the recording session. On September 14, Walt wrote to Roy and Ub: "We are using a seventeen-piece orchestra and three of the best trap drummers and effect men in town. They get ten dollars an hour for this work. It will take

three hours to do it, plus the time the effect men put in today."
Later in the same letter he says that there would be about thirty-
five men on the job, but this may have included technicians.
At all events, the first recording session was a disaster. Disney's
team had developed a system of indicating—probably by flashes
on the screen—the tempo to which the orchestra should play.
Thus the film could be projected and serve the same function
as a metronome. Unfortunately this system was a little crude,
and Edouwards did not feel inclined to have his tempo determined by such a coarse mechanical device. Disney was forced to
cable California for more money and try again. Roy sent out
enough money to proceed with a second session but not, it
would seem, without some qualms. Walt, convinced that he had
the problem licked, wrote back suggesting that he try to borrow
another five thousand dollars so that they could be ready to go
into full production. "I am firmly convinced," he insisted, "that
it will be far cheaper in the long run to go into it in the proper
manner. . . . Let's do things in the proper way and not try to
save a penny here and there."

In the same letter (like the others, it is addressed to both
Roy and Ub) he says, "We have all been working like the devil
on the picture. . . . The orchestra leader and myself completely
revised the Score. . . . I finally got him to see it my way (he
thinks he thought of the idea). The fact is that he just saw what
I have been telling him for the last two weeks. . . . They are
very clever in their line—but want too much beauty and too
many Symphonic effects. . . . They think comedy music is low
brow. . . . Believe me, I have had a tough fight getting them
to come down to our level. . . . I wish you knew the whole story
and I know you would sympathize with me. . . . I feel positive
we have everything worked out perfect now."

One improvement was that instead of sticking with the
crude flashing device that had been used at the first session,
Disney had had the film reprinted with the addition of a bounc-
ing ball system, to indicate the accents as well as the beat, making it much easier for Edouwards to follow. Fewer musicians
were used at the second session, and everything went off without
a hitch. *Steamboat Willie* now had a sound track and Mickey
Mouse was ready for his debut.

Finding a distributor was not easy, however. Still in New
York, Disney took his sound cartoon from screening room to
screening room, but the industry remained in a state of confusion and the response he met was discouraging. Eventually,
Harry Reichenbach, then managing Manhattan's Colony Theater,
saw *Steamboat Willie* and offered Disney a two-week run for

SCENE #3:

       Horse and cow in bathing suits. Horse puts his fingers in his mouth and whistles to attract the attention of Mickey and Minnie. Pantos, "watch me!" Runs out to left along a dock.

Typical gags from
1931 Mickey Mouse shorts:
The Beach Party, left,
and *Mickey Cuts Up*

SCENE #5:

       Mickey uses Pluto for a pump to inflate the inner tube. Gag of Pluto letting go to bite at a flea, tube goes down, and Mickey bawls him out. Pluto gets back to work again, and when the tube is blown up, Mickey takes it, puts it on over his head, and runs down to the beach and into the water. The dog stops on the beach.

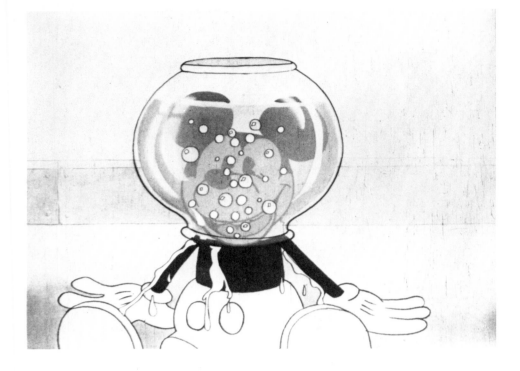

Scenes from *The Birthday Party*,
1931, top, and two 1932 cartoons,
Barnyard Olympics and *The Grocery Boy*

SCENE #43:

     Pluto drags Mickey into a pedestal
holding a statue of Napoleon. The statue
falls and lands over Mickey's head and shoulders.
Pluto runs on out of scene with turkey.

This story sketch for *The Grocery Boy* shows how the scene is to be laid out. Different stages of the action are indicated in a single drawing

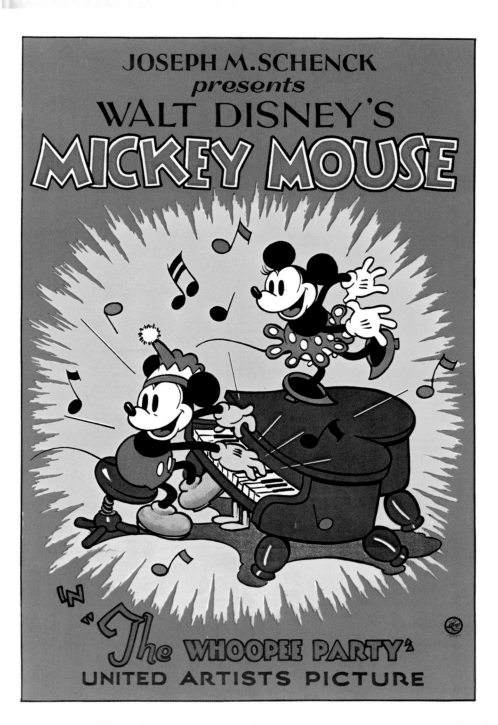

Poster, 1932

This camera—adapted in the late twenties to shoot animation—is still in use today

Walt Disney at his desk, c. 1931

In 1930, Carl Stalling, seen here at the piano, composed "Minnie's Yoo Hoo" as a theme song for Mickey. Seated alongside Stalling are Jack King and Ben Sharpsteen, two of the animators Disney had imported from New York. Standing, left to right, are Johnny Cannon, Walt Disney, Burt Gillett, Ub Iwerks, Wilfred Jackson, and Les Clark

the film. After some hesitation—he was hoping for a national distributor—Disney agreed. Reichenbach had made his reputation as a press agent and, when *Steamboat Willie* opened at the Colony on November 18, 1928, he saw to it that it received excellent coverage in the news media. This, combined with the fact that audiences roared with laughter at Mickey's adventures, encouraged the prestigious Roxy to book the movie. Pat Powers re-entered the picture and offered to distribute Disney's cartoons on a States Rights basis (this was an old system of distribution that allowed an independent producer to bypass the major studios, which controlled most of the theaters at that time). The deal that Powers offered was not perfect, but it was the best offer Disney had received. He signed up for one year. He then busied himself with adding sound to *Plane Crazy* and *Gallopin' Gaucho.* A fourth Mouse cartoon, *The Barn Dance,* was already animated, and work began on still another, *The Opry House.*

The Mickey Mouse who hit the movie houses in the late twenties was not quite the well-behaved character most of us are familiar with today. He was mischievous, to say the least, and even displayed a streak of cruelty (which soon disappeared), but from the very beginning he had that little germ of real personality we have remarked on, and this prevented him from seeming to be just another callously cruel cartoon animal. At times—when confronted by Pegleg Pete (the perennial villain who co-starred in both *Steamboat Willie* and *Gallopin' Gaucho*), or when forced to defend Minnie's honor—he was even capable of heroic behavior. His heroism, however, was usually the heroism of the little man; it resembled the intermittent nobility of Charlie Chaplin's tramp. Chaplin undoubtedly provided Disney with one of his most important models, and we may say that Mickey and his gang provided for the sound era the kind of entertainment that Chaplin and the Mack Sennett comedians had provided for an earlier generation. Since this *was* the sound era, Mickey had to have a voice. Several people, mostly from the Studio, had a shot at immortality as the Mouse's voice, but Disney was not satisfied with any of them. He knew just the kind of squeaky falsetto Mickey should have, and it soon became clear that only he could speak for the Mouse (he continued to fill this role for twenty years).

Minnie was with Mickey from the very first. In *Steamboat Willie,* after Pete has chased Mickey from the bridge of the riverboat on which he is employed as a deck hand, Minnie is discovered on shore, about to miss the boat. The ship is already moving downstream when Mickey manages to snag Minnie's patched panties with a boat hook and haul her aboard. Later, on the deck, they cavort with the cargo of livestock, using the various animals as musical instruments on which to improvise "Turkey in the Straw."

This sequence is by far the most interesting in the movie in that it contains the seeds of much that was to come. It is also marked by a kind of humor Disney was later to abandon on grounds of taste. Mickey, for example, stretches a cat's tail so that it becomes a stringed instrument; the cat gives vocal expression to its displeasure at this misuse of its anatomy. A good deal of music and laughter is milked out of a cow's udder (later, the Hays Office was to insist that Disney cows be udderless and, indeed, it was actively suggested that they find some suitable form of apparel). Minnie cranks a goat's tail, transforming the unfortunate beast into a hurdy-gurdy, while Mickey plays xylophone riffs on a cow's teeth (the xylophone was a much-used instrument in the sound tracks of these early shorts, providing good opportunities for visual puns; almost any more or less regular group of solid objects—the rib cage of a skeleton, for example—could double as a xylophone).

We might note that the callous attitude displayed by Mickey and Minnie toward other animals made it quite clear that, although not human, these were not ordinary mice. They were creatures invested with special powers. They wore clothing and acted out roles that parodied the habits of men and women. In this respect they belonged to a tradition that goes back to Aesop and Aristophanes. Audiences were fascinated to see this tradition come to life on the screen, and if the gags were a little rough-and-ready, they were certainly effective. The way the action was tied to music and sound effects was unlike anything anyone had ever experienced before. *Steamboat Willie* was both a success and a major breakthrough for the animation industry.

Since *Plane Crazy* and *Gallopin' Gaucho* were made as silent films and then had sound added to them, they are not so interesting from the technical point of view. *Gallopin' Gaucho* has a plot that parodies Douglas Fairbanks melodramas (Mickey, in the Argentine, rescues Minnie from the clutches of Pegleg Pete). The animation, and most of the situations, are strongly reminiscent of some of the things in the Oswald series. *Plane Crazy,* the first Mouse cartoon produced, has considerably more to recommend it. The plot is topical. Mickey fancies himself a second Lindbergh (studying a picture of the aviator, he musses his hair and adopts a boyish grin) and, after some mishaps set in a barnyard, an automobile is converted into an airplane. Mickey offers to take Minnie for a spin. She climbs aboard but, before he can join her, the motor starts and the plane takes off

What appears to be clowning probably had a serious purpose. The two dancers are trying out a pose for the benefit of other animators. Those involved are, left to right, Burt Gillett, Norm Ferguson, Ted Sears, Fred Moore, Gilles "Frenchy" de Trémaudan, Tom Palmer, Ben Sharpstee Walt Disney, and Jack King

This photo of the production staff was taken in 1932, after Disney had won an Academy Award—his first—for the creation of Mickey Mouse

Recording the sound track for *The Beach Party* at the Hyperion Avenue studio, 1931. The girl at the microphone is Marcellite Garner, the voice of Minnie Mouse

on a crazy trajectory across the countryside, narrowly avoiding disastrous collisions with various items of livestock, farm machinery, and a passing car. Mickey catches up with the plane just as it is about to become airborne. Once clear of the ground, Mickey attempts to engage Minnie in a passionate kiss. She takes umbrage at his advances and bails out, using her panties as a parachute. Back on the ground, Mickey laughs at her disarray and Minnie floors him with a horseshoe. *Plane Crazy* was animated in its entirety by one man—Ub Iwerks—making it something of a tour de force. The whole thing moves along at a lively pace, and parts of it still seem funny even after almost half a century.

When *Steamboat Willie* was released, Walt Disney was twenty-six years old. His operation was still a very small one by Hollywood standards, but he had his foot on the first, perhaps even the second, rung of the ladder. Jack Cutting, now head of the Disney foreign department and responsible for such matters as the dubbing of Disney films into other languages, joined the Studio the following year and still remembers the atmosphere vividly.

"I had to leave the Otis Art Institute and look for a job. I had heard about a small cartoon studio near Glendale, so I went around to 2719 Hyperion without an appointment, walked in off the street with a few samples, and was hired that same

From the very first, the Silly Symphonies ▶
touched a wide variety of subjects and moods.
Examples illustrated here are, top to bottom,
from *The Merry Dwarfs,* 1929; *Winter,* 1930;
The China Plate, 1931; *Midnight in
a Toy Shop,* 1930; and *Pioneer Days,* 1930

In 1929, Disney launched a new series of cartoons which he called
Silly Symphonies. The first of these was *The Skeleton Dance,*
which featured some imaginative animation by Ub Iwerks
set to a macabre score devised by Carl Stalling

day in August, 1929. I had just turned twenty-one and most of the nineteen fellows on the staff were very young, with the exception of one or two—Roy must have been about thirty-five and the oldest on the staff was an animator named Burt Gillett, who may have been thirty-eight. I soon found being part of what was going on in that little studio very exciting. Walt was determined to develop the art of animation far beyond the level at which it was practiced in those days. He did it by being persuasive, by convincing everyone that his ideas and dreams for the future were exciting and worth believing in.

"During the early Mickey days, Walt was only taking fifty dollars home a week and Roy thirty-five. Some of us, like myself, who were just out of art school, were making eighteen dollars a week. We worked eight hours a day, six days a week, and we'd often come back nights to help get the work out. We didn't get paid overtime but that didn't matter if you were under the spell of the animated cartoon business as I was in those days. I came to the Studio without any experience in animation. A few of the older members of the staff, whom Walt had imported from the East, were experienced animators and, of course, Ub Iwerks was the Studio's top animator at that time. When you came in green, like I did, you learned to do a bit of everything. We began by inking cels, then we were taught in-betweening; we would come back at night and Ub would explain the principles of animation to us. The Studio was very small and the atmosphere informal. Most of us had a key to the front door.

"If you were an animator's assistant, after you did the in-between drawings for a scene you had to shoot a pencil drawing test. [In-betweens are the drawings used to fill in the gaps between the key drawings made by the animator. There must be an image for every frame and the animator supplies perhaps just one in three or four. Pencil testing, a way of checking out the animation on a scene before it is inked and painted onto the cels, was a Disney innovation.] After hand developing the test and putting it in a revolving drum to dry, you went back to the drawing board. When it was dry, you spliced it into a loop and ran it for the animator. We all had a chance to try our hands at different phases of the work."

Cutting recalls that Disney and Wilfred Jackson were both directing at the time he joined the Studio. Two shorts would be in production at any given time (they cost an average of about five thousand dollars apiece to make), and, in addition to supervising Jackson's work, Disney would always be working on ideas for new cartoons. From the very beginning, gag confer-

Silly Symphony posters, 1932

ences were held. Everyone on the production staff was expected to attend and invited to contribute jokes or other ideas that would enable the animators to get the most out of each story. Disney was also passionately interested in audience response, convinced that everyone at the Studio could learn a great deal about humor by studying the reactions of a group of laymen.

"When a picture was finished," Cutting reports, "Walt would take the first print from the laboratory to the Alexander Theater in Glendale and tip the projectionist to run it between the first and second shows. We all paid our way to get in and, directly after the cartoon was run, we would meet outside in front of the theater and Walt would evaluate the audience reaction and we would discuss why certain gags didn't go over and why others got such a big laugh."

The Disney brothers were working hard for their first modest success. An account book, written in Roy's hand, survives and indicates that Cutting's estimate of their take-home pay is quite accurate. Accurate, that is, except for the weeks when there was not enough cash to go around and the brothers' pay shrank to less than that of the lowliest apprentice animator.

A number of new Mickey Mouse cartoons appeared in 1929, sporting titles such as *The Karnival Kid, Mickey's Choo Choo,* and *The Jazz Fool* (this last a take-off on Al Jolson). Mickey acquired, within the space of a few months, gloves, shoes, and a more endearing manner. There were other developments too. The sound tracks became increasingly sophisticated, and in most cases they were now recorded before the animators began work. That is to say, once a story line was established, a score was prepared to fit the action; it was recorded and the animators worked to the rhythms and accents contained in the sound track. This system allowed for greater flexibility.

To handle the music side of the business, Disney called in an old acquaintance from Kansas City, Carl Stalling. Stalling had had years of experience in the theater pit, providing music for silent movies—a background which left him well equipped for his new career. Already the Disney team was becoming extremely adept at synchronizing sound and action, and several of the earliest Mickey Mouse pictures—*The Opry House,* for instance, and *The Jazz Fool*—took music as the main substance of the plot. The director always had a piano in his office so that, at story conferences, the composer could illustrate the melodic and rhythmic lines the animators would have to follow (for this reason the director's room became known as the music room, a designation it retained for many years). Most of the music used was—like "Turkey in the Straw"—in the public domain, meaning that no royalties would have to be paid. Stalling was quite capable of producing original material, however, and soon came up with "Minnie's Yoo Hoo," which served for some time as Mickey's theme song (it has recently been revived as the signature tune of television's *The Mouse Factory*).

This emphasis on music led in the same year, 1929, to quite a new kind of animated film—the Silly Symphony.

It seems likely that some of the credit for the concept of the Silly Symphonies should go to Carl Stalling. An account of how the series came about was given by Wilfred Jackson in the magazine *Funny World* dated Spring 1971. Talking of the Mickey Mouse cartoons, he recalls that there were often arguments between Disney and Stalling when "Walt would want more or less time for the action than could fit the musical phrase." The rest of the staff would sit in the next room, enjoy-

6

Flowers and Trees

This 1932 cartoon has a special place in
the history of animation as the first to be made
in full color. From this point on, all Silly Symphonies
were produced in Technicolor

Three Little Pigs

In 1932, Walt Disney produced *The Three Little Pigs*—a cartoon
which had an extraordinary impact on the American public.
Its hit tune, "Who's Afraid of the Big Bad Wolf?"
swept the nation. Many people saw this film
as Disney's comment in fable form on
the Depression era. Whatever his motives for making it,
it did display a marked advance in terms of
storytelling and character development

From 1932 to 1934, the
Silly Symphonies evolved a new range
of subtleties. Shown here are
scenes from, left to right,
Babes in the Woods,
The Grasshopper and the Ants,
Father Noah's Ark,
The Tortoise and the Hare,
and *The Wise Little Hen*

ing the whole thing but glad they weren't involved ("Walt could be pretty stiff"). Eventually a solution was arrived at. Walt decided that, so far as Mickey was concerned, the music must be made to fit the action, but that another series would be launched in which the action would be keyed to the music.

Stalling, interviewed in the same issue of *Funny World,* claims he was responsible for the idea of a series of musical cartoons. These were to be not merely illustrated songs, but films in which music and animation were combined to provide a totally new experience. The name Silly Symphonies was selected for the series, and work began on the first of them, *The Skeleton Dance* (Stalling indicates that the subject was his choice).

The Skeleton Dance opens as cats, howling in a cemetery, are disturbed at midnight by four skeletons who emerge from their graves. The skeletons go through some fairly elaborate dance sequences and then, at dawn, scurry back to their resting places. The whole thing is set to suitably sepulchral music, a composition of Stalling's which utilized elements from Grieg's "March of the Dwarfs" (many film historians have erroneously reported that the music used is Saint Saëns' "Danse Macabre"). Despite the success of the Mickey Mouse shorts, theater owners were a little nervous of the reception that would be accorded this new kind of cartoon entertainment, and so *The Skeleton Dance* and its successors were released under the byline "Mickey Mouse Presents a Walt Disney Silly Symphony."

These first Symphonies were received well enough for the series to continue. Certainly they were very original in concept, but they now seem rather less interesting than the early Mouse shorts. Mickey gave his pictures a central core around which the action could develop. The Symphonies had no such core. Each of them was constructed around a rather generalized theme—*The Merry Dwarfs, Winter,* and *Spring* are typical early titles—

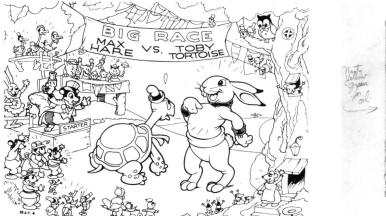

which had to be stated before it could be explored; with the techniques available in 1929 and 1930, this was quite a challenge. In a Mouse cartoon, however, you had only to catch one glimpse of Mickey to know exactly what to expect, and this allowed the animators to take much more for granted.

For the first year or two of their existence, the Symphonies had no real focus. But we must emphasize just how significant it is that Disney instituted them and then persisted with them when it would have been far easier to exploit Mickey for all he was worth. Before long, the Symphonies would have an invaluable role to play in the development of the art of animation. We should lay to rest, too, the idea that the classical music content of these cartoons showed Disney displaying pretensions toward high culture in this series. All the evidence suggests that he saw himself as making motion picture entertainment for the general public. If he persisted with the Silly Symphonies, it was because he wanted to give his animators an opportunity to extend the range of subject matter they were dealing with. He was, as usual, looking to the future.

In 1930, another personnel crisis hit the Studio. Ub Iwerks and Carl Stalling quit the Disney operation.

The loss of Iwerks resulted directly from the fact that Disney's contract with Powers was due for renewal. It would seem that Powers had, at the beginning, thought of these cartoons as little more than a novelty that might help promote his Powers Cinephone system; but Mickey (and *The Skeleton Dance* too, by dint of a successful run in New York) had proved that there was a real long-term potential for this kind of entertainment. Meanwhile, the Disneys had not been entirely happy in their relationship with Powers. They had been unable to get detailed financial reports from him, his method of doing business

Lullaby Land, 1933, top, presents a
child's dream adventures in a landscape
metamorphosed from the patchwork quilt that
covers his bed. Center and bottom:
the following year, in *The Goddess of Spring*,
Disney artists attempted to revive
the myth of Pluto and Persephone

This layout drawing for ▶
Old King Cole, 1933, gives some idea
of the detail that went into every scene
of the Silly Symphonies

Another layout drawing, this one for ▶
The Wise Little Hen, 1934, illustrates the scene
in which Donald Duck made his debut.
He is discovered dancing a hornpipe
on the deck of a somewhat decrepit
barge, right. When the Wise Little Hen
asks a favor of him, left, he feigns
a tummy ache, establishing himself
as a somewhat unreliable and
disreputable character from the very outset
of his career

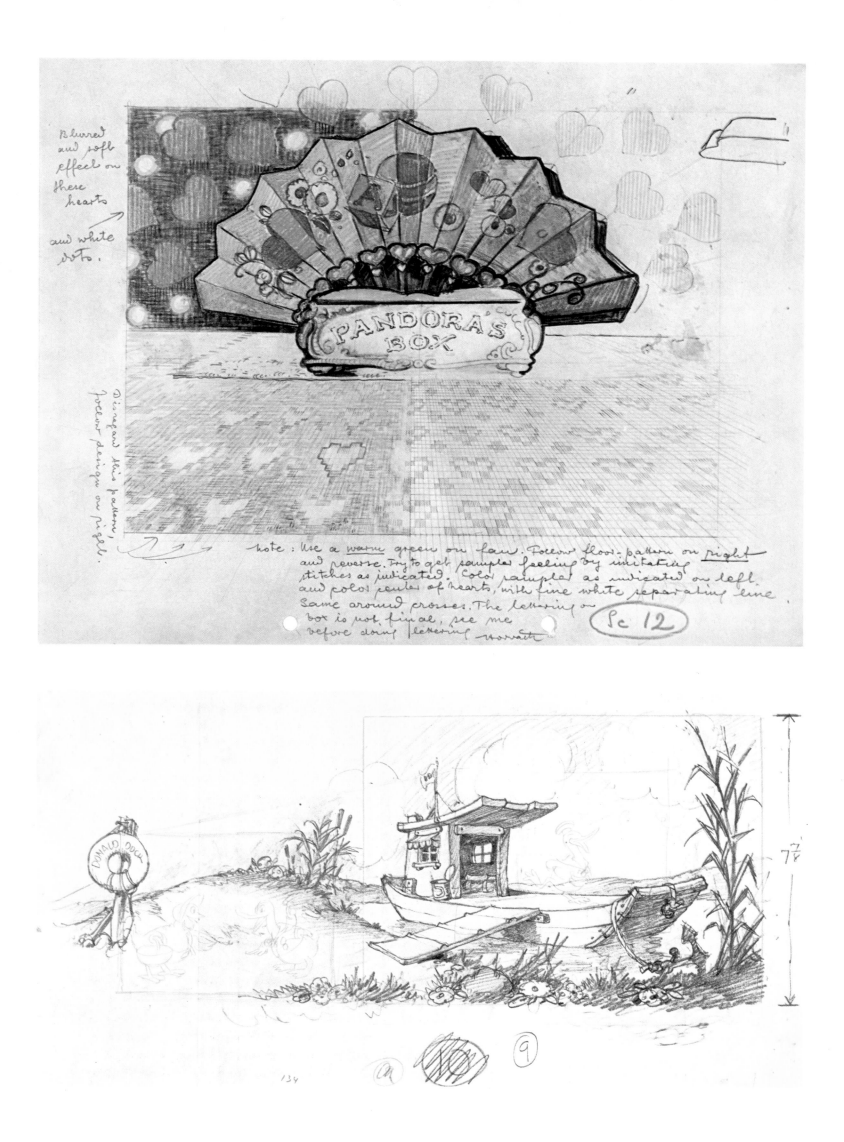

being to send them money from time to time—just enough to keep the Studio operating. Powers must have been aware that the Disneys might be disinclined to renew their contract, and so decided on tactics for the upcoming negotiations. Behind the Disneys' backs, he approached Ub Iwerks and offered him a series of his own. Not unnaturally (and not suspecting Powers's true motive) Iwerks accepted the offer. The distributor then confronted the Disneys with the *fait accompli,* but promised to tear up the Iwerks contract if they would renegotiate. He made an offer of a guaranteed $2,500 a week, which sounded like a great deal of money, but the Disneys refused to sign with Powers and instead negotiated a distribution agreement with Columbia Pictures (Harry Cohn made the deal at the suggestion of director Frank Capra, who had been greatly impressed by the originality and vigor of Disney's cartoons). Iwerks found himself out on a limb. We can only guess at the personal feelings that must have been stirred up by Powers's unethical maneuverings, but the end result was that Iwerks sold out his partnership to the brothers for $2,920, and then, backed by Powers, set up his own studio. He produced, among other things, a series called Flip the Frog, which never attained any real success. Iwerks did not have either the story sense or the business intuition of Walt Disney.

He was, however, a great animator, and as such had been an enormous asset to the Studio. His work on Mickey alone would have been enough to establish his importance, but he also contributed inventive work to practically all the early Disney cartoons. Not only were his drawings of absolutely top quality, he also turned them out at a phenomenal rate—according to at least one source, as many as seven hundred a day. He had also provided invaluable assistance in training young artists and had been the resident technical genius, adapting most of the equipment used in the production of the early pictures. Next to Walt Disney himself, Ub Iwerks had been the most important single figure in the development of the Studio. Small wonder that Powers had figured he would not be an easy person to replace (like Charles Mintz before him, Powers was underestimating Disney's own importance).

Some ten years later, Iwerks returned to the Studio and re-established himself there as a special-effects innovator, developing—among other things—the Xerox camera that has been used in recent Disney animated films and the matte process that lent Mary Poppins some of her magic powers.

Stalling left at about the same time, mainly, it would seem, because he thought that without Iwerks the Studio had little future. He remained in the animation industry, eventually becoming musical director for Warner Brothers' Looney Tunes —Merry Melodies.

Both these losses, then, were serious, but they do not seem to have caused Disney to so much as break stride. He quickly replaced Stalling with Bert Lewis. Iwerks could not be replaced by any one man, so Disney coped with this loss by building up his stable of animators in two different ways: he brought in a number of apprentices and he imported experienced animators from New York. Certainly the Disney product did not seem to suffer. Mickey, by the end of 1930, had become an international celebrity. Known in Italy as Topolino and as Miki Kuchi in Japan, the Mouse continued his adventures, saving Minnie from immolation by fire and worse, confronting Pete in various exotic situations, and performing to audiences of exuberant animals whose taste in music ranged from ragtime to violin concertos. A simple-minded bloodhound made an appearance in a 1930 picture called *The Chain Gang* and developed, before long, into Mickey's faithful companion Pluto. As Mickey's career unfolded in the thirties, other characters such as Horace Horsecollar and Clarabelle Cow began to enjoy the status of co-stars, but their personalities offered relatively little for the animators to work with and, as the pictures became more sophisticated, their roles became less significant and eventually vanished entirely.

By 1931, Mickey was important enough for *Time* magazine to devote a feature article to him. Another feature, printed in *Motion Picture Daily* (June 20, 1931), tells us that the production staff, including assistants, had grown to more than forty. Several of the animators—Dave Hand, Ben Sharpsteen, Rudy Zamora, Tom Palmer, and Jack King, for instance—had experience in New York studios, as had story men like Ted Sears and Burt Gillett. Other animators—such as Les Clark, Jack Cutting, Dick Lundy, Gilles "Frenchy" de Trémaudan, and Johnny Cannon—had learned their craft with Disney. Emil Flohri, a former newspaper cartoonist and art director, was painting backgrounds and Frank Churchill had joined Bert Lewis in the music department (both of them, like Stalling, had received their training in theater pit orchestras during the silent era). Floyd Gottfredson was drawing the daily Mickey Mouse comic strip (and has continued to do so ever since) while Hazel Sewell, Lillian Disney's sister, headed up the ink and paint department. Wilfred Jackson was directing and contributing to story. Still listed as assistants were Webb Smith, soon to be an important member of the story team; Roy Williams, who later attained fame on television's *Mickey Mouse Club;* and Fred Moore, who would become one of the very best animators of his generation.

The New York animators were employed, to a large extent, in a stopgap capacity. Their experience was needed by the Studio at that point, but their approach to animation differed somewhat from that which had been established by the Disney artists under Iwerks's tutelage. Les Clark explains that Disney-trained animators usually worked from key pose to key pose—that is to say, they picked out the signal poses in any action, established those first, then filled in the gaps afterward. The New York animators had been trained to animate "straight-ahead"—in other words, they started at point a of any action and worked their way through to point z. The New York animators were very good at this (Clark recalls his amazement as he watched Zamora animate the flight of a butterfly by the straight-ahead method), but in the long run the key-pose style of animation was much more efficient and flexible. Apart from anything else, it fitted in perfectly with the Disney system of animating to music (key poses being made to correspond with rhythmic accents). Gradually, Disney-trained animators took over, but the experience of the New York imports was not wasted. Dave Hand, Ben Sharpsteen, and Jack King all had important careers ahead of them at the Studio as animation directors.

It is interesting to note that there was, by 1931, a full-fledged story department. This was not like any other story department, because everything was worked out in visual terms (all the story men were competent draftsmen). At about this time, or shortly after, the first "story boards" made their appearance. The story board was an important innovation. It is difficult to attribute its invention with any certainty to any one person, but Disney himself always credited it to Webb Smith. Until then, stories had been worked out comic-strip fashion in notebooks or on loose sheets of paper (generally there would be three or six drawings to a page, sometimes accompanied by a written description of the action and dialogue notes). Smith, possibly in collaboration with other people, hit upon the idea of making each of the drawings on a separate sheet of paper and pinning them all, in sequence, to a bulletin board. The story for an entire short could be accommodated on a single board and thus the director, or anyone else concerned with the production, could see the plot of an entire movie spread out in front of him. If changes had to be made, drawings could be moved or taken down and replaced by others. It was the ideal system for developing cartoon stories and it soon came into general use throughout the Studio (it is still in use today and has been adopted not only by other animation studios but also by producers of live-action films and commercials).

A general view of
the Hyperion Avenue studio, c. 1933

A group photograph taken at
the Studio in the mid-thirties, about
the time that staff expansion was
picking up momentum

Walt looks on as Mary Moder,
Pinto Colvig, and Dorothy Compton rehearse
"Who's Afraid of the Big Bad Wolf?"
Composer Frank Churchill is
at the piano

A promotional vehicle and theater marquees advertising Mickey Mouse

Disney himself must have been delighted by this innovation. The story board enabled him to participate even more closely in the development of his cartoons, allowing him to walk into a music room and see at a glance exactly what needed to be done.

Dick Huemer was working for Charles Mintz at this time and he recalls that everyone in the industry figured that Disney must have some trick—a gimmick or secret of some kind—that made his films so superior.

"Whenever we met a guy like Ted Sears or Ben Sharpsteen, we'd say, 'Oh, come on now—what is it that Walt does that we don't do?' and they would simply say something like, 'He analyzes.' Analyzes! So do we—we think! But we didn't and Walt did. He did chew everything over, did prepare beautifully, so the director could just take it and give it to the animator and then look at it and correct it."

By the end of 1931, Disney's demand for constant improve-

ment had driven the cost of a single cartoon to above $13,000. The Studio was barely breaking even and in 1932 another innovation drove costs still higher. In that year, Disney released a Silly Symphony called *Flowers and Trees*. This cartoon caused a sensation in the industry. It was in full color.

Technicolor had introduced a two-color system as early as 1929, but it had been used sparingly by the major studios which, with good reason, thought it had little more than novelty value (its chief limitation was that the color values were somewhat distorted). By 1932, however, Technicolor had a three-strip system ready which offered far more accurate color reproduction, and Disney at once saw its advantages. *Flowers and Trees* had been partly made as a black-and-white film. This footage was scrapped and the whole thing was done again in color. It was premiered at Grauman's Chinese Theater in Hollywood along with Irving Thalberg's production of *Strange Interlude*.

By today's standards, *Flowers and Trees* is a strange mixture of charm and absurdity. A romance between two young

Lillian and Walt Disney at home
with their pet chow

trees is disrupted by a crabby tree stump who initiates a fire that
threatens the whole forest. Birds puncture clouds so that rain
falls and douses the fire. The stump is destroyed and the two
young lovers are married, with a glowworm for a wedding ring,
while neighboring flowers celebrate their nuptials. Whatever
weaknesses or strengths this cartoon may have had were
overshadowed by the fact that it was in color. Color made it a
valuable property and, from that point on, all Silly Symphonies
were fully chromatic. Disney made an advantageous deal with
Technicolor which gave him exclusive rights to the three-color
process, as far as animation was concerned, for the next two
years. For the time being, the Mickey Mouse cartoons continued
to be in black-and-white—they were successful enough not to
need the extra boost—but the Symphonies took full advantage
of the new possibilities. Almost at once they became more inventive. *Flowers and Trees* was followed by *King Neptune* and

Left: Walt and Mickey pose
with Will Hays.
Right: lunch at the Paramount
commissary, 1934. Disney
is seated with veteran animator
Walter Lantz. Standing are
Gary Cooper, left, and Walter Winchell

Babes in the Woods, both of which display tighter structure and livelier action than anything previously seen in this series.

One factor which contributed to their inventiveness was the addition to the staff, in 1932, of Albert Hurter. Hurter, a Swiss-born artist, had learned the art of animation at the Barre studio in New York. After spending some time in the Southwest (he was passionately devoted to the desert landscape), he set up a commercial art studio in Los Angeles and then, probably at the instigation of Ted Sears or one of the other New York exiles, joined the Disney staff. From the very beginning of this association Hurter had a very special position at the Studio, Disney realizing that his gift was for producing what became known as "inspirational drawings." This is to say that he spent his time developing visual ideas for future projects and improvising on themes which might trigger the imaginations of story men or animators. Neptune's court in *King Neptune* and the gingerbread house in *Babes in the Woods* both reflect his influence. He was trained in Europe and his drawings were imbued with the spirit of the gothic fairy tale. This added another dimension to the native American vigor of the Disney product. As the Stu-

Disney's growing success abroad
can be gauged from this French comic
and this Russian poster

dio continued to evolve, Hurter's influence was felt more and more strongly.

In 1933, Hurter designed the settings and main characters for what turned out to be the greatest Disney success up to that time—the famous *Three Little Pigs*. It is hardly necessary to recapitulate here either the plot or the success of Frank Churchill's hit tune, "Who's Afraid of the Big Bad Wolf?" The movie was a smash. Theaters retained it week after week and its impact reflects the fact that it went far beyond any of the earlier Symphonies in terms of plot and character development. The story line is so strong that social commentators have seen it as a parable about the Depression (Disney insisted that it was intended as entertainment and nothing more, but the film had such an archetypal ring to it that it invited interpretations of this sort). The animation was excellent and the characters had a real existence of their own—something which, to that date, had only been achieved with Mickey and Minnie. Just one thing marred it. In one section of the movie, the Big Bad Wolf approached the brick home of the Practical Pig in the guise of a Jewish peddler. Humor at the expense of racial stereotypes was not uncommon in Hollywood at the time, but this gag was an unfortunate lapse in taste and later, when *Three Little Pigs* was re-released, this section of the movie was revamped to eliminate this element.

The following year, 1934, saw the production of several excellent Silly Symphonies including *The Tortoise and the Hare, The Grasshopper and the Ants,* and *The Wise Little Hen*—all of which were moral fables and showed just how proficient the Studio had become at structuring a story and establishing character. *The Tortoise and the Hare* put Aesop into modern dress as the rakish hare loses his race to the tortoise against a milky landscape that is typical of these early color cartoons. This milkiness—at times it resembles smog—resulted from the fact that Emil Flohri mixed a great deal of white pigment with his colors, lightening tones this way rather than by thinning his paint with water. In *The Grasshopper and the Ants,* the grasshopper is a particularly well-established character (his theme song is "The World Owes Me a Living") keyed to the voice talent of Pinto Colvig. Colvig—a former circus clown—was a musician and a member of the gag team, but his greatest claim to fame is that he provided the voice of Goofy, who had had his first supporting role in a 1932 cartoon, *Mickey's Revue.*

The Wise Little Hen introduced another voice talent and a new character who was, within a year, to challenge Mickey as

These stills from *Mickey's Surprise Party,* a commercial made for the National Biscuit Company, show that by the end of the decade Mickey and Minnie had developed a certain nonchalant sophistication and Pluto had come into his own

For *Playful Pluto,* 1934, Webb Smith devised and Norm Ferguson animated a scene in which Pluto becomes entangled with a strip of flypaper. A classic of its sort, this sequence demonstrates how Disney artists could take a simple situation and build on it in such a way that the humor arose directly from the personality of the character

In *Orphan's Benefit*, 1934,
Donald Duck came into his own.
His efforts to entertain
a group of children are frustrated
by the malicious behavior of
the audience, which causes him to
dissolve into helpless rage

LARGER

Disney's star attraction. This character was, of course, Donald Duck, and the man who provided him with a voice was Clarence "Ducky" Nash. Until Disney discovered him, Nash had worked for a milk company, entertaining children with his animal imitations. One of these imitations evolved into Donald's ill-tempered quack and made his voice known all over the world.

Donald Duck had a relatively modest role in his first screen appearance. He debuts as a miserable creature, living on a ramshackle houseboat, who feigns a bellyache every time the Wise Little Hen asks him for assistance (in this first incarnation he was drawn by Art Babbitt and by Dick Huemer, who had finally joined the Disney animation staff). Donald's bill was a little longer than it is today, but he had the same voice, the same sailor suit, and the same irascible temperament. He quickly made the jump to co-starring roles in Mickey Mouse pictures such as *Orphan's Benefit,* irritating everyone on the screen but endearing himself to audiences. Many animators found the Duck difficult to work with, but two in particular—Dick Lundy and Fred Spencer—had a way with him and they must be given much of the credit for developing him into a star.

We might remark at this point that the idea of animators being "cast" for certain characters was becoming quite common. Animators tend to think of themselves as actors who "perform" with their pencils and, given this concept, it was only natural that some animators should have a better touch with certain roles and certain types of action than with others. Just as Ub Iwerks had given Mickey his initial impetus, so Donald found benefactors in Spencer and Lundy, and Pluto and Goofy began to develop as major characters largely because certain artists had strong feelings about them and the way they should behave. Pluto owed much of his growing importance to Norm Ferguson. For a 1934 cartoon, *Playful Pluto,* Webb Smith devised a sequence in which Pluto becomes entangled with a sticky ribbon of flypaper. Ferguson took this sequence and turned it into a classic of comic animation. The man who had a real feeling for Goofy was Art Babbitt. Babbitt knew how to make the most out of any situation that the Goof might find himself in, and this led to more and better situations being invented for him. In this way the Goof developed from a bit player with a funny voice into the full-fledged idiot star of the mid-thirties.

Mickey, meanwhile, had become virtually a national symbol, and as such he was expected to behave properly at all times. If he occasionally stepped out of line, any number of letters would arrive at the Studio from citizens and organizations who felt that the nation's moral well-being was in their hands. It was

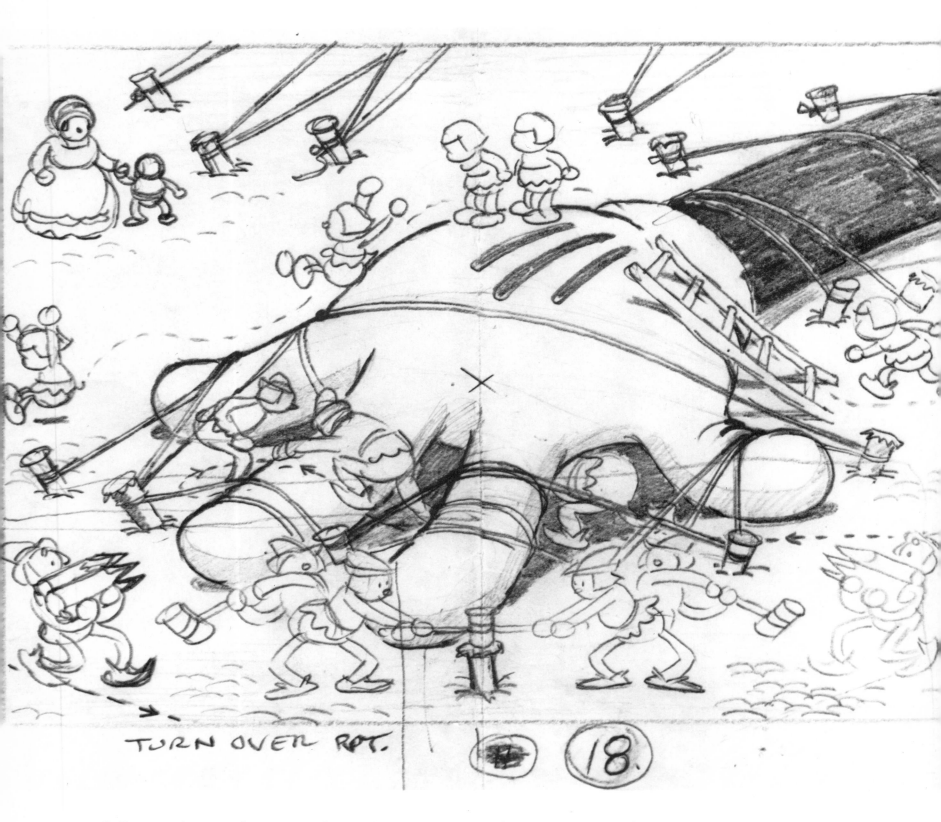

TURN OVER ROT.

18.

Gulliver Mickey, 1934, is one of several cartoons that make Mickey the hero of a children's classic

In this layout drawing ▶
for *Gulliver Mickey,*
Mickey's dream self takes leave
of his sleeping body

becoming harder and harder to find comic situations for Mickey that would not give offense in some quarter. Eventually he would be pressured into the role of straight man, but the gradual change had not yet eroded the core of his personality, and the Mouse cartoons of the mid-thirties were consistently inventive while becoming increasingly sophisticated. The strides made by the Disney Studio between 1928 and 1934 were quite extraordinary. The story department came up with better and better ideas and the animators were implementing them with more and more skill. They had learned that for a character to seem real he had to have real weight—had to be seen to obey the laws of gravity (or to deliberately defy them if that was what the situation called for). This was not an easy thing to achieve. To make Goofy, to take just one example, seem to have real weight, one had to understand exactly how gravity would affect his own particular walk—part lope, part shuffle.

In Mickey's early days, he had expressed his reactions in terms of elaborate "takes"—throwing his whole body into a response so that there could be no doubt about the fact that he was surprised, angry, happy, or whatever. By the mid-thirties, Disney artists had learned how to convey a shift in mood by a subtle change of expression on a character's face or by an almost imperceptible alteration of physical attitude. And as the Disney team perfected its skills it continued to expand, drawing to itself talented young men who were attracted by the spectacular advances that had already been made.

One nonaesthetic factor made the Disney Studio especially attractive to young artists in the 1930s. The Depression was at its height, and there were not too many markets they could turn to. Ward Kimball's story is typical:

"I was going to art school in Santa Barbara and I thought I wanted to be a magazine illustrator. . . . This was the Depression and you had to make a little bread anywhere you could find it, so on Saturday mornings I would pick up four or five dollars at the local Safeway store. I'd have to get there at 5 A.M., rain or shine—or rather fog—and hack lettuce. . . . After I thawed out my fingers, I'd go back and paint showcards. . . . When I was through with this, about 9:30, I'd go across the street and up a block to the Fox Arlington Theater which, every Saturday morning, featured the original Mickey Mouse Club. . . . I was paid three dollars to rehearse and lead about ten kids who played instruments and did a short band march number at the beginning of the program. . . .

"About this time, I saw my first Disney color cartoon—

In the early thirties, Mickey and
the other Disney characters were already
being adapted for use in all kinds
of merchandising operations.
Dozens of companies manufactured items
under license from the Studio.
At least two were saved from bankruptcy
by their Disney franchises
(see also overleaf)

Father Noah's Ark, a Silly Symphony—and I was amazed at the movement and the artwork. Rarely did you see a Technicolor live-action picture—maybe John McCormack singing partly in color—but here was this full-color *Father Noah's Ark.* Wow! I began to see that this was no ordinary, run-of-the-mill cartoon stuff. The Disney gags were funnier and there seemed to be one every few seconds.... The Disney cartoons had a realism that no others had—the giraffes ran like giraffes and the chipmunks and squirrels scampered like chipmunks and squirrels. Not only that, the faster animals caught and passed the slower ones—which I had never seen done before.

"Then along came *Three Little Pigs* with its hit tune which was played over and over on the radio.... Many of the other studios were reaching into their bag of old silents and re-releasing them with new sound tracks by people like Jelly Roll Morton and Fats Waller, to which they would add a few ratchets and honks and slide whistles—and that was supposed to be a sound cartoon—but Disney cartoons made a real honest attempt to integrate sound and picture.

"In 1934, when I'd been going to art school for two years and money was real tight, one of the instructors at school said, 'Kimball, you make a lot of funny drawings and it seems to me you ought to work for a man like Walt Disney.'

"Well, to drive all the way to Los Angeles during the Depression was tough—gas was twelve cents a gallon. So my mother says, 'Okay—I'll take you into Los Angeles and bring you back just this once.' So I loaded my portfolio with paintings and sketches. Well, nobody had ever come to Disney's with a portfolio of his work before. So I come in and here I am, just turned twenty, and I come to the front office on Hyperion Avenue and ask for a job."

Kimball began work as a Disney apprentice on April 2, 1934. Within five years he would become one of the Studio's top animators.

The expansion of the Studio can be illustrated in another way. In 1929 and 1930, additions were made to the front, rear, and one side of the original building on Hyperion Avenue. In the spring of 1931, a two-story animators' building and a sound stage were built (Disney moved his office to the second floor of the new building). From 1929 to 1933, the Studio grew from 1,600 square feet of floor space to 20,000 square feet.

A 1934 group gathered around a story board: left to right, Webb Smith, Ted Sears, Harry Reeves, Walt Disney, Pinto Colvig, Bill Cottrell (partially hidden), and Albert Hurter

3 Six Cartoon Classics

Once Hollywood had come to terms with the challenge of sound, the industry began to explore the avenues that had been opened up. The filmed musical, for instance, offered possibilities that had been totally beyond the grasp of silent cinema, and this new genre presented the theater-goer with varied and novel experiences. There were, for example, the Warner Brothers' musicals—tinseled epics like *Forty-Second Street* and *Footlight Parade*—with Busby Berkeley's spectacular choreographic symmetries punctuating the fictional show-business careers of stars such as James Cagney, Joan Blondell, Dick Powell, and Ruby Keeler. Maurice Chevalier sang his way into French high society in Rouben Mamoulian's quasi-operatic *Love Me Tonight*; the movie fan could also indulge himself, by proxy, in the silk-hat sophistication of Fred Astaire. It all helped keep the Depression at bay. There had been gangster movies in the silent era, but sound lent them a new dimension. Screeching brakes and the rattle of Thompson submachine guns thrilled audiences from Inglewood to Istanbul as Cagney and Edward G. Robinson stalked arrogantly through histories of carnage with titles like *Little Caesar* and *Public Enemy*. The film-maker learned to terrify his customers with such simple devices as the sound of footsteps in foggy alleyways. The cries of victims could be blanked out by the clang of shunted boxcars in a railroad siding.

FROSTING FOR DECORATION

The Cookie Carnival

This bizarre little masterpiece is full of humorous invention. As the title suggests, it
concerns a holiday in Cookie Land, the high point of which is the election of a queen.
The contestants include such lovelies as Miss Banana Cake and Miss Licorice, who are
paraded past the judges on confectionery floats. Just as the proceedings are getting under
way, a hobo cookie arrives in town, riding a boxcar in true thirties fashion. On the
outskirts of the carnival he discovers a heartbroken cookie—the Cinderella of the
piece—who has been left out of the parade because she does not have a suitable costume.
The hobo soon remedies this with the aid of a little whipped cream and frosting and a
few deftly placed candies. The transformed young lady appears before the judges and,
dazzled by her charms, they declare her queen. Once she has ascended the throne, she
is asked to select a consort. Various male cookies—rum cakes (suitably tipsy), saintly angel
cakes, and other tasty morsels—compete for her favors. She politely declines them all and
picks her hobo.

This outline hardly does justice to the film, which comes across as a quick-fire
sequence of hilarious visual puns. The animation is superb, and much credit must go to
the story team and layout artists. The wittily baroque imagery probably owes a great deal
to the imagination of Albert Hurter. The movie is so beautifully paced, and so much
is packed into its plot, that it is hard to believe it lasts only eight minutes

Who Killed Cock Robin?

Disney gives the old nursery rhyme a new twist. Robin, it turns out, is not dead, but has merely been wounded by Cupid's arrow. Even Walt Disney himself seems to have been satisfied with this polished and sophisticated little production, and it is said to have influenced him to go ahead with *Snow White*.

The triumph of the cartoon is Jenny Wren, the object of Robin's passion, who is a thinly disguised caricature of Mae West

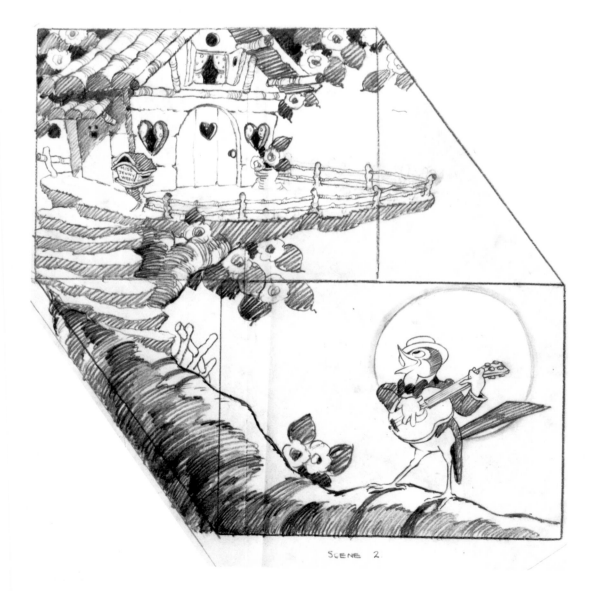

Sound changed the character of comedy too. A few of the old stars—Harold Lloyd and Laurel and Hardy, for example—made the transition to talkies, while Charlie Chaplin experimented in his own unique way with the possibilities of music and pure sound. More significantly, sound enabled talented vaudeville-trained comedians to reach the larger audiences that the cinema had to offer. W.C. Fields began to croak his asides to audiences from a rich assortment of bars and poolrooms, while the Marx Brothers brought chaos and disrepute to any number of previously respectable institutions. Mae West, despite the attempted strictures of the Hays Office, managed to blend humor with sexual innuendo, as, at a more sophisticated level, did the great Austrian-born director Ernst Lubitsch in such films as *Trouble in Paradise.*

The melodrama and the historical epic had long been in favor with Hollywood producers. Sound did little to alter their basic appeal, but audiences were soon subjected to musical scores which literally led them by the ear to the appropriate heights of ecstasy and depths of despair. The words of dying heroines could now be inflected with all the pathos that Hollywood money could coax away from the Broadway stage. Westerns also stayed with their old formulas, but now hoofs thundered across the boulder-strewn hillsides of the Fox ranch and bullets that ric-

Broken Toys

This cartoon makes even more explicit use of caricature than *Who Killed Cock Robin?*
W.C. Fields and other Hollywood characters appear in the guise of discarded dolls. The
main plot involves a sailor doll who performs an emergency operation to restore the sight
of a dainty little creature who has lost her eyes. A neatly constructed little film, it is
typical of Disney productions during the mid-thirties

ocheted off the timbers of back-lot saloons seemed to whine into the auditorium.

Most important of all, sound brought a galaxy of new stars and amplified the magic of a few older ones. People would go to their local movie houses just to hear the distinctive voice and delivery of a Gary Cooper, Cary Grant, Clark Gable, Spencer Tracy, Claudette Colbert, Carole Lombard, Jean Harlow, Marlene Dietrich, or Garbo.

What is incredible is that, in this time of plenty in the motion picture industry, Walt Disney was able to reach a position of high eminence—matching that of the greatest stars and producers—with a modest output of animated films, none of which ran for longer than eight minutes! He was not yet a major economic force in the industry—in fact his operation was very humble by the standards of MGM or Paramount—but he was an international celebrity and, by 1935, the Studio had at least two "stars"—Mickey and Donald—who ranked with any live actors who ever embraced beneath an art director's branch of apple blossom or led an army of extras into battle.

Disney achieved his position with a unique blend of talent and professionalism. Not only had his artists learned how to make drawings perform incredible feats, but also—and this is where Disney himself made his own greatest single contribution—they had learned how to pack as much real dramatic action into the confines of their eight-minute format as ever Cecil B. De Mille did in the most gargantuan of his epics.

Nowhere is Disney's talent as a great story editor more apparent than in the shorts of the mid-thirties. He knew how to take a simple gag situation and squeeze every last drop of humor out of it. And then he would find a way of topping that with a situation even funnier than the one preceding it.

For practical reasons, an animated cartoon is usually broken down into very short segments (different animators being assigned to each of these), so that the effect, on the screen, is of very rapid cuts from one character to another. Disney learned how to take advantage of this as a storytelling device. He badgered his story men, his layout men, and his animation directors into the realization that every cut had to be meaningful, that each short segment of the film must contribute to its overall pace. No decision was implemented without his approval, and he was constantly on hand with fresh ideas to spur flagging imaginations. Each cartoon was planned down to the last detail.

Dozens of people might be involved in this, but the entire process was controlled by Disney himself. By the time segments of action were assigned to individual animators, Disney had an

Background paintings for *Music Land* ▶

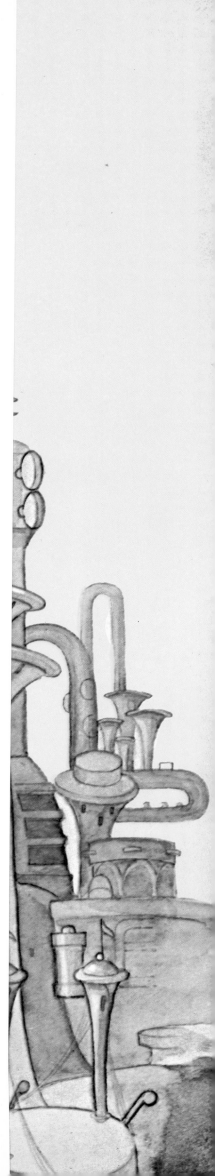

Music Land

In this twist on the Romeo and Juliet story, the son of the King of the Isle of Jazz falls in love with the daughter of the Queen of the Land of Symphony. There is bad feeling between the two monarchs, and while on a clandestine visit to his sweetheart, the Prince of Jazz is captured and imprisoned in a masonry metronome. War breaks out and the metronome is blown to bits. The Prince escapes and takes to the Sea of Discord, accompanied by his love. When both monarchs realize that their offspring are in danger of drowning, they call a cease-fire and set off to the rescue. All ends happily. The Prince and Princess are plucked from the waves and soon join their parents in a double wedding. A Bridge of Harmony unites the reconciled kingdoms.

The cartoon gets by without conventional dialogue—the characters speak with the voices of musical instruments. The Land of Symphony blasts its rival with Tchaikovsky's *1812 Overture,* blowing holes in the rococo saxophone skyscrapers. Hurter's influence is felt once more, especially in the humanized instruments (see also overleaf)

almost complete knowledge of how the final product would look on the screen. The one factor that he could not control was the animation itself. Here he had to rely on the talents he had gathered around him and, by 1935, they were quite considerable.

Apart from the experienced animators we have already mentioned—men like Ferguson, Babbitt, Huemer, Clark, and Lundy—a number of other artists were making their presence felt. Three of exceptional ability were Ham Luske, Fred Moore, and Bill Tytla. Luske was not an outstanding draftsman, but he had strong ideas about the best ways in which to develop character, and these were very close to Disney's own. Moore and Tytla were probably the two best draftsmen ever to work for the Disney organization. Moore, as we have seen, had been an assistant in the early thirties and he quickly rose to a position of importance on the staff. His facility with a pencil was such that one of his contemporaries remarked that "his brains were in his fingertips." We can characterize his work by saying that everything he did had charm. He was incapable of drawing a line that did not have inherent grace and rhythm. His finest work was to come in Disney's early feature-length films, but in the mid-thirties he was bringing his sense of style to Mickey and other stock characters. In contrast to Moore, Tytla's draftsmanship emphasized strength and muscularity. Moore's line had energy, but it was a kind of nervous energy controlled by the fingers. Tytla was an altogether more physical draftsman. The energy of his line seemed to come from the shoulder, from the entire body. Like Moore, his best work would be done for the early features. Usually he was assigned villains and already, in 1935, he was responsible for an outstanding one in the person of the prizefighting rooster in *Cock of the Walk.*

By this time, the young men who would provide Disney with his next wave of key animators—Ward Kimball, Eric Larson, Woolie Reitherman, Marc Davis, Milt Kahl, Frank Thomas, Ollie Johnston, and John Lounsbery—were with the Studio. Most of them were still apprentices, but two of them, Larson and Reitherman, were already full-fledged animators and the others were not far behind. The story department was still dominated by men like Ted Sears and Webb Smith. Art direction and layout were in the hands of skilled artists like Charles Philippi and Hugh Hennesy. Frank Churchill and Bert Lewis continued to run the music department and another young musician, Jim MacDonald, took over the sound effects department, to which he brought a touch of eccentric brilliance.

This represents only the cream of the talent that was available to Disney in the mid-thirties. The Studio had expanded

(SUPER-SPEED ACTION →) 26 28

Mickey's Service Station

This was the last Mickey Mouse cartoon to be made in black-and-white. Pegleg Pete, the perennial villain, brings his car in for a check-up because he has been hearing a squeak. Mickey, Donald, and Goofy rip the car apart looking for the source of the offending noise. It turns out to be a cricket which has concealed itself in the vehicle, but our heroes do not discover this until the car has been reduced to wreckage.

A typical enough plot, it affords all the main characters ample opportunity to display their usual foibles. Mickey is doggedly persistent in an ineffectual sort of way, Goofy is characteristically incompetent, and Donald's propensity for rage is tempered only by his latent cowardice. Pete is as nasty as ever and receives his inevitable comeuppance

The Band Concert

Generally recognized as one of the classics of Disney animation, *The Band Concert* was the first Mickey Mouse cartoon to be made in Technicolor. Mickey is discovered in the park of a small Midwestern town, directing an orchestra through a program of popular classics. He embarks on a spirited version of *The William Tell Overture,* but several factors conspire to disrupt the performance. A roving bee creates an irritating distraction for Mickey and his musicians. Worse still, Donald Duck, in the guise of a street vendor, again and again leads the orchestra astray by playing "Turkey in the Straw" on an unending succession of fifes which are concealed about his person. Mickey, understandably outraged, destroys these instruments one by one, but the Duck seems to have an inexhaustible supply.

As the orchestra approaches the storm section of the *Overture,* a more serious problem arises. A tornado, which seems to have been conjured up by the music, approaches the town. The twister picks up the entire orchestra—along with Donald, a farm house, and assorted vegetation—sending everyone and everything spinning in the air. Mickey doggedly continues to conduct his musicians, even as he and they are tossed about like leaves. He holds the performance together by sheer will power, and the piece comes to a rousing finale, with musicians hanging from trees and anything else that has been left standing. Mickey's triumph is ruined, however, when a fife appears from a fallen tuba and the film ends on Donald's impertinent rendition of "Turkey in the Straw."

It is interesting that the Duck plays this particular tune, which was Mickey's theme in *Steamboat Willie.* It is almost as if this signifies that the Duck has taken over the role of mischief-maker which Mickey has outgrown

considerably and was continuing to grow as Disney prepared for his next great project, a feature-length animated movie. Within a year or so, most of the major talent would be transferred to full-time work on this, but there was a brief period during which it was all distilled into the limited format of the one-reel cartoon short. The result was an astonishing outburst of concentrated energy and invention in a group of little comedies that compare in quality with the Chaplin shorts of the 1914–17 period.

During 1935, Disney released eighteen cartoons. At least half of them are gems. A good deal of valuable visual material has survived from this period, and this chapter is illustrated with story continuity drawings and other art work relating to six of these movies. Four of them (*The Cookie Carnival, Music Land, Who Killed Cock Robin?* and *Broken Toys*) are Silly Symphonies. *Mickey's Service Station* was the last Mouse cartoon to be produced in black-and-white; *The Band Concert* was the first to be made in color.

Each of these six cartoons generated its own very special atmosphere and exploited it to the hilt. What all of them have in common is that they are jam-packed with action, imagination, and wit.

Mickey Mouse and
Mary Pickford

4 Hyperion Days

On January 12, 1936, the *New York Times* published an interview headlined "H.G. Wells in Close Up." The author of *The Invisible Man* and *The History of Mr. Polly* had a few comments to make about the film industry. "Many do not realize that all Hollywood studios are so busy that they keep very much to themselves. Consequently, Chaplin never visited the Disney studios. Imagine, Charlie and Walt Disney, those two geniuses, never met! I took Charlie there. Disney has the most marvelous machinery and does the most interesting experiments. Like Chaplin he is a good psychologist and both do the only thing in film today that remains international."

Four days after the *Times* story, on January 16, René Clair was reported by the New York *Journal* as saying that the outstanding figures in the movies at that time were Charlie Chaplin and Walt Disney. "The reason is," he explained, "that they have no outside interference. They act as their own producer, director, and even attend to their own stories and musical scores. Their artistry is sublime."

Two months later, on March 13, the Tulsa *Tribune* quoted Thornton Wilder as telling a lecture audience, "The two presiding geniuses of the movies are Walt Disney and Charlie Chaplin." Ten days after that, Mary Pickford told a reporter for the

Walt Disney with Will Rogers   Disney with the Barrymores

Boston *Post*, "There is only one Walt Disney.... He is the greatest producer the industry has ever turned out."

On May 25, the New York *Journal* carried some outspoken opinions expressed by the composer Jerome Kern. "Cartoonist Walt Disney," said Kern, "has made the 20th century's only important contribution to music. Disney has made use of music as language. In the synchronization of humorous episodes with humorous music, he has unquestionably given us the outstanding contribution of our time. In fact I would go so far as to say it is the only real contribution."

Harper's Bazaar, dated November 1 of that same year, printed an article titled "Boom Shot of Hollywood" by Janet Flanner (better known as "Genet"—Paris correspondent for the *New Yorker*). "Certainly the sanest spot in Hollywood," she observed, "is that studio exclusively devoted to the creation of delicate deliriums and lovely lunacies—the fun factory of Mickey Mouse, Miss Minnie and Mr. Walt Disney, Incorporated. Visitors are rarely admitted. Withdrawn to a safe distance from the rest of the movie maelstrom, the Disney plant is remotely located in one of those endless suburban settings of Barcelona bungalows, pink roses and red filling stations that makes southern California so picturesque. The studio looks like a small municipal kindergarten with green grass for the children to keep off of and, on the roof, a gigantic glorious figure of Mickey to show them the best way.... With hysteria the seeming law for movie making, it's a wonder Mickey and Silly Symphonies succeed in this world at all, since the place where they're made is as sensible as a post office. Law and order reign there, without

Disney with Stan Laurel and
Oliver Hardy

seeming unattractive, side by side with Minnie, Madam Clara
Cluck, Donald Duck and Elmer the Elephant who, all Rabelai-
sian in spots but solidly moral at heart, are doubtless easier to
get along with than the other big stars in the movie game."

Disney, then, did not lack for influential admirers, and the
list could easily be extended. Toscanini, for example, saw *The
Band Concert* six times and invited its producer to visit Italy.
Sergei Eisenstein, the greatest of Soviet directors, pronounced
Mickey Mouse America's most original contribution to culture.

Mickey, though still a star, was rapidly becoming a symbol, representing some concept of comedy that was to all appearances universal. In 1934 Harold Butcher, New York correspondent for the London *Daily Herald*, had written, "After a quick
trip around the world . . . I have returned to New York to say
that Mickey Mouse has been with me most of the way. On the
Pacific, in Japan and China, at Manchouli—suspended precar-
iously between Siberia and Manchukuo . . . "

From England, in 1935, came the report that the Queen
and the Duchess of York had selected Mickey Mouse chinaware
as gifts for six hundred children. That same year, Mickey Mouse
cartoons were used to test RCA's television system and the
League of Nations voted its approval of Mickey.

The Disney merchandising operation was by now a
multimillion-dollar enterprise. The *American Exporter* informed
its readers that, "beside the 80 licensees in the U.S. who are
manufacturing merchandise bearing the likeness of Mickey
Mouse or some other of the Walt Disney characters, there are
15 in Canada, 40 in England, 80 on the European continent and
15 in Australia. Kay Kamen, Inc., representing Walt Disney
Enterprises, has branch offices in Toronto, London, Paris, Copenhagen, Milan, Barcelona, Lisbon, and Sidney.

"U.S. exporting manufacturers who are now exporting merchandise under Walt Disney license include Hickok belts, Lionel
electric toys, Ingersoll watches, Dennison paper goods, Seiber-
ling latex rubber dolls and Oak toy balloons.

"England is making a Mickey Mouse marmalade. Other
products include cutlery, soap, playing cards, candy, bridge
favors, wristwatches, toothbrushes, socks, shoes, garters, slip-
pers, umbrellas, hot water bottles, lamps and sheets."

The same publication estimated that exports of Disney li-
censed products would exceed $5,000,000 for 1935. The New
York *Telegraph* reported that total sales were up to $35,000,000
a year. Cartier offered a diamond bracelet bearing the likeness
of Mickey for a mere $1,150. More significantly, both Lionel
trains and Ingersoll watches were virtually saved from bankrupt-

126

cy by their Disney franchises (2,000,000 Mickey Mouse watches were sold in a single eight-week period).

Donald was by now seriously challenging Mickey's pre-eminence and, when the Studio announced his first birthday, the *New York Times* devoted a serious editorial to the growing popularity of the irascible duck, wondering if he might not replace Mickey in our affections. Dozens of other papers echoed the question.

As for Disney himself, he was learning to field the questions that come with fame. Always he was suitably modest. "I do not draw, write music or contribute most of the gags and ideas seen in our pictures today," he told the *Times*. "My work is largely to supervise, to select and shape material, to coordinate and direct the efforts of our staff."

Another reporter asked Disney how it felt to be a celebrity. "It feels fine," he replied, "when being a celebrity helps get a choice reservation for a football game.... As far as I can remember, being a celebrity has never helped me make a good picture, or a good shot in a polo game, or command the obe-

Thru the Mirror, 1936, is a witty improvisation on one of the Lewis Carroll themes that had fascinated Disney since the time of the Alice Comedies. Dick Lundy's animation drawings for a sequence in which Mickey impersonates Fred Astaire show clearly how flexible Mickey's body had become

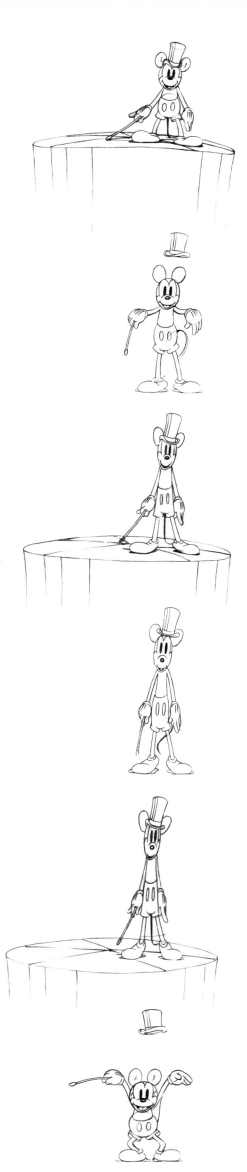

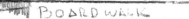

Moving Day, 1936, provides Goofy with some of his finest moments, pitting him against a piano with a mind of its own. This sequence, animated by Art Babbitt, is a sustained and inspired piece of nonsense. Comedy is distilled from the situation with a close regard for character that would have been unthinkable even two or three years earlier

dience of my daughter, or impress my wife. It doesn't even seem to help keep fleas off our dogs and, if being a celebrity won't give one an advantage over a couple of fleas, then I guess there can't be that much in being a celebrity after all."

So much for Disney the public figure, but what of Disney the man? How did his colleagues see him?

Jack Cutting recalls that Disney seemed mature beyond his years and, at times, very serious. "I always felt his personality was a little bit like a drop of mercury rolling around on a slab of marble because he changed moods so quickly. I believe this was because he was extremely sensitive. . . . He could grasp your ideas and interpret your thought rapidly. You didn't have to give Walt a five-page memo—he understood the point right away. . . .

"Although Walt could exude great charm if he was in the mood, he could also be dour and indifferent toward people—but this was usually because he was preoccupied by problems. Sometimes you would pass him in the hall, say hello, and he would not even notice you. The next time he might greet you warmly and start talking about a new project he was excited about. You

Moving Day also presents Mickey with a number of problems, including a struggle with a trunk that will not stay closed

Moose Hunters, 1937, presents Mickey, Donald, and Goofy in a series of typically disastrous confrontations with wildlife

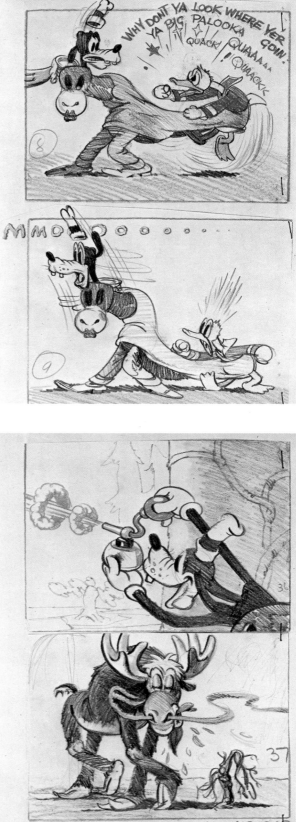

Mickey's Amateurs, 1937,
offers a blend of entertainment
and near catastrophe

Pluto co-starred in such movies as
The Beach Picnic and *Society Dog Show*,
both released in 1939.
The top drawing is by Fred Moore

Top: *Mickey's Circus*, 1936, presented Mickey in a role that was a natural for him—the ringmaster. Right: a Fred Moore study for *The Brave Little Tailor*, 1938. Bottom: a scene from *A Gentleman's Gentleman*, 1941. For a brief period during the early forties, Mickey was given ears that worked in perspective

might not understand what he was talking about at first, because he didn't always give you a preamble on the subject. If you didn't pick up on his chain of thought quickly, he would sometimes look at you as though you were slow-witted, because when he was excited about an idea it was clear to him and he assumed it was to everyone else.

"The people who worked best with Walt were those who were stimulated by his enthusiasm. . . . More than once, when he was in a creative mood and ideas were popping out like skyrockets, I have suddenly seen him look as if he had been hit in the face with a bucket of cold water. The eyebrow would go up and suddenly reality was the mood in the room. Someone in the group was out of tune with the creative spirit he was generating. Then he would say it was difficult to work with so-and-so."

These creative moods were often exercised at the "sweatbox" sessions which were so essential a part of the Studio routine (the projection rooms at Hyperion Avenue were not air-conditioned—hence the name sweatbox). As soon as a sequence was animated and shot as a pencil test, it would be run in one of these projection rooms. Disney would be in attendance along with animators, story men, the director, and anyone else directly concerned (sometimes people from outside the production team would be invited in to give a layman's opinion). The sequence under consideration would be subjected to an intensive analysis in an effort to see if it could be improved in any way before it was sent off to the inking and painting department. Sometimes, instead of pencil tests, it would be a "Leica reel" that would be under consideration. The Leica reel (another Disney innovation) provided a way of projecting story continuity drawings in synchronization with whatever part of the sound track had been prerecorded, thus giving at least a rough idea of how the final movie might look and sound. In any case, Disney would always lead these discussions and generally had valuable contributions to make.

"He always had the answers," says Dick Huemer. "He would go right to the middle of the problem and there would be this nugget that he'd pull out. Damnedest thing! You'd kick yourself and say, 'Why didn't I see it? There it is!' But he had an instinct for it, and I think the instinct was based on the fact that he always considered the common man's viewpoint. . . . Aside from his genius, he was just a down-to-earth guy."

Marc Davis is one of the many Disney artists who has emphasized his employer's readiness to gamble everything on an idea as one of the key factors in the growth of the Studio. "He

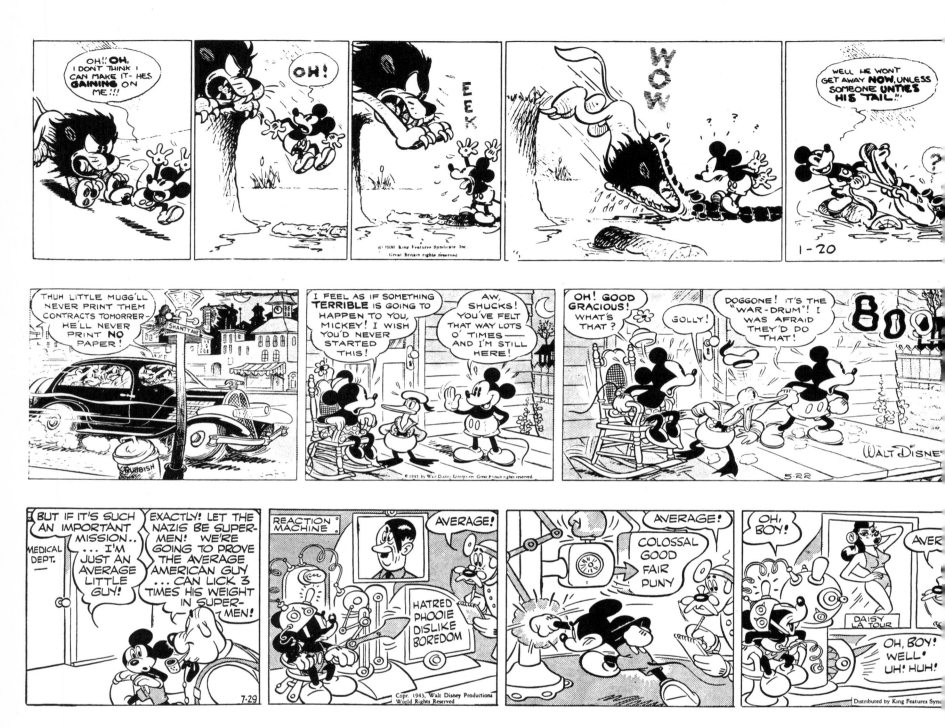

was not afraid to risk every penny, go into hock, hire 150 people and wonder how he was going to meet the payroll. He did this all his life. He felt money is good only because of what you can do with it. Without him, I can't see animation having become much of a business because, for the most part, the other studios were either followers or they were just filling up programs. Almost anything they did that was half-way good was acceptable. But Walt was trying to make a little jewel out of each one of these things."

Of course, if you were a young and inexperienced animator you were not privy to the vital sweatbox conferences. "Word would

The Mickey Mouse daily comic strip was launched in January of 1930. The first eighteen episodes were drawn by Ub Iwerks. Win Smith took over from him but was replaced, in April of that same year, by Floyd Gottfredson, who has drawn the strip ever since. The first example shown here, top left, is from the original Iwerks set. The others, dating from 1935, 1943, 1949, 1960, and 1970, are all by Gottfredson

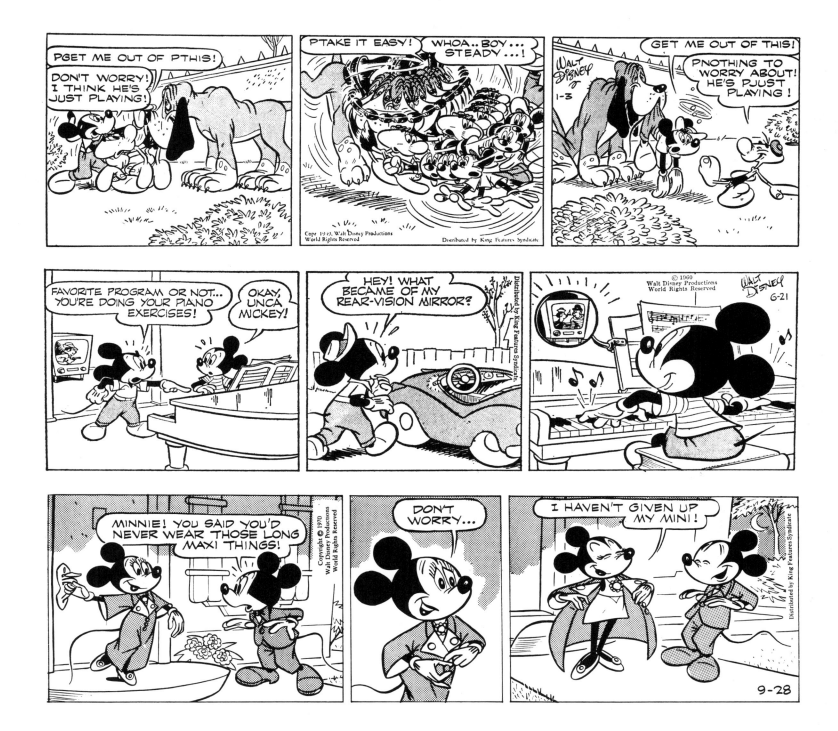

dribble down to you," Frank Thomas remembers, "that someone had decided to do such-and-such to your scene. Milt Kahl and I once wrote a song—'If I Should Die, Please Bury Me in Sweatbox Four'—because that's where all the big meetings were held and then we could find out what was going on."

Young artists joining the Studio usually started by learning to do in-between drawings. Ward Kimball remembers that the Studio was still a small place in those days. "The in-betweening department was down in the semibasement. . . . We called it the bullpen and in the summer you had to strip to the waist, it was so damn hot. . . . By five o'clock I was always exhausted. . . . I would get on a Big Red streetcar and, on those hot summer

Studying penguins as an aid to animation: standing, left to right, Walt Disney, Albert Hurter, Leigh Harline, Frenchy de Trémaudan, Clyde Geronimi, Paul Hopkins (behind Geronimi), Hugh Hennesy, Art Babbitt, Norm Ferguson, and Bill Roberts. Seated, Dick Huemer and Wilfred Jackson

Frank Churchill conducts a recording session. Disney and Wilfred Jackson are seated at the extreme left. The clarinetist to Churchill's left is Pinto Colvig

Ted Sears

Disney listens as three members of
his story team display their versatility:
Webb Smith, piano; Ted Sears, violin;
and Pinto Colvig

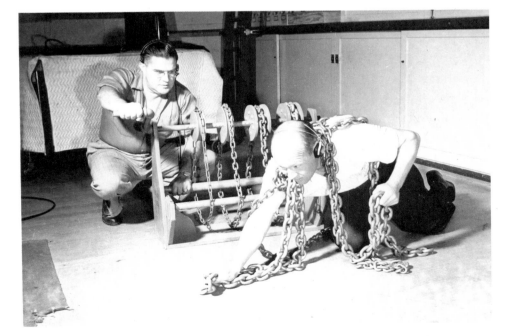

Jim MacDonald and Ed Forrest
record sound effects

Above: a pastel drawing for *Water Babies,* 1935. Opposite, top: a scene from *Cock of the Walk,* 1935, a Silly Symphony which includes clever parodies of Hollywood dance routines. Opposite, bottom: a story continuity sketch for *Toby Tortoise Returns,* the 1936 sequel to *The Tortoise and the Hare*

evenings, I sometimes would fall asleep leaning on the window and watching the loose screws twist in and out of the wooden window frames."

It was not every night, however, that an in-betweener could leave work at five o'clock. Apart from the overtime—which seems to have been plentiful—there were also art classes, which had become an integral part of the Studio schedule. As far back as 1931, Disney had decided that his artists would benefit from further training, and he arranged for some of them to take an evening class at the Chouinard Art School (Les Clark recalls that, since not all of them had cars, Disney himself would often drive them to school). The class these Disney artists attended was taught by a young man named Don Graham, who was soon to have an important role in the Disney organization. Graham remembers that for most of the school year 1931–32 he worked one night a week with a group of about fifteen Disney artists in his regular class.

"Walt, of course, picked up the tab. In the fall of 1932, Art Babbitt, one of the top animators at the Studio, convinced Walt that instead of sending his men across town to Chouinard,

Several Disney shorts exploited caricature, but Will Rogers had to be taken out of *Mickey's Polo Game*, 1936, after his death in a plane crash

Mother Goose Goes Hollywood, 1938, includes portraits of Groucho Marx, Katharine Hepburn, Laurel and Hardy and W.C. Fields

it would be far wiser to conduct classes at the Studio, where there could be more control of attendance.

"On November 15, 1932, the great Disney Art School was born in the old sound studio at Hyperion. First it was just two evenings a week, with some twenty or thirty men each evening. In a matter of three or four weeks, it became necessary to divide these classes. Phil Dike was called in and between us we worked these two evenings a week until 1934. During this period James Patrick, a talented young artist, was also employed for a few months as a teacher. The attendance during these two years averaged better than fifty men a session. . . .

"In 1934, the nature of the school changed its character completely. Dike was put in charge of the color coordination of all production work which went through Technicolor. . . . I was employed on a three-day and two-night basis. During the first year of this period I was trained in the sweatboxes under the direct critical eye of Walt and the directors. The evening school was put on a five-evening-a-week schedule. Eugene Fleury and Palmer Schoppe filled in the evening schedule with me. A new training department was instituted in the daytime. . . .

"At about this time, Walt announced his intention of making *Snow White*, which implied a vast expansion of the animation department. Early in 1935, he came to me and said, 'I need three hundred artists—get them.' And thus began a huge campaign of recruitment. Ads in all the newspapers up and down the West Coast, then on a national basis, and even opening up an office in the RCA building in New York City, where I spent three months looking at portfolios. . . .

"When the new training department was instituted, in

1934–35, the new employees were brought into the Studio in small groups, usually a dozen or so at a time. They were given from six to eight weeks to demonstrate their potential. . . . Usually I would work with them the first two weeks, every day, eight hours a day, utilizing a human model. Then their day would be devoted a half day to drawing, a half day to production problems. They were also encouraged to attend the evening school, which soon became extremely active, with a nightly attendance of about 150. Under George Drake's supervision, many authorities on various aspects of animation, drawing of characters, layout and background problems, et cetera, were called in to lecture and instruct."

Typical of the kind of instructional material used was a book assembled by Ted Sears and Fred Moore. This contained model sheets, indicating how the main characters should be drawn, photographs of humans and animals in action poses, and detailed analyses of the personalities of Mickey, Donald, Goofy, and Pluto. The following, written by Sears, is a typical example:

"Mickey is not a clown . . . he is neither silly nor dumb.

"His comedy depends entirely upon the situation he is placed in.

"His age varies with the situation . . . sometimes his character is that of a young boy, and at other times, as in the adventure type of picture, he appears quite grown up. . . .

"Mickey is most amusing when in a serious predicament trying to accomplish some purpose under difficulties, or against time. . . . When Mickey is working under difficulties, the laughs occur at the climax of each small incident or action. They depend largely upon Mickey's expression, position, attitude, state of mind, etc., and the graphic way that these things are shown. . . .

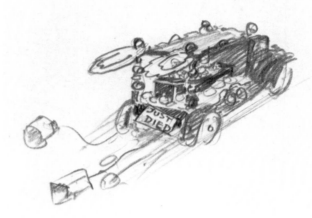

Leda and the duck

Albert Hurter's contributions to
specific movies have already been mentioned,
but he spent much of his time producing
casual drawings like these—
drawings which would be circulated
among directors, story men,
and animators on the chance that
they might spark an idea for a gag
or even for an entire cartoon

A title card for the 1935 cartoon *On Ice*, top,
and a background painting for *Mickey's Fire Brigade*,
also released that year

Many fine artists—Charles Philippi, Hugh Hennesy, Tom Codrick,
and others—made layout drawings for Disney during the thirties.
Their work often displays a high standard of draftsmanship,
as in these examples from a 1935 release, *Mickey's Garden,* opposite,
and from *Thru the Mirror*

Clock Cleaners

Mickey, Donald, and Goofy worked against these spectacular backgrounds
in a 1937 short, *Clock Cleaners*

Three Blind Mouseketeers

Pan shots—takes in which the action moves across a
panoramic background—necessitated elongated paintings like this one
for *Three Blind Mouseketeers*, 1936

150

"Mickey is seldom funny in a chase picture, as his character and expressions are usually lost."

Before giving hints on how to draw the Mouse, Fred Moore adds his own thoughts on Mickey's personality:

"Mickey seems to be the average young boy of no particular age; living in a small town, clean living, fun loving, bashful around girls, polite and clever as he must be for the particular story. In some pictures he has a touch of Fred Astaire, in others of Charlie Chaplin, and some of Douglas Fairbanks, but in all of these there should be some of the young boy."

Moore's drawing hints include the following suggestions:

"The body to be drawn as somewhat pear-shape, fairly short and plump.... The body should be pliable at all times.... If Mickey were taking a deep breath we would give him a chest. If he were sad, we would loosen chest and droop shoulders, etc. The body should be thought of as having a certain volume, so when it is stretched it should grow thinner....

"The shoes are fairly large and bulky—a medium between hard and soft—flexible enough to help animation, but stiff enough to be shoes.... Mickey is cuter when drawn with small

Background paintings for *Modern Inventions*, top left and right,
and for two other 1937 cartoons, *Pluto's Quinpuplets* and *Don Donald*,
the latter of which was Donald's first solo vehicle

shoulders, with a suggestion of stomach and fanny—and I like him pigeon-toed."

Moore added some suggestions to be kept in mind when drawing Minnie:

"Minnie seems cuter with her skirts high on her body— showing a large expanse of her lace panties. This skirt should be starched and not hang loose.... Her mouth could be smaller than Mickey's and maybe never open into so wide a smile, take, expression, etc. Her eyelids and eyelashes could help very much in keeping her feminine as well as the skirt swaying from the body on different poses, displaying pants. Carrying the little finger in an extended position also helps."

Clearly, these hints are rather elementary and were intended mainly for the recruits being processed by Don Graham's training program. The fact that so much critical attention was being lavished on these apprentices did not mean, however, that the senior animators were being ignored. Their work was always subject to the appraisal of Walt Disney himself. He had, some time earlier, instituted the practice of issuing credit ratings on many of the cartoons. These would be sent to the director and to each of the animators. Individual scenes would be rated "A," "B Plus," and so on, and these ratings would be accompanied by extensive comments in which Disney indicated where and how he thought each sequence could have been improved.

In December, 1935, credit ratings were issued for a Silly Symphony titled *Cock of the Walk*. This film was directed by Ben Sharpsteen, to whom Disney addressed the following remarks:

"The direction is fine from a technical standpoint. Some of the technical scenes and setups were well planned but the direction of the action is very poor from a personality and interest-building angle. The main fault with the story lies with the director and the story men. Without a doubt the animators would have gotten a better result if the story had been properly worked out and if the director had taken the story and treated it from a fantastic comical angle . . . instead of having so many scenes that paralleled human actions."

The following are extracts from some of the comments aimed at animators who worked on this film:

"The actions, as they were given by the director, have been carried out, but the true spirit of the character of the hens is lacking. Instead of waddling, they run. There are certain things which, if handled properly, would have made the action typical of a humanized hen and would have expressed more personality and interest to the audience...."

Backgrounds for some 1938 shorts:
Polar Trappers, above and opposite top,
Boat Builders, far right center and bottom,
and *Ferdinand the Bull*

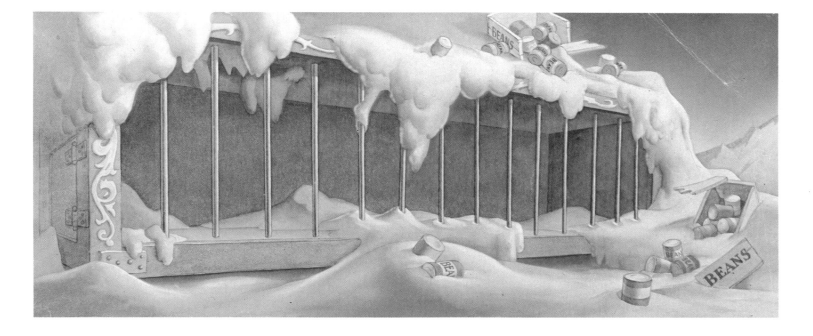

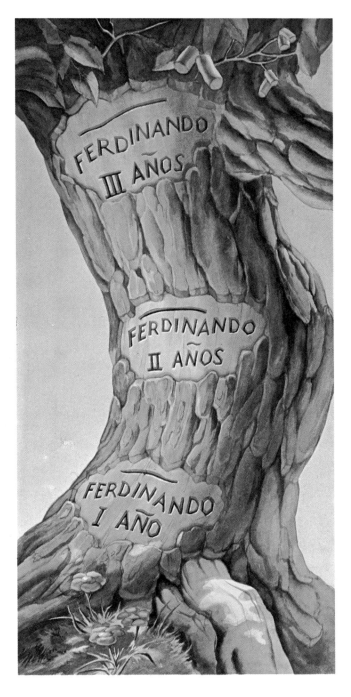

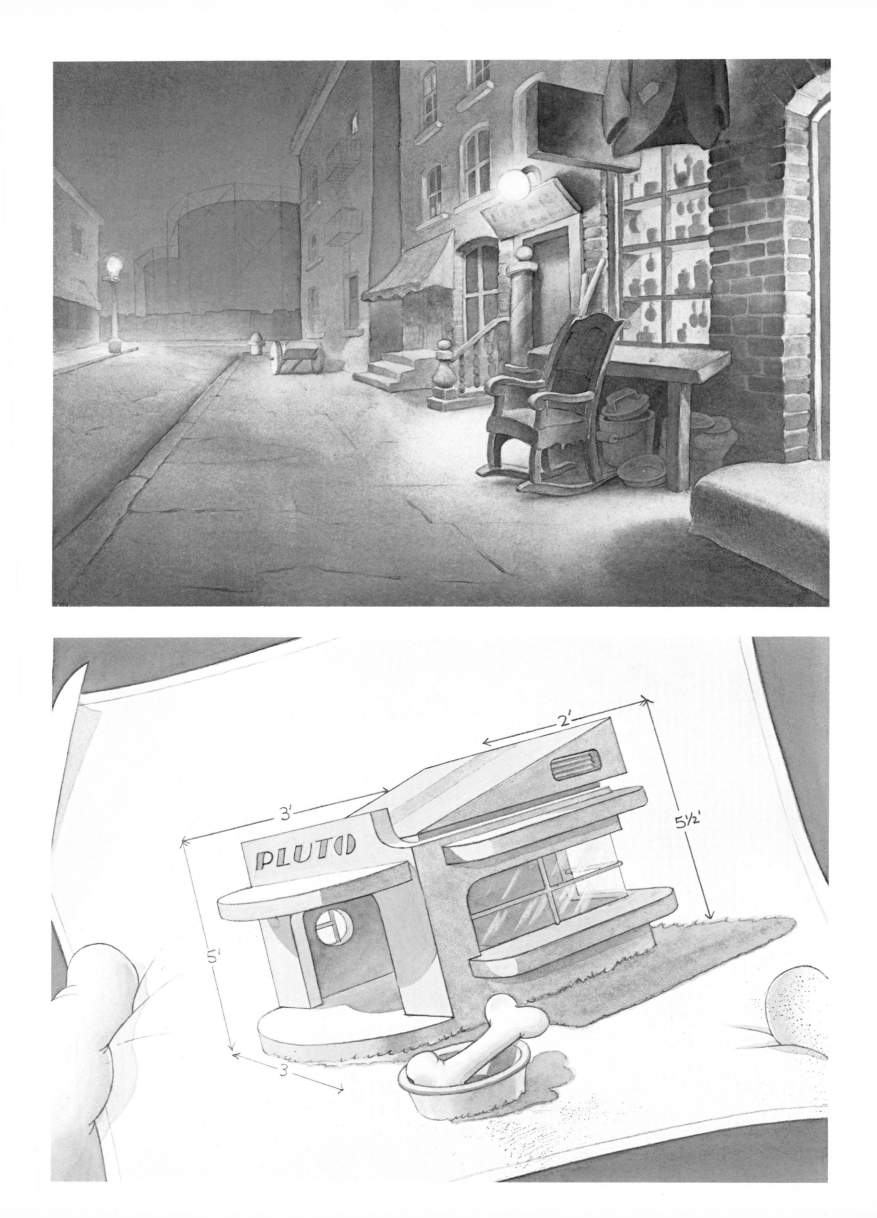

Caricature was practically
a way of life at the Studio.
Above is T. Hee's version
of Norm Ferguson

Aurie Battaglia's caricature of
layout artist Ken O'Connor

Walt Kelly, of *Pogo* fame, was a Disney
artist for several years. In this drawing he
portrays, left to right, an invented character,
himself, Ward Kimball, and Fred Moore

◄ Paintings for a 1939 release,
Donald's Lucky Day, and
for *Pluto's Dream House*, 1940

"I would suggest that you concentrate more on caricature, with action; not merely the drawing of a character to look like something, but giving your character the movements and actions of the person you are trying to put over. Remember, every action should be based on what that character represents. . . .

"Something was started in this scene which is what we are striving for. This is doing things in the dance which humans are unable to do. I mean the pullet on the rooster's muscles and the juggling from side to side, but it was passed over before we had a chance to build it up into anything funny."

Seen today, *Cock of the Walk*, with its brilliant parodies of Busby Berkeley dance routines, seems one of the best cartoons of its period. In view of this, the severity of Disney's remarks seems extraordinary, but we must keep in mind the fact that he was trying to make each one of these films into a little jewel. He believed in pushing his animators as far as he would push himself. We should note, too, that he was by 1935 deeply involved in planning *Snow White* and was, therefore, very concerned with establishing the standards that would be required to make a success of his first animated feature.

Considering the level of activity maintained at the Studio, it is amazing that anyone found any time for leisure. In fact, a nearby vacant lot provided Disney employees with a suitable

By the late thirties, Donald had
all but eclipsed Mickey in popularity.
Examples here are from two 1938 shorts,
Donald's Golf Game, top, and *The Fox Hunt*, center.
At bottom is one from the following year,
Donald's Cousin Gus

Donald's Nephews, 1938, introduced
the indefatigable Huey, Dewey, and Louie

After a cartoon was completed, ▶
story continuity drawings were stapled into books—
often with surprising results.
This group from *Fire Chief*, 1940,
gives a marvelous sense of movement

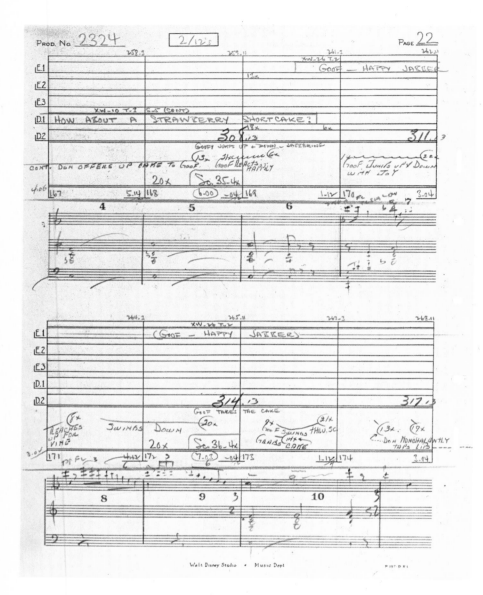

playing field for softball games, which, with volleyball, became popular lunchtime activities. Disney seldom joined in these sports but, apparently because of his friendship with Spencer Tracy, he did take up polo.

Jack Cutting, who played with him, recalls that he went about taking up polo by first finding out who at the Studio could ride a horse. He then hired Captain Gil Proctor, formerly a cavalry officer and a member of the Army team, to coach his recruits. After some reading and blackboard instruction, they began to practice on a field in the San Fernando Valley. At first practice was held two mornings a week, very early, so that everyone could be at the Studio by 8 A.M. In the summer there were further sessions after work, and then serious competition on weekends. Initially the play was between two Studio teams, but eventually Walt and Roy (who also played) bought a string of

Some idea of the complexity of making an animated film can be gathered from these "bar sheets," which govern the entire sound track of a movie, showing exactly where every accent should fall. At different times they have taken different forms, but this example is quite representative.

Above each bar, the film footage is noted, providing a convenient general reference. The three upper staves—E1, E2, E3—are devoted to instructions for the three effects tracks. Immediately below these—D1 and D2—are staves carrying the words to be spoken on the two dialogue tracks. A description of the action that will be seen on screen occupies the center section, along with scene numbers and other material, while the music is transcribed onto the lower half of each bar sheet

CU: Don looks down at chair; looks o.s. to
right, goes into double take.

Left, top: *Donald's Lucky Day,* 1939;
bottom: *The Autograph Hound,* 1939;
above: *Donald's Vacation,* 1940

Goofy in *Mickey's Amateurs*, 1937

A 1939 cartoon, *Goofy and Wilbur,* above,
was the Goof's first solo outing.
Later he starred in a series of comic instructional
films such as *The Art of Self Defense,* 1941,
top right, and *How to Swim,* 1942

SCENE 17 - Goof enters gym thru door, broad
shouldered, wears towel wrapped around head,
bathrobe on. Removes three bathrobes, last
one on coat hanger, and towel, is disclosed
with narrow shoulders, etc.

The Studio polo teams: Walt Disney's team
in the light jerseys, Roy's in the dark

At the old Riviera Polo Grounds:
Walter Wanger, left, and Walt Disney,
right, 1934 or 1935

Left to right, Spencer Tracy, Walt Disney,
James Gleason, and Frank Borzage

Spencer Tracy and Walt Disney

quality ponies and began to play with Tracy, Will Rogers, and
others in the movie colony.

Aside from family life, polo seems to have been Disney's
only form of recreation at that time. The Disney family, like
the Disney Studio, was growing. By 1936, Disney had two
daughters—Diane and Sharon.

II
FEATURE
ANIMATION

5 Snow White:

The First Feature

The initial success of Mickey Mouse and the Silly Symphonies did not satisfy Disney for long, and as early as 1934 he began to think seriously about making a feature-length animated film. Two important considerations prompted him to this line of thought. One was a question of simple economics, namely that no matter how successful the short cartoons were, they could never make very much money. They might share billing with the main feature—they often did—but film rental was determined by running time, not popularity, so the revenue from these shorts would always be limited. Beyond this, Disney was anxious for an opportunity to work within an expanded format—a structure that would allow for more elaborate and leisurely character development, that would give him a chance to evolve more complex plot ideas and greater naturalism. In 1926, Max Fleischer had made a five-and-a-half-reel cartoon titled *Einstein's Theory of Relativity*, but nobody had made an animated feature that could compete on equal terms with live-action pictures, and most people in the industry thought that to do so successfully would be virtually impossible. After all, the reasoning went, the kind of cartoon antics that can make us laugh for seven or eight minutes would become very boring if we were exposed to them for eighty or ninety minutes at a time. Disney

Before embarking on their first feature-length film, Disney artists needed experience in animating the human figure. A 1934 Silly Symphony, *The Goddess of Spring,* was designed to test their skills in this area. Meanwhile, rough versions of characters for *Snow White* began to appear at the Studio

was, as usual, at least one jump ahead, and had no intention
of merely extending his established gag routines to fit into a
larger format. He was planning to take a fairy story and bring
it to the screen with a kind of magical realism that was beyond
the reach of live-action movies.

As everyone knows, the story Disney chose for his first feature was *Snow White and the Seven Dwarfs* (we may recall here
that the first movie he had ever seen, on a newsboys' outing in
Kansas City, was a silent version of *Snow White*). At first he
referred to his new project as the "Feature Symphony," and to
some extent it was an extension of the Silly Symphony concept,
music playing an important part in its structure. But it was
much more besides. No one can say just when Disney began to
think about *Snow White,* but by the summer of 1934 his ideas
were beginning to take concrete form. An exploratory outline,
dated August 9, includes the following discussion of the dwarfs:

> The names which follow each suggest a type of character
> and the names will immediately identify the character in
> the minds of the audience:

Scrappy	Doleful	Crabby
Happy	Wistful	Daffy
Hoppy	Soulful	Tearful
Sleepy	Helpful	Gaspy
Weepy	Bashful	Busy
Dirty	Awful	Dizzy
Cranky	Snoopy	Snappy
Sneezy	Goopy	Hotsy
Sneezy-Wheezy	Gabby	Jaunty
Hungry	Blabby	Puffy
Lazy	Silly	Strutty
Grumpy	Dippy	Biggy
Dumpy	Graceful	Biggy-Wiggy
Thrifty	Neurtsy	Biggo-Ego
Nifty	Gloomy	Jumpy
Shifty	Sappy	Chesty
Woeful	Flabby	

The same outline elaborates some of the possibilities seen for the
dwarfs:

> SLEEPY: Sterling Holloway. Falls asleep in midst of excite-
> ment, in middle of sentence, and so forth . . .

> HOPPY-JUMPY: Portrayed by Joe Twerp, the highly excita-
> ble, nervous radio comic who gets his words mixed up
> (flews nashes ry bichfield). He is in constant fear of being
> goosed but is not goosed until the last scene.

BASHFUL: Portrayed by Buelow, a unique radio personality with a very funny bashful laugh, halting delivery and very funny way of misplacing the word "though" . . .

HAPPY: Portrayed by Professor Diddleton D. Wurtle, whose wild Ben Turpin eyes are reinforced by one of the funniest tricks of speech in radio . . .

SNEEZY-WHEEZY—GASPY: Asthmatic inhalations and exhalations of every breath. . . . Dapper . . . nimble dancer—quick movements stopped in midair by embryonic sneeze. . . . Always trying nutty cures and diets . . .

BIGGY-WIGGY—BIGGO-EGO: Portrayed by Eddie Holden, in his character of Hipplewater. A pompous, oily-tongued know-it-all . . .

AWFUL: The most lovable and interesting of the dwarf characters. He steals and drinks and is very dirty . . .

These ideas were probably dictated by Disney. Anyone familiar with *Snow White* will realize that the dwarfs were destined to go through many changes before they reached the screen, but we can see that certain characteristics were already beginning to take shape (we should point out that not all the performers named in these descriptions contributed to the eventual movie—but they did provide Disney with a concise way of describing a personality). This early manuscript also lists a number of possible songs for the film—including "Some Day My Prince Will Come"—indicating that a good deal of thought had already been devoted to this aspect of the subject. The outline differs from the final version in a number of ways so that, for example, Snow

BASHFUL DWARF ALWAYS TYING BEARD IN KNOTS—SNOW WHITE UNTIES IT FOR HIM—

As *Snow White* went into production, Disney artists were asked how they thought the dwarfs might look and behave. These sketches are representative of the suggestions they made

White is envisaged passing through a whole sequence of enchanted places before the woodland animals lead her to the dwarfs' cottage. These include the Morass of Monsters and the Valley of the Dragons, which are self-explanatory, as well as Upsidedownland or Backwardland (where birds fly tail first and trees have their roots in the air) and Sleepy Valley ("vast poppy fields, slumbrous music from the wind soughing through the trees"). The Queen is described as being "stately, beautiful in the way of a Benda mask." We are told that she is cool and serene. Only in her emotional climaxes does she erupt to full fury (a note in parentheses urges study of Charles Laughton in *The Barretts of Wimpole Street*).

Another outline, this one dated October 22, 1934, includes a complete breakdown of the cast of characters. We can see from this how quickly things were beginning to develop:

SNOW WHITE: Janet Gaynor type—14 years old.

THE PRINCE: Doug Fairbanks type—18 years old.

THE QUEEN: A mixture of Lady Macbeth and the Big Bad Wolf—Her beauty is sinister, mature, plenty of curves—She becomes ugly and menacing when scheming and mixing her poisons—Magic fluids transform her into an old witchlike hag—Her dialogue and action are overdramatic, verging on the ridiculous.

THE HUNTSMAN: A minor character—Big and tough—40 years old—The Queen's trusted henchman but hasn't the heart to murder an innocent girl . . .

PRINCE'S HORSE: This gallant white charger understands but cannot talk—like Tom Mix's horse Tony—The Prince's pal.

MAGIC MIRROR: The Queen's unwilling slave—Its masklike face appears when invoked—It speaks in weird voice.

This outline also includes another set of descriptions of the dwarfs—not dissimilar to the earlier one except that the names have become more settled. Already they include Happy, Sleepy, Doc, Bashful, and Grumpy. Sneezy has been temporarily ousted by Jumpy, and Dopey has yet to be christened.

By the fall of 1934, then, the cast was already pretty well established in Disney's mind. A story team was being built up, and we may presume that Albert Hurter and Joe Grant were beginning to work on character design. Very soon more detailed outlines began to circulate—mimeographed sheets that dealt with specific scenes and situations. These kept everyone in touch with progress and doubled as invitations to submit ideas and gags that would contribute to the development of the plot.

For the cartoon shorts Disney had introduced a bonus system whereby anyone suggesting a gag that was used in a picture received five dollars and anyone providing an idea that formed

the basis for an entire cartoon received a hundred dollars. This system was adapted to the new situation and an outline dated November 2, 1934, includes the notation, "We shall distribute, from time to time, various sequences and situations to be gagged up as the story develops.... The following sequences between Snow White and the dwarfs are now open for ALL POSSIBLE SUGGESTIONS AND GAGS."

Parts of the plot had already taken recognizable shape, as the following extracts show:

> Snow White is going through the woods alone, discovers the home of the Seven Little Dwarfs, who are all away working in a mine—digging for gold and jewels. OPPORTUNITIES OFFER THEMSELVES HERE AS TO HOW SNOW WHITE MIGHT BE LED TO THE HOUSE BY BIRDS. *SUGGEST TYPE OF HOUSE YOU SEE THE DWARFS LIVING IN* . . .
>
> Snow White proceeds to straighten up the house. We show her picking garments off the floor, making beds, washing the dishes. THE BIRDS MIGHT HELP. THEY COULD BRING IN FLOWERS AND VASES, CARRY OUT COBWEBS FROM THE CEILING OR RAFTERS. *SOME GOOD GAGS COULD BE USED HERE TO SHOW SNOW WHITE AND THE BIRDS BUSY FIXING UP THE HOUSE FOR THE DWARFS' RETURN* . . .
>
> All props and the interior of the house want to be of a quaint, old-time nature, such as the dwarfs would have about them. The proportion of the dwarfs to Snow White is about one-half her size, so be governed by that in using utensils, chairs, tables, and so forth. . . .

The circular continues in this vein and ends with the reminder, *"PLEASE DRAW UP ALL SUGGESTIONS AND GAGS READY FOR COLLECTION, THURSDAY, NOVEMBER 8, 1934."*

On November 19, members of the production staff received a two-page memo which was headed, "Time and general sequences of *Snow White* as described by Walt." This gives a synopsis that conforms quite closely to the version that eventually appeared on screen, diverging from the final form mostly in that it includes several episodes that were later eliminated. That same day, another circular went out, accompanied by a letter from Disney which read, in part, as follows:

> GAG OUTLINE sequence DWARFS DISCOVER SNOW WHITE.
>
> Please read through the following outline carefully. . . . Study the gag action and dialogue possibilities of each section of this sequence and try hard to give some helpful sug-

As ideas began to clarify, model sheets and puppets were prepared

gestions. If you don't like any particular section of business, *please say so* and, at the same time, try to suggest something that might be better. . . . There are good gag possibilities through this sequence — let's see if we can't make the most of it.

Thanx, Walt

What followed was a series of notes and questions relating to how the dwarfs might react to finding Snow White asleep in their house. So far as one can gather, the response to these invitations was usually enthusiastic. Someone, for instance, might come up with suggestions of possible dialogue for Doc ("You're a pot-bellied old Hop Toad" "He's a I'm a whose a belly potted old flop load—a hop todied old—a hop jellied pot pode—a jot jellied—a . . ."). Ideas were gathered and weeded out, then marshaled into some kind of usable structure. Within a matter of three or four months, *Snow White* had developed from the embryonic stage and was beginning to take shape as a viable endeavor.

The story at least was taking form. There was, however, a great deal more than story involved in a pioneering project of this kind. The Disney artists would be dealing with problems that neither they nor anyone else had confronted before.

There were, to start off with, several purely technical problems. All animation drawings up to this point had been made on sheets of paper measuring 9½ by 12 inches—layouts and backgrounds also being geared to these dimensions. The drawings were then traced and painted onto celluloid sheets of exactly the same size and sent to the camera department, along with the appropriate backgrounds. The camera could be adjusted to photograph the entire setup—minus the margins—or a small part of it if a close-up effect was required. The area to be photographed was designated as the "field" (rectangles drawn on many of the layouts illustrated in this book are indications of field size). The size of the animation paper determined the largest possible field size, which was known as "five field." As soon as production of *Snow White* got underway, it became evident that this field size would be inadequate for much of the animation involved. A scene in which Snow White was to appear with all seven dwarfs, or with fifty animals, would—if they stuck with the old animation paper—mean that each character had to be drawn on a minute scale, making the animator's task extremely difficult, if not impossible. To overcome this problem, a new field size—"six-and-a-half"—was introduced, which meant that a complete new series of animation boards, sliding

Albert Hurter's studies were vital to the concept of the story that began to emerge

The opening scenes of *Snow White* establish the movie's theme and atmosphere with great economy. The Wicked Queen, her magic mirror, the Prince, and Snow White herself—little better than a servant in her stepmother's palace (see overleaf)—are all introduced. The threat to the little princess's life is introduced without delay and made graphic by a close-up of the box in which her heart is to be placed

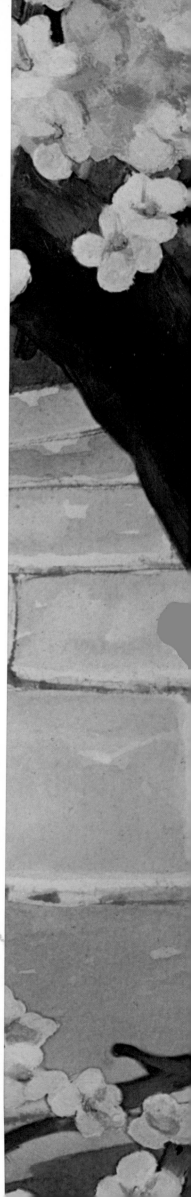

As Snow White flees into the forest, trees and fallen logs become monsters that seem to threaten her. The Disney artists tried to see the world through her frightened eyes, turning it into a nightmare

The Queen entru
of murdering Sn
however, he is
innocence and
forgiveness. Cle
angles adds to t

cel boards, checking boards, and inking and painting boards had to be designed, built, and installed; and animation cameras had to be adapted to shoot this new field size. Even so, certain long trucking shots demanded characters who would appear so small on the screen at some point that even this modification would be inadequate to the animator's needs. To get around this, a method of reducing drawings photographically was devised—a mechanical solution that allowed the artist to work on a convenient scale.

Another limitation that animation had run up against was its inability to produce a real illusion of depth. When a camera moved into a setup which consisted of a painted cel held tightly against a flat background, scale distortions were inevitable. Take, for example, a situation where a character stands in a meadow with mountains in the background. In reality, as one approaches that character he will appear to become bigger, but the mountains will remain about the same size because they are so far away. When the camera moves in on a flat representation of the same scene, both the character and the mountains will appear to increase in size at exactly the same rate. In the short cartoons this had not presented a serious problem because such situations seldom arose, and when a little distortion did creep in it was not really noticeable in the context of quick-fire gags that were sweeping the audience along; but feature films required a much greater regard for naturalism. Flat backgrounds might still be adequate for most scenes, but from time to time a real illusion of depth would be necessary. William Garity, head of the camera department, was given the job of developing a multiplane camera—one that could shoot simultaneously several layers of action and background, layers that were separated in such a way as to produce an accurate sense of depth. (At his own studio, at about the same time, Ub Iwerks was working on a similar idea.)

It is difficult to estimate exactly what kind of schedule Disney had in mind for the production of his first feature. The closing months of 1934 saw great progress in story planning, but was he ready to proceed at full speed? The indications are that the initial burst of energy was followed by a period of more cautious exploration. Technical problems could be solved—we can assume that that aspect of the project did not worry him unduly—but what about the animators? Were they ready to handle the demands that would be placed on them by a movie of this sort?

One serious consideration was that they had had very little experience in animating the human form. Toward the end of

Adriana Caselotti,
the voice of Snow White

1934, several animators were put to work on a Silly Symphony titled *The Goddess of Spring,* which retold the Greek myth of Persephone. The character of Persephone—if not exactly a prototype—was certainly conceived with Snow White in mind. Because of Don Graham's art classes, Disney artists were now better equipped to deal with human anatomy, but animating a young woman still presented great difficulties. Les Clark, one of those assigned to this project, had his sister pose for him as an aid to drawing Persephone, but he was still disappointed with the results. Disney told him not to worry, that it was unreasonable to expect immediate success with so ambitious a project. The experiments continued.

The year 1935, as we have already remarked, saw a high point in the development of animated shorts, and this must have provided the impetus to push *Snow White* into full production. The caricatures of Hollywood personalities in *Broken Toys* were highly sophisticated, and Disney is said to have been particularly happy with the way in which Jenny Wren's character was established in *Who Killed Cock Robin?* These cartoons, and others like them, indicated that the time was ripe. Disney's veteran animators were coming into their prime and younger artists were catching up fast (soon Don Graham's recruiting system would bring many talented apprentices to the Studio). Character design was well advanced by now and the animation team began to take shape. Dave Hand was assigned to the task of supervising director (which meant that he was the man responsible for seeing to it that Disney's instructions were carried out). Bill Cottrell, Wilfred Jackson, Ben Sharpsteen, Larry Morey, and Perce Pierce were named as sequence directors (each of them taking responsibility for specific sections of the movie), while Ham Luske, Bill Tytla, Fred Moore, and Norm Ferguson were made supervising animators (in charge of the quality of the actual animation). Then came the task of "casting" the artists.

We have already noted that animators think of themselves as actors, and the process of casting them for a production of this magnitude was, of course, a sensitive one. Moore, Tytla, Fred Spencer, and Frank Thomas were assigned to the dwarfs (Moore's charm and Tytla's vigor would both be needed for these characters; Spencer had a sure touch with broad comedy and Thomas was one of the most promising of the younger artists). The Queen, as she first appears, was given to Art Babbitt. After her transformation, she would be drawn by Ferguson. Three younger animators—Milt Kahl, Eric Larson, and Jim Algar— were put in charge of the animals who befriend Snow White. Snow White herself, the most difficult and crucial character of

182

all, was consigned to Ham Luske and Grim Natwick. Luske, as we have seen, specialized in character development and thus was a natural for the heroine. Natwick—who also drew the Prince—was a strong draftsman, chosen because of his ability to deal with the human figure.

Layout also presented new problems and the layout team, headed by Hugh Hennesy and Charles Philippi, found itself confronted with a considerable challenge. Layout artists not only determine the spaces in which an animator must work, they are also in a sense responsible for deciding how the film will look when it reaches the screen. They take on many of the tasks which in a live-action movie would be handled by the art director, the director of photography, and the film editor. An animated film must, in effect, be edited in advance, since animation is so costly that one cannot afford to shoot a single bit of extra footage. Every cut is determined at the layout stage (with the collaboration of the director and, sometimes, the story team). Camera angles and lighting are also determined in layout, as are final decisions about the character of the setting in which the action is to take place. This art direction aspect was especially important in *Snow White,* where it was necessary to maintain an atmosphere of fairy-tale quaintness. Most of the preliminary work to this end was done by Albert Hurter—the bizarre furnishings in the dwarfs' cottage, for instance—but it was the layout artists' responsibility to make these inventions work within the final context of the film. Color was an important consideration. In the interiors, it was keyed down to give them an aged look (Gustaf Tenggren's elegant watercolor studies had an important influence on their eventual appearance). Everything had to be carefully designed so that the characters would read clearly against their backgrounds.

By the spring of 1936, production of *Snow White* was in full swing. Story conferences were being held almost every day and each scene was discussed and analyzed down to the last detail. Fortunately, a stenographer was present at all these meetings, so that a complete record exists. The following, for example, are extracts from a session dated Saturday, June 27, 1936. The transcript notes that it lasted from 8:45 A.M. to 1:00 P.M., and that those present were Walt Disney, Frank Churchill, Charles Philippi, Joe Grant, Bill Cottrell, Larry Morey, and Bob Kuwahara. The conference dealt with the sequence in which the Huntsman, having taken Snow White out into the woods, was supposed to kill her. The meeting began with Morey running through the continuity for the scene (we can imagine that the group was sur-

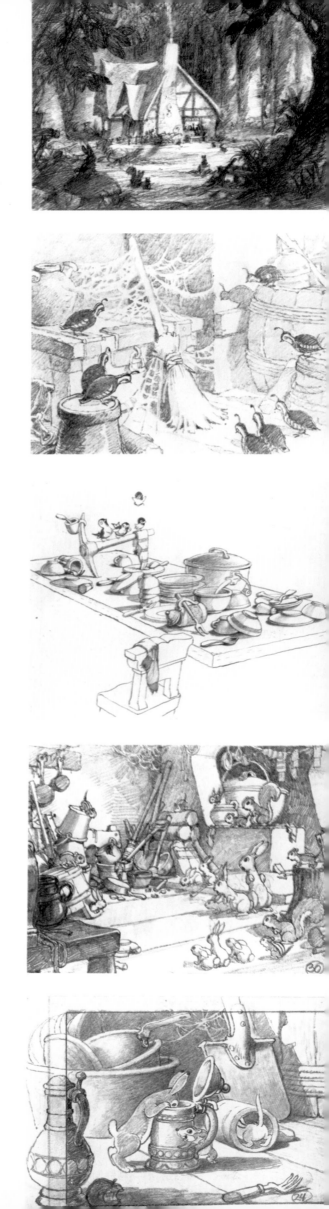

Snow White is befriended by
woodland creatures who take her to
the dwarfs' cottage. Assisted by the
animals, Snow White cleans the
cottage and then—exhausted by
her experiences—falls asleep across
several of the dwarfs' beds

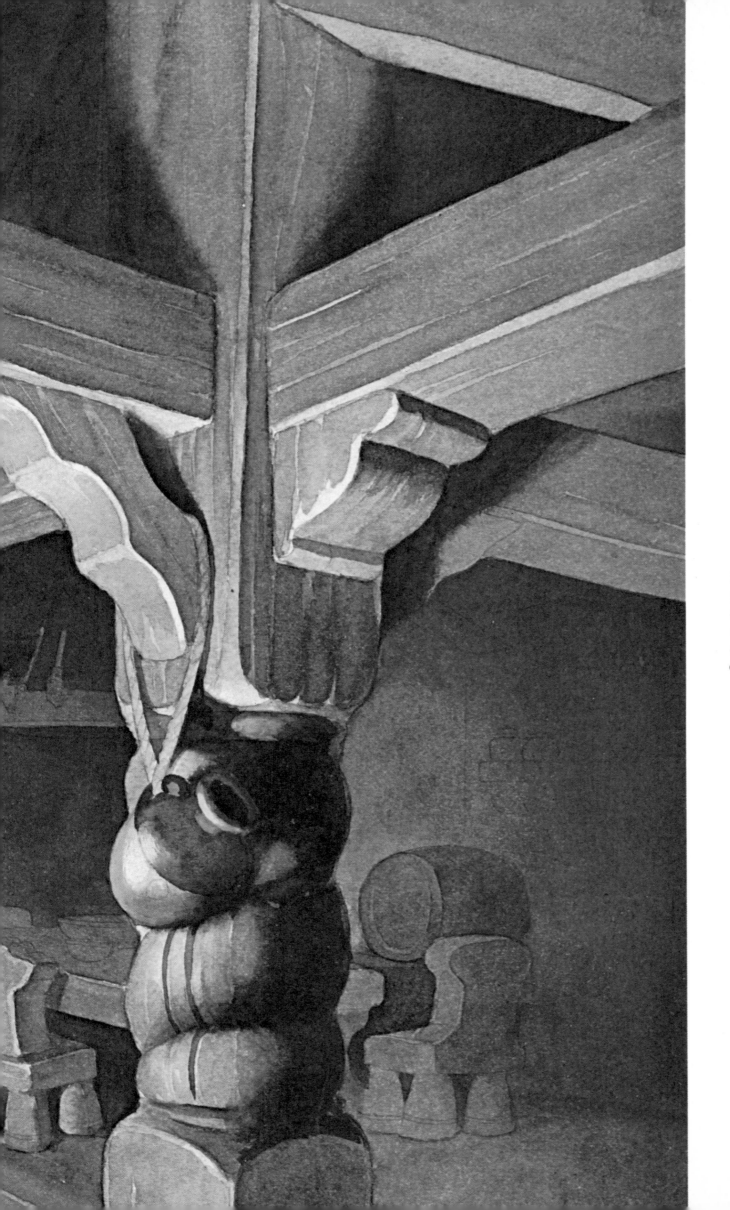

Backgrounds were
painted in low-keyed
colors to emphasize
the antique character
of the cottage
(see also overleaf)

rounded by story boards), while Churchill played the musical score on the piano. Disney then led off the discussion:

"I feel that what Snow White says to the little bird should have a double meaning—such as, 'Are you a little orphan?' In other words, have the conversation with more contact to her present predicament. . . . She is stooped over [this little bird], which gives you a swell position for the knife in the back. Let the menace come in while she is still with the bird—just at that point, with some connection there where she kissed the bird and the bird perked up and flew away—it has a connection for the Huntsman to soften. It would be tying it together. Maybe instead of expressing the menace musically you ought to stay with her and let the menace come in. . . . The Huntsman comes along—he is a threat all during the thing—and Snow White is there with the little bird, which is very innocent—such a sweet girl as she to have picked up a little bird and then someone going to knife her. Get the contrast in there."

At this point, Philippi suggested that the little bird could start chattering and fly away—giving her a reason to turn around. Disney disagreed.

"That is too direct. I want the thought where she has kissed the bird and the Huntsman softens—that is a good contrast."

Disney wanted to develop the scene in such a way that it would show how the Huntsman loses his nerve.

"That is what we want to build. A shot of the bird flying away and the knife is right over her back and—just as she watches the bird go away—the knife drops . . . and she turns on around and looks and he immediately pleads with her. That would be better than a long bunch of dialogue. . . . You have your set-up there—the morning sun and Snow White dressed in her prettiest dress and being taken out into the woods. . . . You know what to expect—you know that he is to kill her."

Clearly the scene under discussion falls into the category of melodrama, but seldom, if ever, had melodrama been subjected to the process of intensive refinement that we can see at work in these story conferences. If we consider Snow White from an artistic viewpoint, what is of special interest is not the fact that Disney selected melodrama as a storytelling form—evidently it was a method he understood and felt was appropriate to the subject matter—but rather that he exposed it to this process of refinement. His overall approach was determined by his own predilections and by the taste of his prospective audience. What gave the film its impact was his obsessive drive for perfection.

Another typical conference was held on December 22, 1936, on

Snow White was the only feature in which transparent colors were employed for the background paintings. Later, gouache became the usual medium

188

MCU: Doc at sorting table - tapping
diamonds - gets sour note - tosses
diamond away - o.s.song continues

MCU: Bashful, Sneezy and Happy.
Bashful: "LOOK OUT - SHE'S MOVIN'!"
Happy: "SHE'S WAKIN' UP."
Sneezy: "WHAT'LL WE DO?"

MLS: Group. Doc: "HIDE!" Group
scrambles under bed - Dopey last.

While Snow White sleeps, the dwarfs conclude their
day's work at the mine and head for home.
Mistaking the princess for a monster, they are set to
kill her, but—just in time—they see that
she is a girl and hide in confusion

At the mine, Dopey places two huge
diamonds over his eyes like spectacles.
The diamonds' facets create this
frightening image

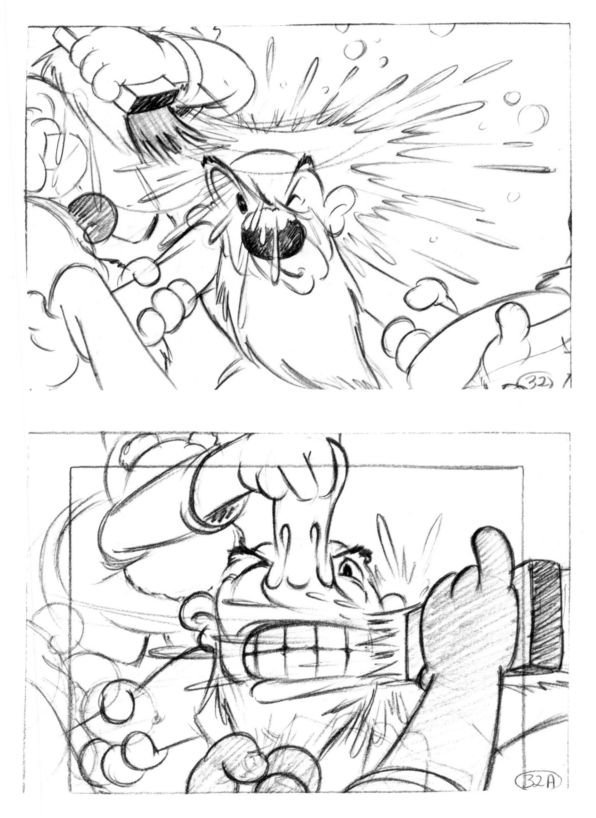

Snow White insists that the dwarfs wash up before they eat.
Grumpy, even more reluctant than the others to submit
to this humiliation, undergoes a forced scrubbing

the Hyperion sound stage. Twenty-nine people—mostly animators and animation directors—were present to discuss the dwarfs' personalities, but the main feature of this meeting—which lasted from 7:00 P.M. to 10:20 P.M.—was Disney's incredibly detailed shot-by-shot description of the movie, which seems to have been a virtuoso performance, as the following extract shows.

"We fade in on the sunset and hear the dwarfs coming home from the mine. They are marching home against the setting sun, singing the marching home song, which is the 'hiho' song that has a whistling chorus. We have a little sequence of these guys going over picturesque spots—mushrooms and roots of trees. There are little gag touches in there. We fade out on this sequence into the next sequence of Snow White, with a candle in her hand, and the animals following her upstairs. . . . She sees all these cute little beds, all seven, and she is pleased. These beds are hand carved and she reads the names on them, and she thinks they are little children. . . . Doc, Bashful, Grumpy, Dopey, Sneezy, Sleepy . . . and when she reads on to Sleepy she says, 'I am a little tired myself,' and lies there on three beds and tries them all out. The animals see her get in bed and cover her up with a sheet as she goes to bed. The rabbits and deer and all the animals get in these beds and settle down for a snooze. You hear the offstage dwarfs singing the marching home song, and the animals dash and look out the window. They immediately scram out of the bedroom, run down out of the house, and hide. They anticipate these dwarfs coming. Then we pick up with the guys coming home, on up to Fred Moore's sequence where they come up to the bedroom to attack this monster."

What we can learn from this meeting is that *Snow White* existed in Disney's head as a very real thing and that he was determined it should reach the screen just as he had conceived it. There can be no doubt as to who was in control. *Snow White* was a team effort, but it is still clearly the creation of one mind.

These meetings were the medium through which Disney exercised his control over the movie, and they permitted him to keep everything under close scrutiny. The musical score, for instance, which would be vital to the total impact of the film, was in the capable hands of Frank Churchill, Ollie Wallace, Leigh Harline, and Paul Smith, but Disney had his own ideas about how it should help move the action along—ideas that were strongly held and remarkably sophisticated. On February 16, 1937, during a discussion of the dwarfs' entertainment, he made the following remarks:

"It can still be good music and not follow the same pattern

◀ After supper, the dwarfs put on an entertainment. In a sequence animated by Fred Moore, Dopey experiences some difficulty while attempting to balance on Sneezy's shoulders

everybody in the country has followed. We still haven't hit it in any of these songs. . . . It's still that influence from the musicals they have been doing for years. Really we should set a new pattern—a new way to use music—weave it into the story so somebody doesn't just burst into song."

By the time *Snow White* reached the screen, its songs were indeed integrated with the story in a fresh and original manner. The way this was done anticipates the ingenuity with which Richard Rodgers and Oscar Hammerstein II incorporated songs into the structure of *Oklahoma!* which premiered in 1943. *Oklahoma!* was hailed as a breakthrough, but it seems that Disney was already moving toward the same goals several years earlier. With music, as with so many other things, Disney was not satisfied to do things the way they had always been done, and he did not want *Snow White* to be a mere imitation of live-action musical comedies. His attention to musical detail can be gauged by the attention he gave to the dwarfs' entertainment. For this sequence he insisted that the music be as bizarre as the characters of the dwarfs themselves, and he instigated experiments in which "legitimate" and "illegitimate" instruments were blended to sound like no orchestration that had ever been heard before. This sequence also involved yodeling, and various performers—described as Swiss, cowboys, and hillbillies—tested for it, but none came up to Disney's standards. Eventually this problem was solved from within the Studio. Someone asked Jim MacDonald, the sound-effects man, to try out, and, though he had never yodeled before, his understanding of music and the demands of the sound track enabled him to provide exactly what was needed.

Voice talent was, of course, an important contributing factor to the success of the whole project. The most difficult voice to cast was the heroine herself, and Disney had a loudspeaker installed in his office so that he could hear singers auditioning on the sound stage without having to see them (he did not want his decision to be influenced by their looks). Eventually Adriana Caselotti—a young lady with some operatic training—was chosen.

Live actors were also filmed as an aid to animation. The problem with animating humans is that everyone instinctively knows how a man or a woman moves, so that the least inaccuracy in the way they are drawn is immediately apparent. Nobody has ever seen a real-life Mickey Mouse, or even a real-life Dopey. Snow White, however—as well as the Prince and the Queen—presented a different kind of challenge. Years earlier, Max Fleischer had devised a method of filming live actors and using the results as a guide for his animators. This system, known as rotoscoping, yielded gestures and mannerisms that could never be invented. Now actors were brought to Hyperion Avenue (the young lady cast as Snow White went on to achieve fame as the dancer Marge Champion), and they would act out a piece of "business" in front of the cameras—often under the direction of the animators themselves. This action would then be transferred to a series of photostats which the animator could use for reference. The artist could, in fact, have simply traced the figures from the photostats, but this was seldom done because the characters had to be adapted in order to be consistent with the remainder of the animation. Instead, a kind of gentle caricature was employed, so that gestures and poses became slightly exaggerated. This system served the animators well, and they continued to use it in later movies.

The character of Snow White was an enormous challenge in many ways. Frank Thomas, recalling just one of the details that went into establishing her screen image, reports that when the cels came back from inking and painting, Snow White looked pale and anemic. "She had no color in her cheeks. So they tried painting color on there—which made her look like a clown. One of the girls said, 'Walt, can we try putting a little rouge on her cheeks?' He said, 'What do you mean?' So she took out her makeup kit and put some rouge on the cel and it looked keen. Walt said, 'Yeah, but how the hell are you going to get it in the same place every day? And on each drawing?' And the girl said, 'What do you think we've been doing all our lives?' He said, 'You mean to tell me you can put that in the same place on the girl's face no matter how she turns?'. . . They just knew where it ought to go and, without any kind of guide, they made Snow White up on each cel—so there's this lovely little tint on there. That's how much we cared."

Disney's perfectionism can be illustrated by another Frank Thomas story. As we have mentioned, Thomas was assigned to work on the dwarfs, and one of his scenes called for Dopey to do a little hitch step to catch up with the others. "This was on the story board, not my idea. So I had him do a hitch step. Walt said, 'Hey, that's good—we ought to use that hitch step all through the picture.' Of course a lot of stuff had been animated by then, so he called all the scenes back for hitch steps to be added. The guys came over to me and said, 'Was that goddam hitch step your idea?' That kind of thing would often happen. You'd be well into a picture when a better idea would come along—and you'd back up and change everything that had been done."

14 ♂   (11)

Grumpy says: "THE QUEEN! SHE'LL KILL HER!
WE'VE GOT TO SAVE HER"

Warned that the Queen (who has used magic
to transform herself into an old hag) has
reached her victim, the dwarfs set off to the
rescue. They are too late to save Snow
White, who has already bitten the poisoned
apple, but they pursue the Queen up into
the mountains, where a storm is raging

The Queen attempts to send a boulder crashing down on the dwarfs, but lightning strikes the crag she is perched on and she is hurled to her death. The dwarfs return to the lifeless body of Snow White and sadly place it in a crystal casket. She remains there through a full cycle of the seasons until, finally, the Prince arrives to wake her with a kiss

At a Disney premiere: ▶
Marlene Dietrich, top,
Judy Garland, center,
and Charles Laughton with
Elsa Lanchester

Although much of the production work on *Snow White* was jammed into the final ten or twelve months, it was the result of more than three years of concentrated effort by Disney himself—three years in which he faced new problems almost daily. The whole venture was an enormous gamble from the very first. The industry was convinced that he had bitten off more than he could chew, and hints of impending disaster were commonplace both in the trade papers and the national press. During this period, the Studio staff expanded to more than one thousand, many of whom were directly involved in the feature project. Some names have been mentioned, but literally hundreds of other artists and technicians were involved in all kinds of capacities, from painting backgrounds to devising special effects. (How, for example, do you make a painted stream look like a stream, or a rain storm look like a rain storm?)

Finally, at a cost of close to $1,500,000, *Snow White* was completed. Four days before Christmas, 1937, it was premiered at the Carthay Circle Theater in Hollywood. The audience was studded with celebrities. It was the kind of opening of which Disney had always dreamed. The reviews were sensational. *Snow White,* justifying all of Disney's hopes for it, was an overnight success—impressing itself on the imagination of the Western world.

Snow White is distinguished by two seemingly opposed characteristics: economy of construction and extravagance of invention. As we have already observed, Disney's training in the field of cartoon shorts had taught him how to tell a story without wasting a single foot of film. There is nothing in *Snow White* that does not contribute either to developing character or to moving plot. (Two scenes—the dwarfs eating soup and building a bed for Snow White—were deleted at the last moment.) Yet this does not lead to a feeling of spareness, because crammed into this framework is a profusion of detail that is almost overwhelming. The fruits of three years' work by hundreds of talents are compressed into eighty-three minutes of action, imagery, music, and dialogue.

The songs are memorable and, like everything else, contribute to the movement of the story. As for the animation, the character of each dwarf is firmly established—each is a distinct individual. The development of the Queen is excellent, both before and after her transformation into the witchlike crone. The Huntsman is effective and the birds and animals function well as a kind of Greek chorus. Snow White occasionally seems a little too much like a twentieth-century co-ed, but she has great

198

charm and easily wins our sympathy. The only real failure is the Prince, who seems wooden and lacks character (Snow White deserves a better consort). Above all, the entire movie manages to sustain the ambiance of timelessness which is so essential to the fairy-tale genre.

Some critics have found the film simplistic and therefore not worthy of serious consideration, but this approach is in itself simplistic. *Snow White* has the elemental quality of folklore—questions of right and wrong are understood in advance—which dictates a certain directness of approach that would be merely banal in most live-action pictures. But the character of animation is quite different from live action in that it permits virtually total control of every detail of every situation that may arise. Nothing need be left to chance and, in the case of *Snow White,* nothing was. Disney lavished such loving care on every aspect of the film that it took on an imaginative density which makes it quite extraordinary.

Other people have charged that *Snow White* is excessively frightening—suggesting that it might have a harmful effect on children. This can be countered by pointing out that many episodes in the fairy tales of Hans Christian Andersen and the Brothers Grimm are far more terrifying, but ultimately it can be justified only if the terror is justified by the nature of the story. It is hard to imagine *Snow White* without the Wicked Queen, and it is hard to imagine the Wicked Queen without having her perform deeds that inspire fear.

Snow White may have provided Walt Disney with his finest moment. There was an element of luck in Mickey's success (admittedly Disney tended to make his own luck) but this first animated feature was a triumph of a different order. No happy accidents were involved. Disney walked into the project with his eyes wide open, knowing the risks involved and convinced that they were worth taking. *Snow White* was a conscious effort on his part to advance the art of animation to a new level of sophistication—a level that everyone else had thought was beyond reach.

Shirley Temple presents Walt Disney with a special Academy Award incorporating one large and seven little Oscars for his production of *Snow White*

6 Pinocchio

Snow White may have provided Disney with his finest moment, but *Pinocchio* is probably his greatest film. It shares in all the qualities that made the first feature such a success, and adds to them a technical brilliance which has never been surpassed.

Pinocchio opens with a stunningly effective shot—the camera pulling back from a large white star, panning across the tiled roofs of a sleepy European village, then closing in on the lighted window of Geppetto's cottage. It is the kind of shot that has become familiar enough in live-action movies since the advent of power-operated zoom lenses, but taken within the context of its own period, and within the history of animation, it is innovative and spectacular. Nor is it just a piece of flashy showmanship. It serves to capture our imagination and draw us into the atmosphere of the story before a single word has been spoken.

Disney's early success had resulted from his grasp of the potentials of the sound film. By the time of these first feature films, he had evolved a method of storytelling which relied primarily on visual means. Next to animation itself, camera movements provided his team with its chief narrative devices. Disney continued to make expert use of music and sound, but his greatest achievement was the creation of a visual language that was totally convincing and extremely flexible.

Some critics have suggested that this visual language is marred by being backward-looking—leaning heavily on the illustrational styles of the nineteenth century. This seems an unreasonable objection since—given the subject matter of films like *Snow White* and *Pinocchio*—what idiom could have been more appropriate? Disney's obsession with naturalism seems anachronistic if one places him alongside Picasso (especially considering that the Spaniard was the senior by twenty years). At the same time, however, Picasso's fidelity to traditional art forms—especially the limitations of the stretched canvas—might be considered anachronistic compared to Disney's pioneering in the art of animation. Disney's great contribution was to break free of the static image. We might have seen interiors resembling Geppetto's workshop in old prints, but never before had we been able to penetrate these spaces and move about within them. Disney's imagination, the skill of his artists, and the technological magic of the motion picture camera made this possible.

The multiplane camera had seen only very limited use in *Snow White,* but *The Old Mill,* a short released in 1937, demonstrated its full potential and it was employed extensively throughout *Pinocchio.* Disney now had the ability to produce a full illusion of depth. The only drawback was the expense involved in operating the multiplane. A single scene—in which the camera zooms down on the village with the school bells ringing and pigeons circling down and down until they are among the houses—cost $45,000 (equivalent to perhaps $200,000 today). The scene lasts for only a few seconds. To offset outlays of this kind, Disney technicians managed to create some simpler devices, which they used whenever they would not detract from the quality of the film. One sequence, for example, shows a steamer crossing an expanse of calm ocean. It was made by pulling a single cel, on which the boat was painted, across a background, with smoke effects trailing behind it and distortion glass over the water. Disney was immensely proud of this scene because it was so simple—no real animation was involved—yet so effective that, at the premiere, it received a round of applause.

More often than not, however, Disney's quest for perfection led to more rather than less expense. Figaro the kitten had a highlight airbrushed onto him on every single cel he appeared in. Most producers would have looked on this as unnecessary, even absurd. Disney thought it might improve his film, so he did it. The result of this attitude was an animated movie of unprecedented lavishness.

Walt Disney in action:
a sequence of photographs taken at
a *Pinocchio* story conference

Geppetto's workshop ▶

One of Gustav Tenggren's watercolor studies for *Pinocchio*

204

Some of Albert Hurter's
early sketches for *Pinocchio*

DRUNKS

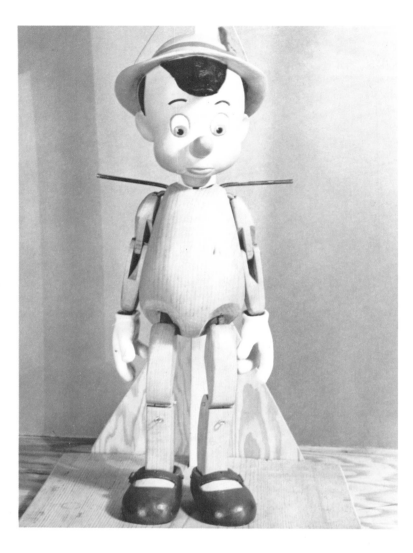

Many models were made to
guide the animators. Live-action footage
was shot for the same purpose;
the example shown here was used
as an aid for a sequence featuring
the Fox and the Cat

Snow White, as we have seen, developed rather gradually. Now Disney seems to have felt that with the experience of one feature behind him, he need not be quite so cautious, and production of *Pinocchio* was put into top gear. Things did not work out according to plan, however, and after six months he called a halt to the project and put everyone on new assignments until the problems had been ironed out.

The primary dilemma centered on the character of Pinocchio himself. Should he be treated as a puppet or as a small boy? Until this issue was settled, very little could be done. Book illustrations of the story tended to show Pinocchio as essentially puppetlike, and this seems to have influenced the animators' first efforts. Frank Thomas, Milt Kahl, and Ollie Johnston were assigned to the character, and they animated about 150 feet of film, using the speeded-up voice of Ted Sears as a sound track. Disney was not happy with the results. After further experimentation, they went ahead with a more boylike version of Pinocchio (except in the scenes, animated by Thomas, where he is still on strings), and found a child's voice which fitted with this interpretation. A further snag was Jiminy Cricket's personality,

This panoramic background ▶
was painted for the opening
of *Pinocchio*

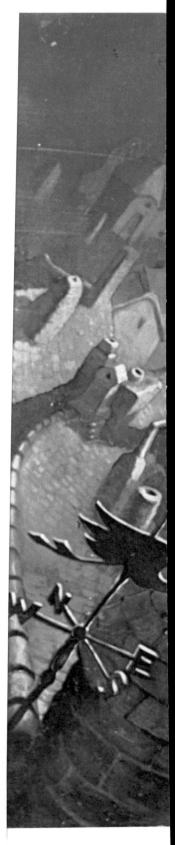

At the beginning of *Pinocchio*,
the Blue Fairy brings the hero
to life and appoints
Jiminy Cricket to be
his conscience

Jiminy Cricket in Geppetto's workshop

which became more and more important as the story developed, until he had usurped many of the functions intended for Pinocchio. The nominal hero of the film was soon reduced to speaking dialogue that did not go far beyond "Why?" and "Why not?" He was a total naive—the Blue Fairy had brought him to life and he had the innocence of a baby. The animators had to show that everything was a completely new experience for him, and this had to be evident in every movement he made. The success of the film hung on their ability to handle this considerable challenge.

Jiminy Cricket, animated by Ward Kimball, Woolie Reitherman, and Don Towsley, presented another kind of challenge. Being a very small character (his physical size contrasts with the importance of his role in the film) made him difficult to deal with except in close-ups. The animators rose to the challenge, making him so expansive a character that he seems larger than life. In contrast to the Cricket stands one of the villains of the piece, the puppet master Stromboli. Stromboli, animated by Bill Tytla, is an enormous, muscular presence who fills the screen with his infamy. His every gesture is a threat. Tytla, as we have remarked, was an exceptionally gifted animator, and this was an ideal assignment for him. It is probable that no one else could have built this character to the same point of menace. Stromboli is a man whose anger combines with physical strength

Geppetto, delighted with ▶
his new son, sends Pinocchio off
to school. Before he gets
there, however, Pinocchio is
sidetracked by the Fox and the Cat,
who persuade him that
the theater offers more glamour.
Soon he finds himself co-opted
into Stromboli's puppet troupe

Stromboli, animated by Bill Tytla,
is perhaps the greatest of Disney
villains—totally consumed
by rage and evil

Stromboli shuts Pinocchio in a wooden cage.
The Blue Fairy rescues him, but not before
he tells her a series of lies—only to
discover that, with each lie, his nose
grows longer and longer, eventually sprouting
branches and leaves

Succumbing to temptation ▶
once more, Pinocchio, accompanied
by the jaded street urchin Lampwick,
finds himself on Pleasure Island

to keep him in a constant state of explosive agitation (at the pre-miere, W.C. Fields was heard to say, "He moves too much," but Fields was noted as a harsh critic).

Perhaps more likable, but in the villains' camp nonetheless, are the Fox and the Cat, who are slyly determined to lead Pinoc-chio astray for the sake of a fast buck. Animated by Norm Fergu-son and John Lounsbery, these characters—like Stromboli—seem to be in constant motion, but it is motion less governed by rage. The cunning of the Fox and the stupidity of the Cat turn them into a kind of vaudeville team that keeps moving to hold the attention of the audience. The Fox knows just when to throw a knowing glance and the Cat is a malicious innocent with an instinct for mischief. Neither is subject to the eruptions of sheer evil that determine Stromboli's personality. They are self-made villains. He is a force of nature.

Geppetto, handled largely by Art Babbitt, is the least in-teresting of the main characters. He is asked to function on a single, fundamentally sentimental emotional level, thus presenting the animator with very little challenge. Fred Moore was luckier in his assignment, treating Lampwick, the cocky street kid, as something of a self-caricature. Monstro the whale is suitably fearsome and two smaller creatures, Figaro the kitten and Cleo the goldfish, add a touch of charm to the proceedings. Live-action footage was shot as an assist to the animation of several characters, notably the Blue Fairy, whose brief appearances are very effective.

Once again, Albert Hurter's influence is felt throughout the film, both in terms of character design and in the profusion of quaint detail that crowds the background of almost every scene. Gustav Tenggren contributed many line-and-wash studies which greatly affect the look of the movie. The multiplane camera and the visual complexity of the film as a whole presented the layout team with great opportunities which they eagerly seized. Under the direction of Charles Philippi and Hugh Hennesy, with important contributions by Ken Anderson, the art of layout was carried to new heights of inventiveness. Many of the layout drawings are extremely beautiful, and the same can be said of the background paintings. For *Snow White,* backgrounds had been painted mainly with transparent washes, but in the case of *Pinocchio,* while something that *looks* like a classic watercolor technique is adhered to, opaque pigment came into general use. For multiplane shots, all but the bottom layer was painted onto glass, and oil paint was used for this purpose.

Many character models, some fashioned from clay and some from wood, were made to assist the animators. The artist could

◄ Pinocchio and Lampwick engage in an orgy of self-indulgence which comes to a sudden end when the two revelers discover they are turning into donkeys

Chastened by his experiences, Pinocchio sets out to find Geppetto—a search which takes him under the sea

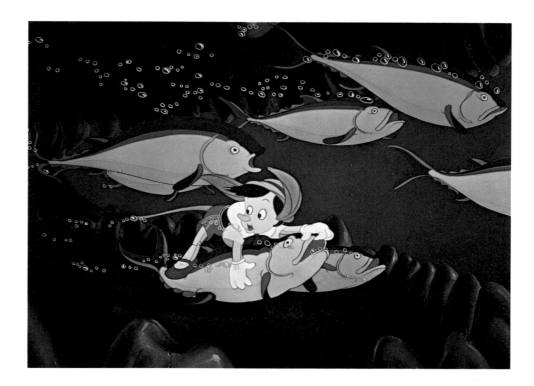

Eventually Pinocchio and Geppetto are reunited in the belly of Monstro the whale

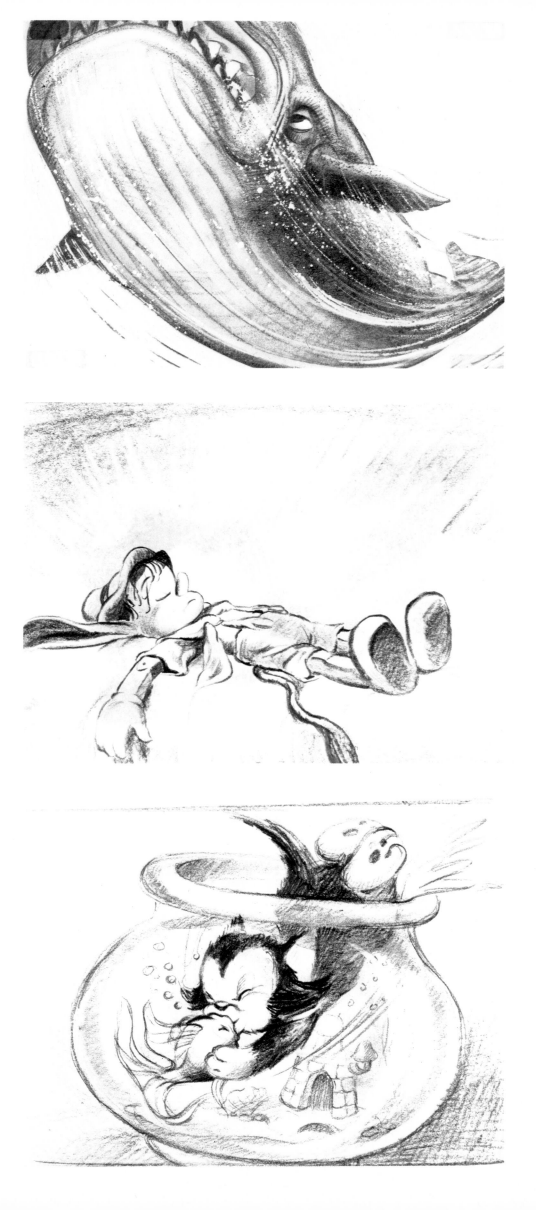

Escaping from the whale, who
gives furious chase, Pinocchio
is washed ashore, seemingly dead.
But he recovers, and,
having proved himself brave,
truthful, and unselfish, is soon
changed into a real boy
by the Blue Fairy.
Joyfully, Figaro the kitten dives
into the fishbowl and kisses
Cleo the goldfish

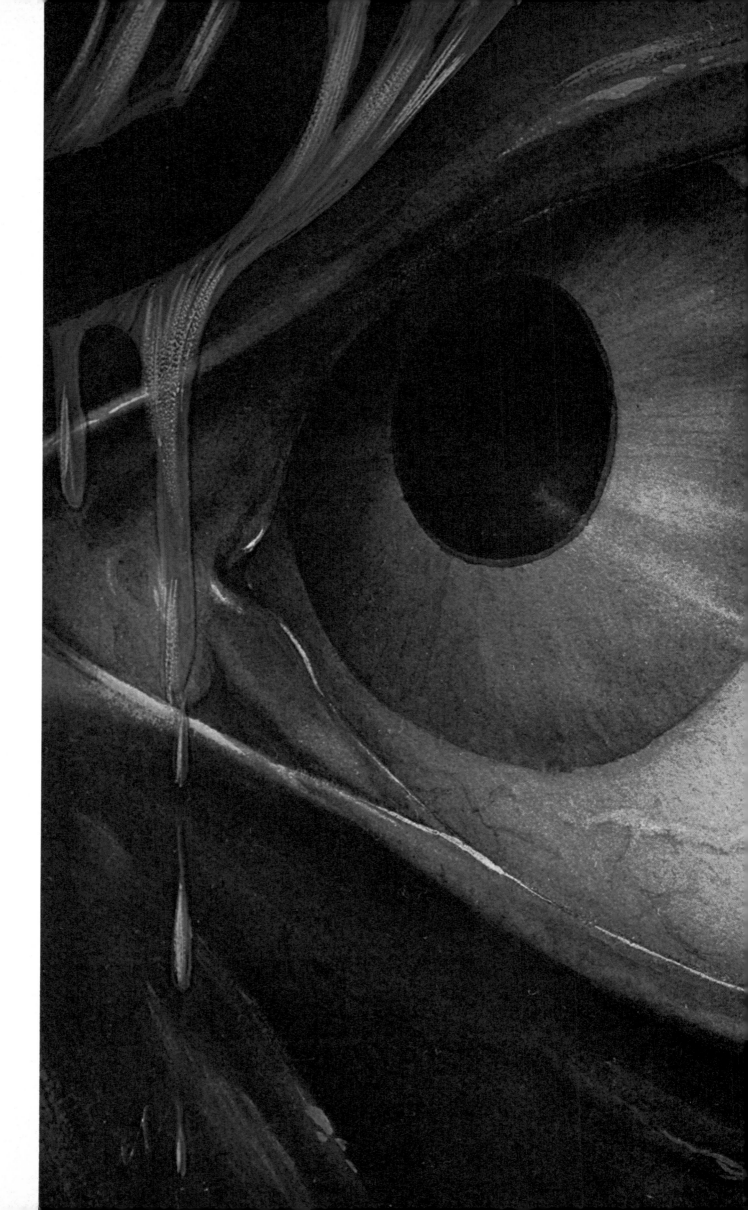

Jiminy Cricket
and the whale's eye

NOTE TO PAINTER- ADD SPIDERWEBS AS INDICATED IN SC. 26-28 ETC.

◀ The layout drawings for *Pinocchio* were made with great attention to detail. Often more than one artist worked on a single layout, the first making an outline drawing and another adding the tonal rendering

Although never intended for public display, many of these drawings are very beautiful

refer to these models, turning them so that they could see at a moment's notice just how Jiminy Cricket, for example, would look from such an angle (in this respect the models served a purpose similar to that of the live-action footage, and they could be used for characters who could not be shot in live action). The special effects in *Pinocchio* are particularly striking. Live-action rain is incorporated into one scene, for example, and one cannot overlook the impact of the musical score, highlighted by such songs as "Give a Little Whistle" and "When You Wish upon a Star"—both composed by Leigh Harline with lyrics by Ned Washington.

The plot of *Pinocchio* required extensive adaptation to make it suitable for the screen—far more radical changes than were necessary for *Snow White*. Once again Disney was charged with frightening children, but compared with Collodi's original, his version of *Pinocchio* is quite restrained. He kept just enough of the element of horror to make the story effective—certainly the scene in which Pinocchio's nose grows longer as a result of each of his lies triggers a deep response, as does the sequence in which he and Lampwick are transformed into donkeys.

Although the reviewers welcomed it with enthusiasm, *Pinocchio* was not an immediate box-office success. The film was released in February, 1940, five months after the outbreak of war in Europe, and it may be that the public was not in the mood for a fable of this sort. Not that *Pinocchio* was a frivolous movie. On the contrary, despite the happy ending, it presents the blackest vision of any Disney feature. But perhaps the reality

Background paintings, opposite and overleaf,
followed the letter and spirit
of the layout drawings, left,
adding the dimension of color

of world events had made the fabulous temporarily redundant. To this day, *Pinocchio* has never reached the numbers of people who have seen some other Disney films. This is unfortunate, for it is Disney's masterpiece.

Pinocchio was not the only thing on Disney's mind during the period from 1938 to 1940. Two more major film projects—*Fantasia* and *Bambi*—were already under way, and, in addition to this and a full schedule of short cartoons, Disney had decided to build a new studio. On August 31, 1938, a deposit was made on a fifty-one-acre site in Burbank, near the Los Angeles River, in the same general area as the Columbia Ranch and the studios of Warner Brothers and Universal Films. New buildings were erected and others were brought from Hyperion Avenue. The

The atmosphere of *Pinocchio* owed a great deal to the effectiveness of the background paintings

Operating the multiplane
camera crane. The technician at
the upper left is
Card Walker, now president
of Walt Disney Productions

move to Burbank began in August, 1939, and was completed
by the following spring.

When the new studio was nearly ready, Walt Disney took
his father on a tour of the premises. Elias, the former carpenter
and contractor, was evidently a little disturbed by what he saw.
"Walter—what can it be used for?" he asked. Disney, taken
aback, said, "It's a studio—where I work." Elias persisted: "No,
Walter, what can it be used for?" Suddenly it dawned on Disney
that what his father wanted to know was what the property
could be used for if the Studio failed. "Now this would make
a perfect hospital," said Disney, improvising. For the rest of the
tour, the Studio became a hospital. Walt showed his father
where the operating rooms could go, extemporized upon the advantages of the wide corridors and the advanced air-conditioning
system. His father left, a happy man.

Elias's worries were not entirely unfounded. In April of
1940 Walt had been forced to offer stock to the public for the
first time; thus an artistic high in his career corresponded with
perhaps his most serious economic low.

But Disney was not the kind of man to cut back his productions because of considerations of this kind, no matter how
serious they might seem to everyone else. He was completely
sure of himself.

7 Fantasia:

The Grand Experiment

The new emphasis on feature film production did not mean that Disney had lost his special affection for Mickey Mouse, but Mickey was losing ground to Donald and this prompted Disney, in 1938, to plan a comeback for him. The vehicle he chose for this purpose was *The Sorcerer's Apprentice,* an ancient fairy-tale motif which Goethe had used in a very popular poem; Disney's immediate inspiration was Paul Dukas's orchestral work of the same title, written in 1897. This popular piece of program music seemed to provide Disney with the perfect score for his project. Its running time made for a film about twice the length of the average cartoon short, thus allowing for leisurely storytelling and substantive character development. Disney, anxious to lend this production as much prestige as possible, was fortunate enough to obtain the services of Leopold Stokowski. Stokowski, who conducted the Philadelphia Orchestra, had long admired Disney's work and was delighted to make himself available. In fact, he involved himself so intensely in the project that it soon began to develop into something far more ambitious.

The idea that evolved was for a full-length feature film which would take the form of a concert of orchestral pieces conducted by Stokowski and illustrated by the Disney artists. Eventually, in November, 1940, it would be released under the title

Deems Taylor, wearing glasses,
and Leopold Stokowski at the Studio.
With Disney, they discuss
the story board for *The Sorcerer's
Apprentice* and inspect the
multiplane camera. In the right-hand
photograph, they visit the
ink and paint department

Fantasia, but for the time being it was referred to as "the Concert Feature."

The first thing to be decided upon was the program of music that would form the basis of this film. While Stokowski was instrumental in the process of selection, the final choice would have to be dictated by visual considerations, and therefore it was imperative that Studio artists be involved from the first. Disney called in Joe Grant and Dick Huemer (he knew that Huemer was an opera buff and that Grant's experience in character design would be invaluable) and had them listen to hundreds of pieces of music and evaluate them in terms of their potential as a basis for animation. It had been decided that a narrator would be needed to link the various episodes of the film, and Deems Taylor, known to millions as music commentator on the Metropolitan Opera radio broadcasts, was chosen for this role and to assist in the process of selection. The field was narrowed down to a dozen or so possible compositions, and Grant and Huemer began to investigate the story potential inherent in each of these.

Eventually the film was broken down into seven main parts, the first being an introduction which culminated with Stokowski's orchestral arrangement of Bach's *Toccata and Fugue in D Minor.* Next came excerpts from Tchaikovsky's *Nutcracker Suite;* then came *The Sorcerer's Apprentice,* followed by Stravinsky's *Rite of Spring.* The fifth piece was Beethoven's *Sixth Symphony,* the "Pastoral." Then came "Dance of the Hours" from Ponchielli's opera *La Gioconda.* The final selection combined Moussorgsky's *Night on Bald Mountain* with Schubert's "Ave Maria."

There is a tendency to think that in making *Fantasia* Disney was courting the intellectual community, but this does not seem

Left: shooting live action
for *Fantasia;* center: Stokowski in
the Disney paint laboratory;
right: dummy musicians used for silhouettes
in the film are loaded
onto a truck

consistent with the character of his goals. There is every reason to suppose that he was careful to keep his general audience in mind, and if intellectuals liked the film, as they had his earlier ones, that would be an added bonus, nothing more. With the exception of the Stravinsky piece, which was still considered avant-garde in the late thirties, all of the final selections fall into the category of popular classics—tunes with which many people would be familiar. In this respect, *Fantasia* is reminiscent of some of the Silly Symphonies.

Disney did not have pretensions toward high culture. He did not claim any deep knowledge of classical music, but, according to his daughter Diane, he enjoyed it tremendously. He certainly understood fully how music could help him in his movies (the years since *Steamboat Willie* supply ample evidence to support this confidence). *Fantasia* should not be seen as a totally new development—a play for cultural respectability—but as a culmination of everything that had gone before. (This would become quite clear if a selection of the best Silly Symphonies could be seen in theaters today.)

Nonetheless, the concert character of the movie and the fact that Stokowski and Deems Taylor were associated with it raised high expectations, and Disney went to great lengths to live up to these. He planned the movie for a special wide screen, but had to abandon this scheme for financial reasons. He also developed a sound system utilizing seven tracks and thirty speakers, which not only anticipated stereophonic sound but was, in fact, far more ambitious than anything that has been used since. Stokowski handled the sound mixing personally, and the results were, to judge by contemporary accounts, quite spectacular. Unhappily, the system was prohibitively expensive and was installed only in a few first-run theaters. The version of *Fantasia*

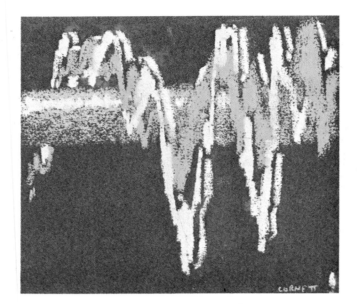

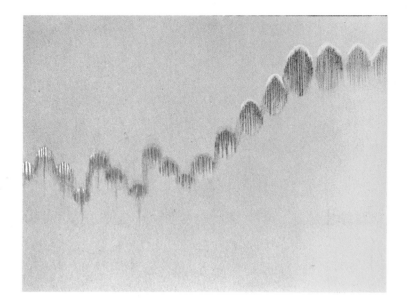

that we are familiar with today has been remixed for more conventional equipment.

Toccata and Fugue

The film opens with a brief introductory section in which Deems Taylor sets the scene; then the *Toccata and Fugue* begins. Visually, this segment provided a field day for the Disney effects department (as did a later interlude which introduced the sound track as a character). When *Fantasia* was in production, more than sixty people worked for the effects department, and they were given the task of interpreting the patterns of Bach's music in terms of abstract and semiabstract forms. This was a new area of experiment for them and, in the circumstances, they did a creditable job. Their notion of abstraction owed more to Art Deco design motifs than to modern painting, but it is consistently inventive. The main criticism that can be made is that whereas the music is very formal and rigorous, the animation is rather lighthearted and stylized, emphasizing the melodic highlights of Bach's themes rather than the harmonic richness. Quasi-surrealistic images are used at times when a more strictly abstract interpretation might have been more appropriate.

Nonetheless, this opening section of the movie does command one's attention and was a bold attempt to do something that had not been done before.

The *Nutcracker Suite* is ballet music, and Disney's artists treated the section of film it underpins as a kind of animated dance sequence. The first two movements of the suite were dropped and the order of the others rearranged so that a continuous story could be constructed, leading off with "Dance of the Sugar Plum

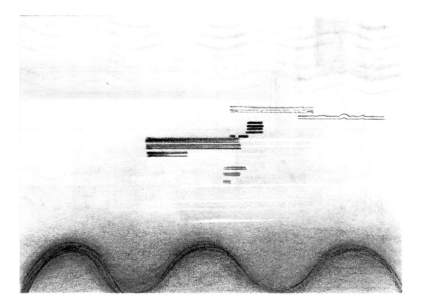

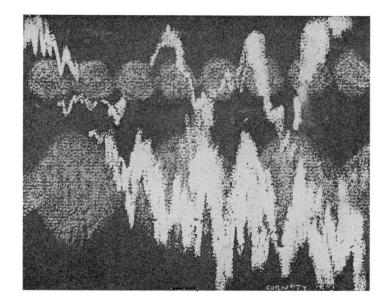

Hundreds of pastel studies were made for the *Toccata and Fugue* segment of *Fantasia* and for the "sound track" interlude, both of which used abstract forms to illustrate musical ideas

Fairy." Dragonfly sprites dart among flowers, touching them with wands so that they sparkle with tiny beads of dew. Buds open and more fairies are awakened. The atmosphere is one of great delicacy (airbrush work and special transparent paint contribute greatly to the sense of lightness).

The next movement, "Chinese Dance"—animated principally by Art Babbitt—is one of the high spots of the movie. A group of humorously choreographed mushrooms move through a solemn routine with almost ritualistic movements. One, smaller than the rest, has great difficulty following the steps of his associates.

"Dance of the Flutes" follows, with blossoms drifting down to the surface of a stream, where they are transformed into tiny ballerinas. A breeze picks them up and sends them skimming out across the surface of the water and among the branches of overhanging trees, until they are swept over a cascade and vanish from sight.

As the fourth movement, "Arab Dance," opens, bubbles rise to the surface from the spot where the blossoms vanished. The camera fades into the depth of the stream and there, among a forest of water plants, exotic fish—some gold and some black—perform an aqua-ballet. As the sequence ends, the light fails and bubbles again begin to rise to the surface.

A thistle in the form of a Cossack bursts from the largest bubble and "Russian Dance" begins. More thistles join in, whirling with orchids that resemble girls in peasant costume. Music and dancing become faster and faster, then freeze to a final tableau.

This segment concludes with "Waltz of the Flowers." Au-

Nutcracker Suite

Disney artists transformed Tchaikovsky's *Nutcracker Suite*
into a nature ballet featuring spectacular effects animation
and delicate airbrush work

tumn fairies move among the trees, touching leaves which take on their fall colors and drift with the wind. The fairies touch milkweed pods which burst, releasing their seeds, which become yet another kind of dancer, complete with bouffant skirts and sleek black hair. Frost sprites appear and skate across the surface of the stream, transforming it to ice as snow begins to fall, covering the landscape.

A technical tour de force, the *Nutcracker Suite* section succeeds admirably within its own terms, allowing the effects department to display its skills and making imaginative use of multiplane shots. It features some extraordinary animation and picks up on the romantic flavor that had colored so many of the Silly Symphonies, transforming that sensibility into something substantial enough to provide a base for bravura performances by all concerned.

Disney had planned *The Sorcerer's Apprentice* as a spectacular showcase for Mickey and it became exactly that, the whole project being developed with great care and attention to detail. Under Jim Algar's direction, nothing was left to chance. Story sketches were made in full color and some of the Studio's top animators were put on this assignment (Bill Tytla, for example, and Les Clark, who had been drawing Mickey for ten years).

Mickey is portrayed as a young magician, the disciple of a great Wizard who, bored for the moment with his own powers, leaves Mickey in charge of the subterranean cavern where he practices his sinister craft. Mickey has been ordered to fill the large water vat in the cavern, but the ambitious apprentice discovers that the Wizard has left his magic hat behind and decides to take advantage of this. Donning the hat, he brings a broom to life and directs it to carry the water. The broom marches to the well, fills a wooden pail with water, and starts on its appointed task. Satisfied with the success of his spell, Mickey settles down in the Wizard's chair to take a snooze. Soon he is dreaming that he is high above the earth, far out in space. His powers have become so great that he can control the paths of stars and planets, and comets change their course at his bidding. Next he is standing on top of a towering crag, conducting the waves of the ocean. With a gesture worthy of Stokowski, he beckons to the breakers to smash against the base of the rock. He repeats the gesture and the waves break over the top of the crag, drenching the dreaming apprentice and startling him from his reverie.

He wakens to find that the cavern is awash. The broom is following his instructions with too great a zeal and has already brought thousands of gallons of water from the well and threat-

The Sorcerer's Apprentice

The Sorcerer's Apprentice
presents Mickey as a neophyte magician
dabbling with spells he cannot control

As *The Sorcerer's Apprentice* moves toward its climax, Mickey finds himself quite literally out of his depth

ens to cause a disastrous flood. Mickey orders it to stop but his magic powers have vanished and the broom mechanically continues its task. In desperation, Mickey attacks it with an axe, only to see the broom split into many brooms, all of which continue with dogged perseverance, sweeping him aside and swamping the cavern. The water gets deeper and deeper. Furniture is afloat. Mickey seeks safety on a gigantic book of spells, which is soon sucked into an iridescent whirlpool. The apprentice seems on the point of losing his life when, suddenly, the Wizard appears at the top of the stairway. A single gesture from him and the waters subside. Everything returns to normal. Mickey, chastened, is left to clean up the mess.

With this story, Disney has certainly come a long way from *Steamboat Willie.* The fantasy of controlling the universe is not something that one would have suspected of Minnie's old sweetheart, not even of the conductor in *The Band Concert.* Yet one of the things that had always given Mickey's personality a certain depth was his true-to-life tendency to indulge in fantasy (and more often than not, his fantasies would clash with some pressing reality). The Mickey of *The Sorcerer's Apprentice* is the same old Mickey, but the circumstances he finds himself in encourage him to indulge in more grandiose dreams. The magnitude of his fantasy and the absurdity of the reality with which

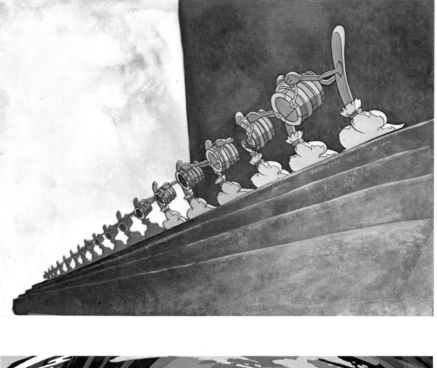

The Sorcerer's Apprentice presents Mickey
at his most Chaplinesque. The mindless
robotlike force of the brooms and pails is
reminiscent of the production-line machinery
in *Modern Times*

he finds himself in conflict enable us to learn something more about Mickey's psychology. As a magician he is a failure, but he succeeds in something much more important—for the first time he becomes a fully rounded, three-dimensional character.

Although told in an amusing way, *The Sorcerer's Apprentice* presents psychological ideas that are very basic to the human condition. Technically, like everything else in *Fantasia,* the segment is superb.

Rite of Spring heralds an abrupt change of mood. Disney saw Stravinsky's ballet music as providing the score for nothing less than a portrayal of the creation of the world (and certainly the insistent rhythms are suggestive of primeval forces). In later years, Stravinsky expressed displeasure with the way his music had been used, but this seems to relate mostly to alterations in the orchestration that may have been made without his permission; there is no reason to suppose that he was dissatisfied with Disney's overall concept. He visited the Studio and saw the story boards that had been prepared, and photographs taken at the time suggest that he was not unhappy with them.

This segment begins with visions of a time when the earth was still a molten mass, and it carries the story of evolution to the point at which the dinosaurs disappeared from the face of the planet. Millions of years are telescoped into a few minutes. We see mountain ranges thrown up by gigantic volcanic convulsions; then primitive forms of marine life emerge from the oceans and learn to live on dry land. Later, huge reptiles roam the surface of the earth and engage in titanic battles to the death. Eventually, a massive drought turns whole continents into deserts.

Unfortunately, all this is not too convincing on the screen. The formation of the earth is treated imaginatively by the effects department, and the emergence of life in the sea is handled with delicacy; after that, however, the story becomes crudely melodramatic. Dinosaurs are transformed into ham actors. When they fight, theatrical lighting is used, as though the action would not seem dramatic enough by itself. The music overpowers the imagery, which finally seems far too schematic.

The next segment, set to the "Pastoral" symphony, is difficult to judge objectively. It has considerable charm, yet its visual character seems to have very little to do with the real nature of Beethoven's music.

This can be explained in part by the fact that the Arcadian scenes which make up this segment were originally intended for a much lighter piece of music—an excerpt from Pierné's *Cydalise*. The rhythms of the Pierné selection proved to be too persistent to support the subject matter (the animators needed some pauses and legato passages). Disney decided to switch to the Beethoven work—apparently against Stokowski's judgment.

Visually this segment owes a great deal to the stylized decorative and illustrative idioms of the thirties—it passes before the viewer like an animated mural for some fashionable Parisian restaurant. The backgrounds are extremely elegant and pleasing (Art Riley, Claude Coats, and Ray Huffine must share credit with the layout team of Ken Anderson and Hugh Hennesy), combining gently curving forms with an innovative use of color.

Rite of Spring

◄ In *Fantasia,* Stravinsky's *Rite of Spring* is used to underscore the story of the earth's prehistory, including the age of the giant reptiles

The best scene comes near the beginning, when flying horses resembling giant butterflies glide in above a lake before settling onto the surface of the water. This has a wonderful sense of poetry which only animation could supply. Much of the action concerns flirtations between centaurs and centaurettes. The former—a hybrid species combining football players and cart horses—seem rather clumsy, but the centaurettes, styled by Fred Moore, display a certain charm, looking like high school co-eds who have undergone some unlikely transformation.

Good comic interludes are provided by Ward Kimball's Bacchus and his drunken unicorn-mule; toward the end, Zeus, aided by Vulcan, stages a thunderstorm for his own amusement. Night falls and Artemis appears in the sky to launch an arrow of fire from the bow of light formed by the new moon.

It is difficult to give an adequate idea of Disney's interpretation of "Dance of the Hours," but we might begin by saying that it is possibly the best—and certainly the funniest—segment of the movie. The animators, who included John Lounsbery, Howard Swift, and Hugh Frazier, were given the task of developing a parody of classical ballet featuring hippos, elephants, ostriches, and alligators. The result is hilarious. A hippo in a negligible tutu does pirouettes as though she weighed no more than a feather. Alligators swoop down from behind pillars, the inherent menace of their species amplified by choreographic fantasy and clever camera angles. Elephants hide timidly behind flimsy architectural elements and ostriches perform *entrechats* with an inspired absence of grace. Gravity and reason are denied in a triumph of insanity. Directed by T. Hee and laid out by Ken O'Connor, "Dance of the Hours" is a classic of comic animation.

Fantasia concludes with *Night on Bald Mountain* and "Ave Maria." As technical achievements they are extraordinary, but emotionally they are unsatisfying. The concept of this segment is a simple contrast of good and evil. To Moussorgsky's dramatic music, witches ride and tormented spirits rise from the grave to join the Devil on top of a jagged, rocky peak. The special effects in these sequences are excellent and Bill Tytla's Devil is realized with enormous vigor. At dawn, the ghosts return to their resting places and, to the strains of "Ave Maria," a procession moves slowly toward a Gothic chapel.

Most of the great monuments of Christianity—whether Chartres Cathedral or the King James Version of the Bible—are the products of years of patient labor. To expect the Studio artists to come up with something even remotely comparable while

243

A pastel drawing for the "Pastoral" segment

From the top down: Disney and
Igor Stravinsky discuss the score
of the composer's *Rite of Spring;*
Disney and sequence director T. Hee
(in shirtsleeves) with Stravinsky and
choreographer George Balanchine;
Julian Huxley inspects a *Fantasia* model,
watched by Disney and astronomer
Dr. Edwin Hubbell;
members of Associated American
Artists visit the Studio—left
to right, George Biddle, Reeves Lewinthal,
Thomas Hart Benton, Ernest Fiene,
Grant Wood, and George Schreiber

working to specifications and under deadline pressure is unfair;
yet anything less in this area does not seem worth attempting.

Fantasia is a film with great merits and great faults. Structurally it owes very little to anything that preceded it in the history of the cinema (*Snow White* and *Pinocchio* were basically conventional narratives), and Disney deserves great credit for breaking so boldly with precedent. His artists deserve credit for some of the finest animation that has ever reached the screen.

It has been said that *Fantasia* was ahead of its time, and in certain respects this is true (the popularity that the film enjoys today bears this out). In other ways it was very much of its time. For the most part, its imagery belongs essentially to

Pastoral   Early studies for the "Pastoral" segment
of *Fantasia* betray influences
reaching back to the nineteenth-century
Symbolist movement

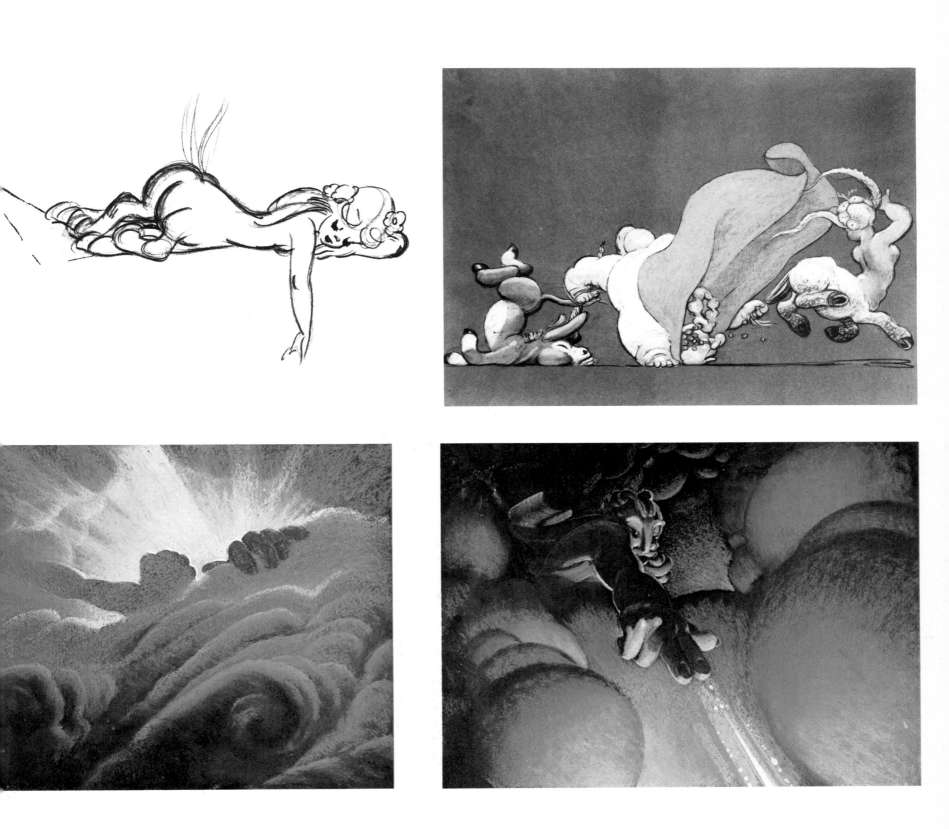

The version of the "Pastoral"
that reached the screen owed
a good deal to Art Deco idioms

◀ The "Pastoral" segment ends as darkness falls
on Arcadia and the goddess Artemis
appears in the night sky

FOLDER Dance of the hours 2004 ①

Dance of the Hours

"Dance of the Hours," as interpreted
by the Disney artists, became
a hilarious parody of classical ballet

252

Night on
Bald Mountain

Fantasia concludes with
Night on Bald Mountain and
"Ave Maria," a presentation
of the conflict between
Good and Evil

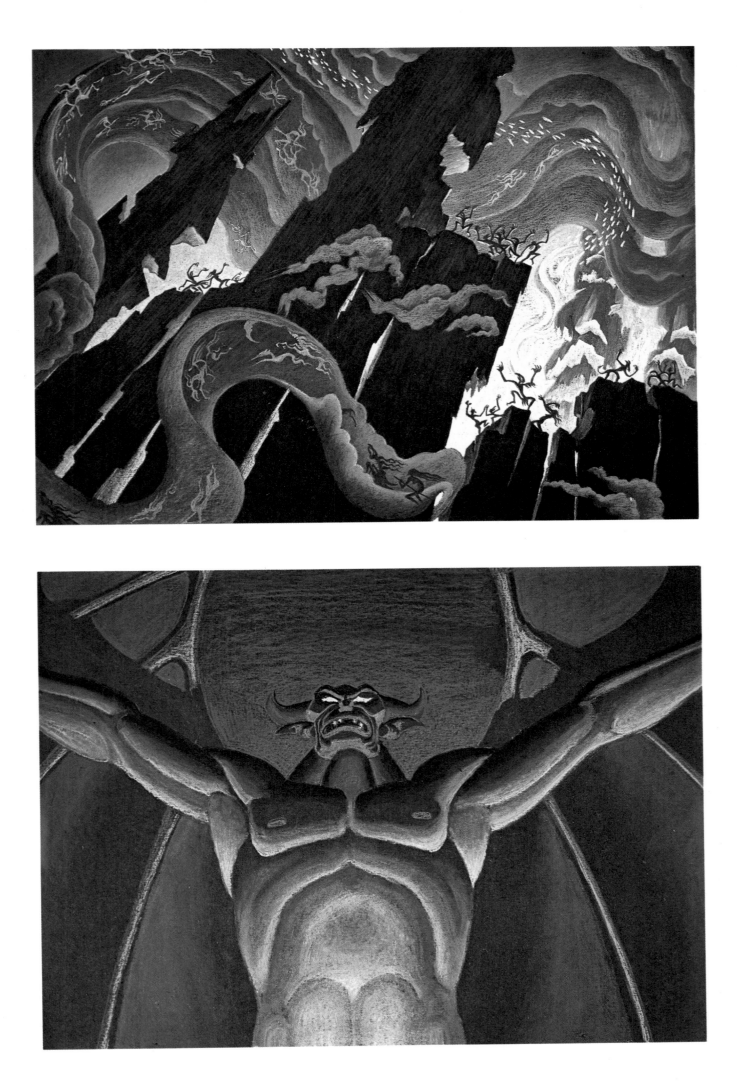

the thirties, as does Deems Taylor's commentary. By stretching out to both the past and the future, *Fantasia* achieved its own kind of uniqueness.

The film has had many critics. Frank Lloyd Wright, the great architect, visited the Studio while it was in production. Invited to lecture the staff as part of the art education program, he was shown sections of the movie and was outspoken in his dislike for it. It was absurd, in his opinion, to illustrate music. He felt that Disney should take a long vacation and reconsider his position.

It was probably inevitable that these two men, both very sure of their own aims, would disagree sharply. Anyone familiar with Wright's strongly stated views on the nature of art will readily understand his criticism. We must understand, however, that Walt Disney was not a man who stumbled into things by accident. He, too, had a firmly held position, and he was capable of defending it with equal fervor.

If we try to assess *Fantasia* objectively, we find that two segments—*The Sorcerer's Apprentice* and the animal ballet of "Dance of the Hours"—have a universal appeal. Each of the other segments has merits of one kind or another, but they are not held together by the aesthetic coherence that is evident in *Snow White* and *Pinocchio*. The viewer is asked to make too many taste adjustments during the course of the movie for it to be a complete success.

Nonetheless, *Fantasia* is an amazing piece of film-making, one that will continue to fascinate audiences. For all its faults, there have been few movies to compare with it in terms of boldness of concept and brilliance of execution. *Fantasia* is truly a phenomenon.

Top: artists Art Riley,
left, and Ray Huffine at work on
Fantasia backgrounds.
Center: Retta Scott, an animator
who worked on the "Pastoral" segment.
Bottom: working on a study for
Rite of Spring, Woolie
Reitherman consults a model
of a dinosaur

8 Dumbo and Bambi

Cinematically, *Snow White, Pinocchio,* and *Fantasia* were blockbusters. The two features that followed—*Dumbo* and *Bambi*—were a little different in character. *Bambi,* except for its final climactic scenes, is a rather low-keyed movie. The Disney artists took great pains to establish the tranquillity that—according to the scenario, at least—prevails in the forest under normal conditions. This led to a lyrical approach which is quite distinctive and separates *Bambi* from all other Disney movies. *Dumbo* is a delightfully unpretentious picture, relying almost entirely on charm and humor rather than on spectacular effects.

Like *Pinocchio, Fantasia* did not have a great financial success at the time of its first release, and *Dumbo* was conceived as a way of recouping some of the losses. It was made for only a fraction of the cost of the two preceding releases, yet its earning potential would be at least equal to theirs. Multiplane shots and other expensive effects were kept to the bare minimum that would assure good production values, and the story was told as simply and directly as possible, with the emphasis placed on humorous character development. In many respects this represented a shift back to the spirit of the cartoon shorts. After the demands of the first three features, *Dumbo* was practically a vacation for the Disney artists, and they clearly enjoyed themselves on this project. It is probably the most spontaneous animated feature that the Studio has ever produced. Audiences responded well to it and the film brought in much-needed revenue (only the fact that its release antedated Pearl Harbor by less than two months prevented it from having an even greater impact).

Dumbo, as everyone knows, is the story of a baby elephant who discovers that he can fly. Adapted for the screen by Joe Grant and Dick Huemer, the film has a number of highlights. The circus parade and the scenes with Dumbo and the clowns have a splashy vigor spiced with the kind of knockabout humor that benefited greatly from the expertise of the veteran animators. The older elephants, caricatured as gossipy women, feature fine animation by Bill Tytla and John Lounsbery. Perhaps the most original sequence in the movie is the one in which Dumbo and his friend Timothy Mouse get drunk and see pink elephants —brilliantly animated by Hicks Lokey and Howard Swift. This leads directly to the scenes in which Dumbo learns that he can fly, a discovery which is prompted by the raucous encouragement of Ward Kimball's quartet of hipster crows.

Disney's own involvement with *Dumbo* seems to have been less intense than it was with the earlier features. This is not to say that he was uninterested in the project—he was, of course, involved in the important story conferences and all decisions were still subject to his approval—but he was not aiming for a new plateau of achievement in this film and clearly felt that much responsibility could be delegated to members of his staff.

All was not well at the Studio, however. Besides continuing financial difficulties, Disney found himself confronted by a strike. Unionization was, by 1941, firmly established in most of the other Hollywood studios, but it had not yet made inroads on the animation industry.

This is not the place to discuss the pros and cons of the dispute that led to the strike against Disney, but we must take note of it since it did have a significant effect on future production. In retrospect, it seems inevitable that some kind of unionization would have come about sooner or later. Unfortunately, the strike was a bitter one and left deep wounds; as a direct or indirect result of it the Studio lost some excellent animators, as well as much of the freewheeling atmosphere that had typified it in the thirties. The Age of Innocence was over.

By coincidence, the theme of *Bambi* focuses on the passing of a state of innocence (man invades the forest, bringing terror and destruction to the animals who live there). Disney had begun

Top: Joe Grant and Dick Huemer at work on the script of *Dumbo*. Center and bottom: while researching Dumbo, Disney artists spent time sketching at the Cole Brothers' Circus

Some of the most inventive
animation for *Dumbo* was done by
Ward Kimball, who drew
the hipster crows

preparatory work on *Bambi* as early as 1937, before the release
of *Snow White,* but for various reasons it did not reach movie
theaters until 1942. By its very nature it was a project that
could not be rushed, and the Studio's economic problems im-
peded the progress of the production. Disney's strongly held
ideas about how *Bambi* should be made dictated that the film
would have to be very expensive and, rather than cut back on
production values, he waited until he was able to make the
movie that he wanted. While *Fantasia* was eating up the company's resources, *Bambi* was cut back to a skeleton crew and
did not go into full production until *Fantasia* was finished.

As we have noted, the prevailing mood of this film (until
the climax, at least) is one of lyricism. Humor is blended with
the lyricism, but it is humor of a very gentle variety and does
not interrupt the mood. The forest becomes a character in the
movie, every bit as important as any of the animals. Its response
to weather (as in the raindrop sequence with its effective use of
multiplane shots) and to season (as in the autumn montage) is
as much a part of the story as any of the things that happen
to Bambi and his friends. Much of the credit for this should go
to Tyrus Wong, who keyed the background styling.

Great emphasis was placed on naturalism in the making of
Bambi. Special art classes—an extension of the existing training
program—were instituted so that Rico LeBrun could instruct the
animators in the finer points of drawing animals. Real deer were
kept on the lot as models for the artists. Books of photographic
studies and innumerable model sheets were compiled, along with
analyses of animal action and thousands of feet of live-action material to be used for reference.

The *Bambi* unit departed from the usual Disney procedure
of casting specific animators for specific characters. This time the
film was simply broken down into sequences and scenes, and any
artist might be asked to draw any character. Because of this, the
art classes and other aids had a special importance.

Technically, *Bambi* has a great deal to commend it. Much
patient work went into it and we might single out the contributions of the art direction team, headed by Tom Codrick, and
the animation of Frank Thomas, Milt Kahl, Ollie Johnston, Eric
Larson, and Retta Scott. But, for all the effort and skill, *Bambi*
is ultimately unsatisfying—especially by the standards Disney
had set for himself in his earlier features. The artists cannot be
faulted. The problem lies with the interpretation of the story,
perhaps with the story itself. In earlier Disney films—both
shorts and features—the fact that animals take on human characteristics and have human voices is not disturbing, since they ex-

Voice talents involved in the making of *Dumbo* included Sterling Holloway,
who played Ol' Doc Stork, and Verna Felton as one of the gossipy elephants

Dumbo

Dumbo follows the career of a young elephant
from the night he is delivered by stork at the winter quarters
of the circus to the day he learns he can fly
and to his "arrival" as a national celebrity

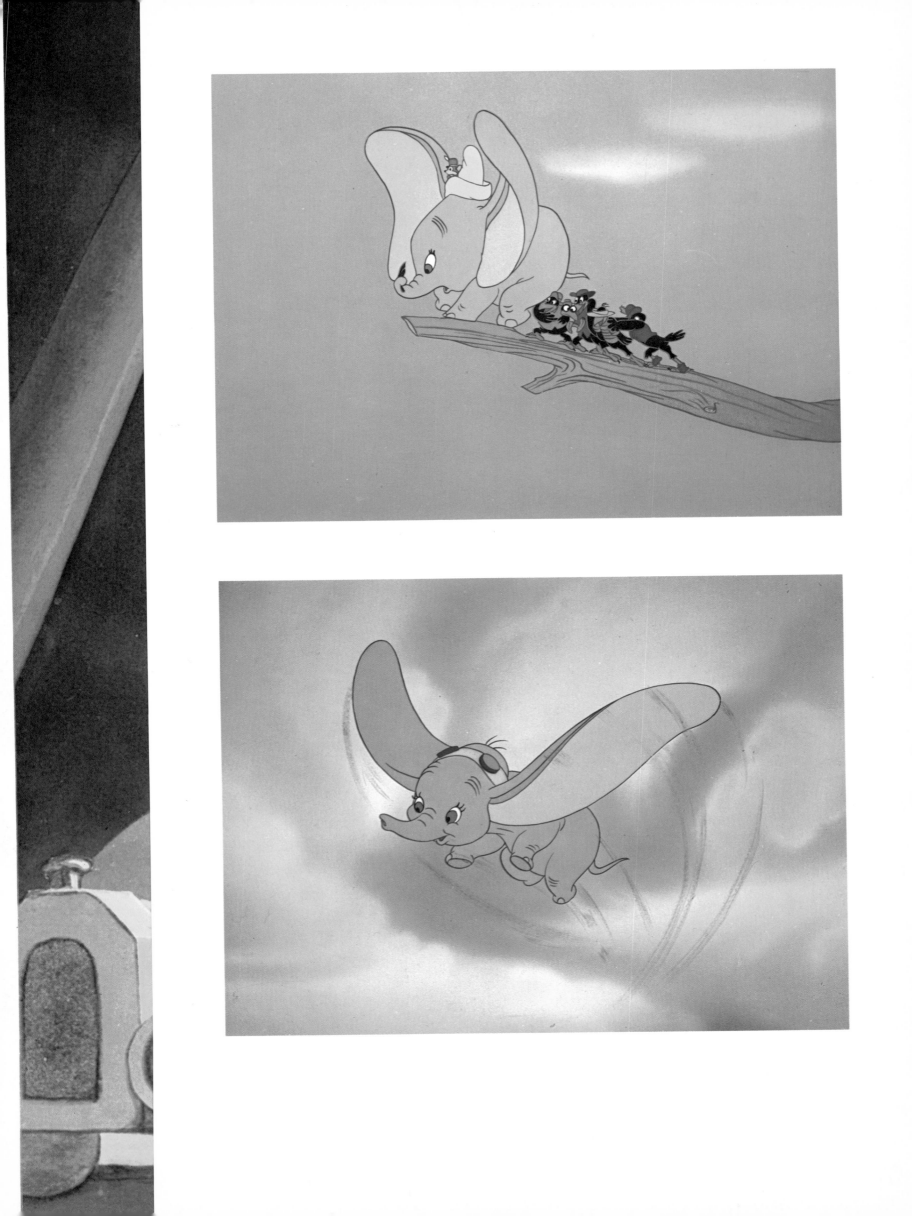

◀ At the end of the film, the circus train carries Dumbo over the mountains and to the bright lights of the big city

Preparatory work for *Bambi* included elaborate studies of animals in action

Bambi

In *Bambi*, Disney artists aimed for
a degree of naturalism quite unprecedented in
the history of the animated film

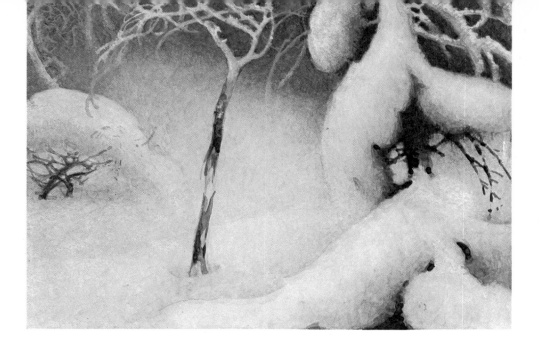

◄ Bambi and his father in the snow

Background treatments
for *Bambi* were conceived to
sustain a lyrical mood

ist in a world of their own which is governed by its own rules (as we have already noted, this links them to a tradition that has its roots in Aesop and Aristophanes). We are not surprised, for instance, when Pinocchio is seduced from the straight and narrow by a fox and a cat, for they are clearly caricatures of human types and the story unfolds in a fantastic dimension which we recognize as a metaphor for reality rather than as a naturalistic portrayal. Even the animals and birds in *Snow White* do not disturb us by their intelligent behavior. Within the framework of the fairy tale it seems quite acceptable, and only relatively small demands are made on them—they are not even asked to speak. Prior to *Bambi,* Disney's use of humanized animals had always been within the limits of established idioms.

Bambi, however, is something quite different. This film aims for a kind of naturalism which falls outside the borders of fantasy and fairy tale—yet it presents an owl on friendly terms with baby rabbits who, in the real forest, would be his victims, and we are asked to believe in deer that speak the language and share the emotions of the humans who are supposed to be their enemies. It is very difficult to reconcile these contradictions.

The most sympathetic characters are those, like Thumper the rabbit and Flower the skunk, who are used mostly for humorous relief. They seem to belong to the Disney mainstream and work well in those terms.

Yet despite its shortcomings, *Bambi* is an important movie. Along with the four preceding feature films and the short cartoons of the thirties, it gave the Studio a tremendous reservoir of idioms and techniques. The Disney artists could now handle everything from the broad stylization of Mickey or the Goof to the naturalism of Faline. They had learned how to create any atmosphere they might need, and the multiplane camera allowed them to use space in new and complicated ways. The Disney paint laboratory had developed hundreds of new colors to extend the possibilities of animation in still another way.

Bambi also marked the end of an era. The expansion that began in the early thirties reached a peak and leveled off in about 1940. By the time *Bambi* reached the screen, the armed forces were already depleting the Studio's ranks. Unionization precluded the possibility of ever building the staff to the level of the early forties, and, in any case, the economic conditions that had made so many artists available in the thirties were a thing of the past. This did not mean that Disney animation had no future—obviously this was far from being true—but it is fair to say that the initial momentum was spent. For a while, the Studio would have to coast—capitalizing on its past achievements, working well within its capabilities, experimenting a little, and waiting for the energies to rise again.

From the top down: special classes for *Bambi* artists were conducted by Rico LeBrun; animators Ollie Johnston, left, Milt Kahl, center, and Frank Thomas, right, pose with Peter Behn, the voice of Thumper; Frank Thomas sketches Faline

9 Interruptions and Innovations

America's entry into the war had an almost immediate effect on Disney Productions. In December, 1941, part of the Studio was commandeered by the military authorities as quarters for seven hundred members of an antiaircraft unit. They took over the sound stage for use as a repair shop and stayed for several months.

Before very long, someone in the Navy realized that animation could be of great value in the presentation of training material. The Studio soon received a series of contracts from military and government agencies and commenced production of instructional films. The variety of material treated can be suggested by listing some of these wartime titles. The 1942 subjects included *Aircraft Carrier Landing Signals, Aircraft Production Processes, Battle of Britain, Food Will Win the War,* and a number of aircraft-identification films. Among later efforts were *The Battle of China, British Torpedo Plane Tactics, Air Masses and Fronts, Defense Against Invasion, Rules of the Nautical Road, Automotive Electricity for Military Vehicles, Basic Map Reading, Tuning Transmitters, Fundamentals of Artillery Weapons,* and *The Winged Scourge* (which concerned itself not with the Luftwaffe but with malaria-bearing mosquitoes). Since economy was at a premium in these productions, extensive and clever use was

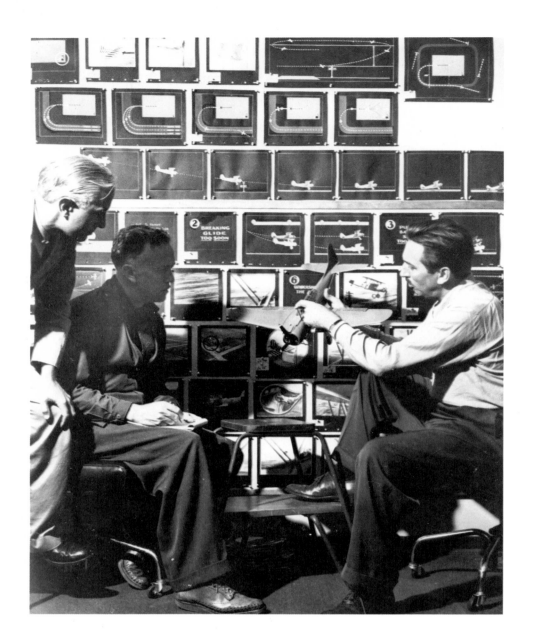

Leaving Burbank for ▶
South America, 1941:
left to right, Hazel
and Bill Cottrell,
Ted Sears, Jim Bodrero,
Jack Miller, Norm Ferguson,
and the Walt Disneys

In front of the story board
for a wartime movie: Commander "Hutch"
Hutchinson, U.S.N., Ub Iwerks,
and Walt Disney

made of limited animation (limited in that camera movements
and other basic devices were substituted for full animation wherever possible). A more ambitious project was *Victory Through
Air Power,* a feature-length film presenting the strategic bombing theories of Major Alexander de Seversky.

Throughout the war period, Disney continued to produce
short cartoons featuring Donald, Pluto, and Goofy (Mickey
Mouse shorts were temporarily discontinued), and a number of
these—such as *Private Pluto, Commando Duck,* and Goofy's
Victory Vehicles—were geared in one way or another to the war
effort. The most famous of these is *Der Fuehrer's Face,* in which
Donald dreams that he is in Nazi Germany, working on a production line in a munitions factory, constantly forced to salute
the likeness of Hitler and other Axis leaders. He awakens from
his nightmare, sees a shadow with a raised arm, and starts to
"Heil" when he notices that the shadow comes from a small Statue of Liberty on his windowsill. He jumps up, dressed in his
red, white, and blue pajamas, kisses the statue, and exclaims,

Walt Disney in Argentina   Walt Disney learns a gaucho dance

"Oh, Boy! Am I glad to be a citizen of the United States of America." As the film ends, a caricature of Hitler is shown. A ripe tomato hits him in the face, obliterating him and running into the letters, "The End."

A still more extraordinary propaganda film was *Education for Death,* which attempted to show how German youth was schooled and disciplined into the military machine. Its high spot is a Wagnerian parody which has Hitler—a knight in shining armor—awakening a grossly overweight but nonetheless playful Germania. This is certainly one of the most bizarre works ever to have emerged from the Disney Studio. Unfortunately, all of the artwork made for it has been destroyed.

The two most important commercial releases of this period—*Saludos Amigos* and *The Three Caballeros*—were themselves indirect products of the war. Europe had been in turmoil since September, 1939, which meant that Hollywood's chief overseas market was wiped out, except for Great Britain and some small neutral countries. Everybody, from the State Department down, was anxious that other markets be expanded, and the most obvious target for this expansion was Latin America (it was no accident that stars like Carmen Miranda rose to prominence at this time). In 1941, Nelson Rockefeller, then Coordinator for Latin American Affairs at the State Department, invited Disney to make a good-will trip to Argentina, Peru, Chile, and Brazil. Disney was not interested in a simple hand-shaking tour but suggested instead that it be combined with a film project. The State Department agreed to underwrite four short films to the extent of $50,000 each.

Disney and his wife, along with a group of Studio artists, made the trip and came back with a mass of material which was grafted onto other ideas that had been developed at the Studio. Four separate shorts were produced, but it was decided that it

Disney's tour of South America
was treated as a major cultural event

Animators Bill Tytla, left, and Fred Moore,
right, with José Oliveira, the voice
of José Carioca

Fred Moore tries out an expressi

would be advantageous to release them as a single package. They were dovetailed into some documentary footage that had been shot on the tour and released under the title *Saludos Amigos.*

The first of the four animated segments is "Lake Titicaca," which illustrates the adventures of Donald Duck in the High Andes. It has some good moments but is no better than any of half-a-dozen Duck cartoons from this period. The second segment, "Pedro," is more interesting, telling the story of a little mail plane which must carry its cargo across the mountains despite foul weather. A remarkable sense of space and depth was achieved for the flying sequences, and both backgrounds and animation are excellent. The third segment, "Aquarela do Brasil," is the most memorable, featuring José Carioca, an energetic parrot who introduces Donald Duck to Rio's Copacabana Beach and to the samba. The action is lively and is helped along by some imaginative effects animation, but what makes "Aquarela" so distinctive is the fact that it has a real Latin flavor and heralds a mood that was new to Disney movies. The final animated segment is "El Gaucho Goofy," starring the Goof as a displaced cowboy. It is amusing but by no means innovative.

Saludos Amigos was released in February, 1943. Two years later, *The Three Caballeros* appeared. In many respects a sequel, it also was aimed at the Latin American market and, like its predecessor, featured a combination of live action and animation. Taken as a whole, it is a disappointing movie—patchy and with no highlights to compare with the best things in *Saludos Amigos.* Donald and Carioca have some lively moments and are joined by a Mexican rooster called Panchito, who sports a large sombrero and an itchy trigger finger. Their energy is not enough

During World War II, ▶
Disney characters were often used
to illustrate matters of
public interest. In *Victory Vehicles,*
1943, Goofy urged people
to save scrap metal and gasoline

to offset the lackluster character of segments such as "The Cold-blooded Penguin" and "The Flying Gauchito."

The package film was not an ideal format for Disney artists to work with, but it did have an economic advantage which remained a major factor as the war came to an end. Reorganization was necessary, and it was important that the Studio have feature-length productions in the theaters to bring in revenues for future programs. A true animated feature would have taken too long to make and would have eaten up too much of the reserves at this point, so other solutions had to be found. *Saludos Amigos* and *The Three Caballeros* had shown Disney that the package movie was one solution, and three more were produced—*Make Mine Music* (1946), *Fun and Fancy Free* (1947), and *Melody Time* (1948).

None of these movies can have satisfied Disney. They were stopgaps and nothing more. To a large extent they capitalized on the vocal and musical talents of performers such as Dinah Shore, Nelson Eddy, Benny Goodman, the Andrews Sisters, Edgar Bergen, Ethel Smith, and Roy Rogers and the Sons of the Pioneers, who introduced various segments and supplied sound tracks for others. *Make Mine Music* combined narrative elements, such as "The Martins and the Coys," with pieces like "After You've Gone," which featured semi-abstract effects reminiscent of *Fantasia*. *Melody Time* follows the same general pattern, while *Fun and Fancy Free* has just two animated segments, "Bongo" and "Mickey and the Beanstalk." In all three there is much that is competent but little that compares with the masterpieces of the thirties and early forties. At times it is hard to believe that these packages were made by the studio that produced *Snow White* and *Pinocchio*.

The other viable alternative to the animated feature was the live-action feature, which can be produced far more cheaply than animation. As we shall see, Disney was forced to diversify his production schedule to adapt to postwar conditions, and one of his first ventures to rely heavily on live action was *Song of the South*, released in 1946. Although real actors carry the main body of the plot, three of the "Br'er Rabbit" stories are included as cartoon inserts, and they undoubtedly represent the best Disney animation of this period. The fox, the bear, and the rabbit are all well-realized characters, drawn with a looseness that was very fresh and which anticipated much that was to come later. In several scenes, live action and animation were combined effectively.

Another live-action feature, the 1949 film *So Dear to My*

Top and center:
Victory Through Air Power, 1943, argued the virtues of strategic bombing.
Der Fuehrer's Face, released that same year, took the form of a nightmare in which Donald Duck found himself working in a Nazi munitions factory

Saludos Amigos

The 1943 package film *Saludos Amigos*
included the story of Pedro the mail plane and
introduced Donald's friend José Carioca

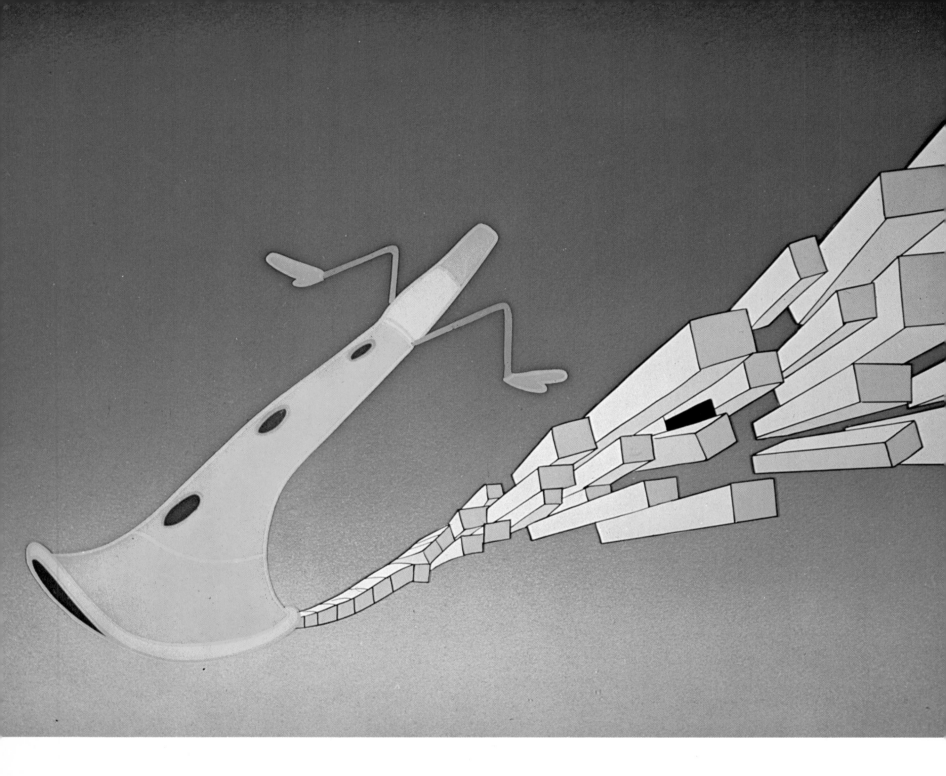

Make Mine Music

"After You've Gone," top,
and "All the Cats Join In," left, are segments
from this 1946 package film

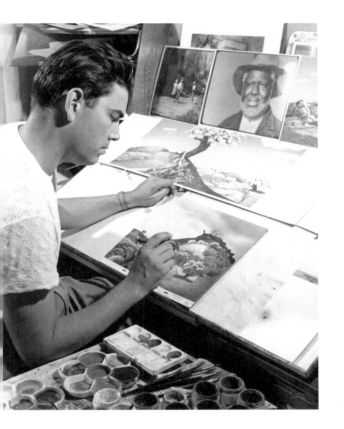

Song of the South

The animated portions of
Song of the South, 1946, brought
the animals of the Uncle Remus
stories to life

Salvador Dali worked at the Disney Studio for several months during 1946. Unfortunately, his project was eventually abandoned

The Adventures of Ichabod and Mr. Toad

◀ Released in 1949, *The Adventures of Ichabod and Mr. Toad* combined screen adaptations of two famous stories

Heart, also included animated inserts, but these, though well conceived and executed, were modest and of no special interest.

That same year, Disney released *The Adventures of Ichabod and Mr. Toad.* This picture falls somewhere between being a package film and a true feature, consisting of two distinct and separate stories which are linked only by the fact that the hero of each segment is prone to disaster. The "Toad" episode is based on Kenneth Grahame's *The Wind in the Willows* and is enlivened by good character animation and some lively art direction. Unfortunately, the story is too compressed for any of the personalities to be fully explored. All the action is there, but not the leisurely pace of the original (it seems that Disney had intended the story to furnish a feature-length film but was forced to settle for this compromise version).

The tale of Ichabod, based on Washington Irving's *The Legend of Sleepy Hollow,* is narrated by Bing Crosby. For the most part it is presented in a rather pedestrian manner, but the final sequences, in which Ichabod Crane, the pathetic school teacher, is pursued by the Headless Horseman, are outstanding, with the drama building to a fine pitch of excitement. *The Adventures of Ichabod and Mr. Toad* is not a great movie, but it was a definite step toward regaining past glories.

The Studio was still producing short cartoons on a regular basis. (It continued to do so until 1956.) Donald and Goofy were now the biggest stars. Formulas had been devised for them which made them easy to write for (Donald's bad temper and the Goof's ineptness provided endless gag possibilities). Pluto was a less flexible character—most of his better situations were still variations of the flypaper routine devised by Webb Smith in 1934. Mickey still made occasional appearances, but he was now used almost exclusively as a straight man. Important newcomers were Chip and Dale, a pair of highly competitive and occasionally pugnacious chipmunks who were often pitted against Donald, driving him to distraction (he had several other antagonists, including a musical bee and an athletic beetle). Besides these "character" shorts, one-shot cartoons were produced from time to time, replacing the Silly Symphonies without ever quite reaching the level of achievement of these at their best. *Morris the Midget Moose* (1950), *Lambert the Sheepish Lion*, and *Susie the Little Blue Coupe* (both 1952) are typical titles. Several directors—Jack King, Jack Hannah, Bill Roberts, and Jack Kinney—were specialists who concentrated on short cartoon production, each with his own unit. Some first-rate animators—Bill Justice, John Sibley, and Bob Carlson, for example—also worked primarily in this field.

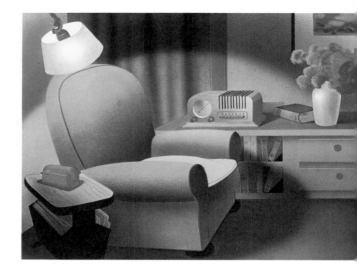

On occasion, short subjects were accorded rather special treatment, as was the case with *Toot, Whistle, Plunk, and Boom* (1953), the first Cinemascope cartoon. Devised by Ward Kimball, it is a highly stylized history of music which makes use of a novel sound track—very simplified and lacking the lush orchestration that had become standard. Its use of limited animation, along with the widened format, gave it a very distinctive character. A similar subject from the same year, *Adventures in Music: Melody,* was used as an experiment in 3D animation.

Meanwhile, in 1950, Disney released his first true animated feature since 1942. This was *Cinderella,* and it was a success both at the box office and as a piece of film-making.

In spirit it harks back to *Snow White,* though with added surface glamour and with a greater reliance on gag routines. An interesting variety of treatments is brought to the human characters. Cinderella, her stepmother, and the Prince are treated more or less naturalistically, while the ugly stepsisters, the Fairy Godmother, the King, and the Duke are essentially caricatures. Surprisingly, they work very well together. The animal characters are excellent. Lucifer the cat is a splendid villain and the mice (who, thanks to the vocal talents of Jim MacDonald, speak a kind of pidgin Latin) are consistently entertaining. The backgrounds for *Cinderella* are less distinctive than those which added so much to *Snow White* and *Pinocchio* (Albert Hurter had died some years earlier and his influence was greatly missed), but they are more than adequate, establishing a kind of French Provincial look in the early scenes. The well-constructed story consists of two parallel plots—one concerned with the human characters and the other with the animals—in which the only real common factor (because of her friendship with the mice) is Cinderella herself. Songs in the film include "A Dream Is a Wish Your Heart Makes," "Bibbidi-Bobbidi-Boo," and "So This Is Love."

Much fine work went into
the short cartoons of the forties, as in
these examples of backgrounds from
Donald Duck and Pluto vehicles

Jack Hannah, director of
one of the Disney shorts units

Top: the 1950 short *Motor Mania*
is one of several that take an ironic look at
the habits of the American driver.
Center: *Two Chips and a Miss*, 1952,
a typical outing for Chip and Dale.
Bottom: *Toot, Whistle, Plunk, and Boom*,
1953, is an experimental short
made in Cinemascope

Slide Donald Slide, 1949

Cinderella succeeds because it remains faithful to the spirit of the original while embroidering it with the kind of business that Disney understood better than anyone else. The next feature, *Alice in Wonderland,* failed because it did not capture the sophisticated atmosphere of Lewis Carroll's book and also lacks, except in a few isolated scenes, the authority of the Disney touch. Disney had first talked of animating *Alice* while *Snow White* was still in production (his interest in the subject goes back even further, of course, to Kansas City and *Alice's Wonderland*). He worked at the idea on and off for years before it finally reached the screen in 1951, but for some reason he never came completely to grips with it. Translating Carroll's highly intellectual verbal humor into visual terms was no easy thing, and *Alice* is perhaps the weakest of Disney's animated features. Occasionally there is a sharp piece of Surrealistic visual invention, and there is one excellent sequence—the Mad Hatter's tea party, which is greatly enlivened by the voice talents of Ed Wynn and Jerry Colonna. For the most part, though, the film is a confusing hodgepodge of disparate elements which, while more or less following the sequence of the original, hardly seem to belong in the same film with one another (curious stylistic inconsistencies crept into the art direction as well). Carroll's story is dislocated by inversions of reason, but it is held together by the insane persistence of its own anti-logic.

Disney blamed the failure of the film on the fact that Alice lacked "heart."

Peter Pan, released in 1953, is an altogether more satisfactory picture. With the exception of Nana, the St. Bernard, and the crocodile, all the main characters are human or have human characteristics (as is the case with Tinker Bell and the Mermaids). We have discussed the special problems involved in animating the human form, but this movie shows just how expert Disney's artists had become at handling them. As in *Cinderella,* they mixed naturalism and caricature without allowing them to clash.

Unlike Carroll's classic, Barrie's play adapted very well to the screen (in certain obvious ways the story is much better suited to animation than to a stage presentation). *Peter Pan*'s chief weakness seems to derive from the fact that there are too many characters to allow for real development. The Lost Boys, for example, are potentially as interesting as the Seven Dwarfs, but they are individualized only in the crudest of ways. Even Peter and Wendy are a little sketchy. Captain Hook, by contrast, emerges as a well-defined personality, and Tinker Bell, though her petulance gets irritating, has an insistent presence.

Cinderella

Cinderella was Disney's first true animated feature since *Bambi*. Released in 1950, it recaptured much of the spirit of the early features, modified by a new lightness of touch and an emphasis on surface glamour (see also overleaf)

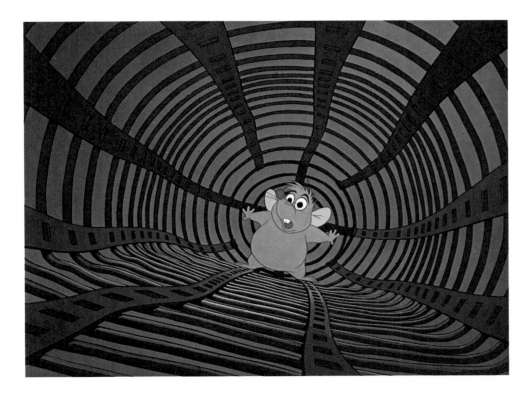

Cinderella's Fairy Godmother prepares her for the ball

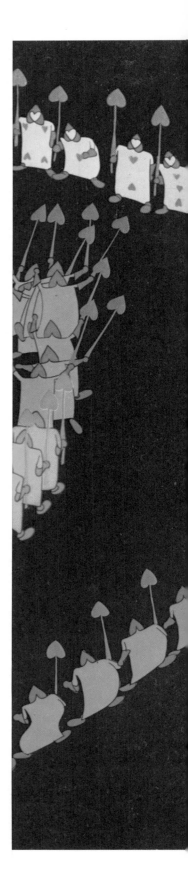

Peter Pan

Disney's version of *Peter Pan*, 1953, is a generally entertaining interpretation of Sir James Barrie's stage classic

Lady and the Tramp

Released in 1955, *Lady and the Tramp* was the first
animated feature made in Cinemascope. More significantly,
it broke new ground in terms of subject matter,
setting a more informal tone for future Disney movies
(see also overleaf)

Sleeping Beauty

Six years in the making,
Sleeping Beauty, 1959, marked
a temporary return to the world of
the fairy tale. Unfortunately, its highly
stylized treatment tended to slow the
action and interfere with character
development

The year 1955 saw the release of *Lady and the Tramp,* Disney's first animated feature to make use of the Cinemascope format. It is innovative in another way too. Set in the recent past, *Lady and the Tramp* deals with a kind of subject matter that had not been encountered at the Studio before, taking us for the first time into a world which is not far removed from our own. *Dumbo,* it is true, is set in the present, but its circus milieu makes it a special case, the atmosphere of the Big Top setting it apart from the everyday world. *Lady and the Tramp* is set largely in the suburbs of a medium-size American city in the early years of the century, an environment compounded from a vernacular that is still familiar today.

Cinemascope itself presented a challenge, especially to the layout artists. With a regular format it is easy enough for a single character to activate the whole screen, and characters can be closely grouped, which makes them easy to handle visually. A sense of space can be achieved by the use of pans, trucking shots, and clever editing. With Cinemascope, the sense of space is ready-made, but the stretched-out format makes it difficult for a single character to dominate. Groups must be well spread out to keep the screen from looking bare. Longer takes become necessary, since the constant jump-cutting that is the norm in animated films would seem busy and annoying.

Considering these problems, *Lady and the Tramp* turned out remarkably well. The animators did a good job of grafting human personalities onto the main characters without losing the nuances of dog behavior that were necessary if the story was to be convincing. Interaction between dogs and humans is neatly handled and there are some well-executed action scenes (Tramp killing the rat is one that springs to mind, and Jock and Trusty intercepting the dogcatcher's wagon at the climax of the movie). The film's humor is low-keyed—outright gag routines would have destroyed the atmosphere—and it features some agreeable songs, including "Bella Notte," "Siamese Cat Song," and Peggy Lee's rendition of "He's a Tramp." The Cinemascope format occasionally slows the pace a little, but in other scenes it is used very effectively. The backgrounds—starting with the opening scene of the city covered with a blanket of snow—are very effective in establishing the well-regulated world that forms Lady's character.

Lady and the Tramp was followed by another wide-screen feature—one that began with high hopes and ended in disaster.

Sleeping Beauty was conceived as the most spectacular of the postwar productions. Eyvind Earle devised background stylings based on early Renaissance paintings, and the characters were designed to blend with these settings. Much care was lavished on planning scenes to make the best possible use of the Technirama 70mm format, and the multiplane camera was to be used extensively.

Unfortunately, *Sleeping Beauty* went into production at a time when Disney was preoccupied not only with live-action pictures but also with his major project of the 1950s—Disneyland. It would seem that he found great difficulty in relating to *Sleeping Beauty* (perhaps he felt that he had done it all before in *Snow White* and *Cinderella*). As always, nothing could proceed without his approval, but because of his other concerns he often neglected the movie for weeks on end. As a result, *Sleeping Beauty* took six years to complete. It finally reached movie theaters in January, 1959, and was greeted with a pervasive lack of enthusiasm.

In all fairness, the film has some excellent moments. The evil fairy, Maleficent, is a well-conceived character and gets sterling support from her army of goons. The Good Fairies are entertaining, and there is some splendid effects animation, especially toward the climax, when the Prince is fighting his way to the castle, facing a fire-breathing dragon and a forest of thorns. Against this must be set the fact that the hero and heroine remain the merest of ciphers throughout the movie—their personalities are wholly compounded from clichés. Also, the backgrounds—though interesting in themselves—are so busy that they distract from the characters. The Technirama format led to some long, static scenes which cause the film to drag, and there is no escaping the fact that the story seems, finally, trite and unsatisfying. One ends up resenting that so much time, technical expertise, and, worst of all, talent has been wasted on so flimsy a vehicle. If we compare it with *Snow White* or even with *Cinderella,* we find a terrible disparity between form and content. The earlier treatments of fairy tales have a much greater intensity—they are substantial enough to be worthy of the gifts of the Disney artists. It was Disney himself who was able to supply this density of concept. When *Sleeping Beauty* was in production, his genius was at work elsewhere.

We must also consider the possibility that the time for fairy tales was past. *Lady and the Tramp* had pointed to another direction that Disney animation could take. The artists had proved that they were not limited to the more traditional forms of fantasy, and the animated features of the sixties would make this still more evident.

An *Alice in Wonderland* story conference: Winston Hibler, Ted Sears, Walt Disney, and Ed Penner

Recording the voice track for *Alice in Wonderland:* Jerry Colonna, Kathryn Beaumont, and Ed Wynn

10 Later Animation

As far as animation was concerned, new formats like Cinemascope and Technirama 70 proved to be more trouble than they were worth. The next feature, *One Hundred and One Dalmatians,* made use of a technical innovation which was to make a more lasting impact. During the fifties Ub Iwerks, now in charge of special processes at the Studio, had been experimenting with Xerox photography as an aid to animation. By 1959 he had modified a Xerox camera to transfer animators' drawings directly to cels, thus eliminating the inking process and preserving much of the spontaneity of the drawings. As a time (and money) saver, this was of enormous importance to the Studio, and it had a major effect on the way future Disney animation would look, since the distinctive character of the Xerox cels would influence the art direction. The Xerox line would now be employed for most backgrounds, too, so that there would be no stylistic clash between character and setting. This has meant that recent Disney films have had a more linear and graphic look—quite different from the tonal renderings that were so typical of the earlier features.

The first picture to make full use of Iwerks's Xerox techniques was a 1960 short titled *Goliath II. One Hundred and One Dalmatians* appeared the following year. Xerox was used

One Hundred and One Dalmatians

One Hundred and One Dalmatians, 1961, was the first feature to use the Xerox camera—a device which gave the backgrounds a more linear and graphic quality and helped preserve the spontaneity of the animators' drawings.
This film provides fast-moving entertainment and many good touches, including "quotations" from old Disney cartoons (seen on television), and Cruella de Vil, who is perhaps the best villainess in Disney's postwar movies

throughout, and the old inking method was resorted to only in a few instances where a colored line was needed.

In fact, the film would have been difficult to make without the Xerox camera. There are scenes in which literally dozens of puppies fill the screen—each of them liberally spotted—and to animate these scenes using traditional methods would have been a herculean task. The Xerox camera allowed the artists to bypass the problem by simply animating one small group of puppies—enough to occupy a fraction of the total area of the cel—and then using the camera to repeat this group across the entire surface, being careful, of course, that the repeat was not too mechanical. This system worked splendidly. Watching the film, one is not aware of any duplication.

One Hundred and One Dalmatians represents more than technical innovation. It is a very good movie. The new process made the artists' task easier and left them free to concentrate on

The Sword in the Stone

Released in 1963, *The Sword in the Stone* brought to the screen Disney's version of the boyhood of King Arthur

the real substance of the film—character development and story. Set in the present, the plot unfolds in London and the surrounding English countryside. The opening sequences, in which true love finds a way, are a little weak, but the moment Cruella de Vil—the villainess of the piece—enters the picture, the pace picks up and never flags again. The treatment is loose and witty, with plenty of action and laughs, and the viewer is given no chance to lose sympathy for the heroes as the story builds steadily to a fitting climax.

The dogs and other animals are, as in *Lady and the Tramp,* human surrogates and work very well as such. Perhaps the most interesting animation in the film, however, is reserved for the humans. They are drawn with a looseness which was new to Disney features, no attempt being made to imitate photographic reality. Elbows and knees are not always where they should be according to anatomy books, but everything works. Roger and Anita, the owners of the Dalmatians, are believable if not memorable, while Horace and Jasper, the two thugs, are excellent, projecting just the right degree of malicious stupidity. But the real triumph of the film is Cruella. Animated by Marc Davis, she is the most sophisticated of Disney bad guys (the plot revolves around her desire for a coat made from the skins of Dalmatian puppies). Her face is a blend of death mask and fashion plate, perfectly expressing her character, which is at the same time evil and laughable.

One Hundred and One Dalmatians is a consistently entertaining film. After the uncertainties of the previous decade, the Studio had recovered its old assurance, and in doing so had arrived at a new idiom. A good deal of the credit for this should go to Ken Anderson, who was responsible for production design, and to Bill Peet, who developed the story.

By the early sixties, the animation staff had been pared down to a fraction of what it had been in the heyday of *Pinocchio* and *Fantasia.* Increasingly, Disney relied on the group he referred to as "the nine old men" (Frank Thomas, Ollie Johnston, Milt Kahl, Eric Larson, Marc Davis, Woolie Reitherman, John Lounsbery, Ward Kimball, and Les Clark). These veterans were the key animators, but their ranks were depleted when Davis switched his attention to designing for Disneyland and Reitherman began to concentrate on directing. As the staff settled into a new rhythm, a policy emerged of having one feature-length movie ready for release every three or four years, punctuating this schedule with occasional special projects.

Unfortunately, the next animated feature was not one of the

The Jungle Book

Voice talents—including George Sanders, Phil Harris, Louis Prima, Sterling Holloway, and Sebastian Cabot—played an important part in the production of *The Jungle Book,* 1967. This adaptation of Kipling's stories also features some of the best animation of the postwar period (see also overleaf)

Studio's better efforts. Released in December, 1963, *The Sword in the Stone* presents the boyhood of King Arthur, concentrating on his education at the hands of Merlin the Magician. The film totally misses the tone of T.H. White's story and, while there are some amusing set pieces and the animation is as accomplished as ever, character development is weak. Merlin, instead of being awesome, is presented as a bungling nincompoop, thus destroying the essence of the plot.

The Jungle Book was the last animated film that Walt Disney ever produced. In the late fall of 1966, a medical checkup revealed that he was suffering from advanced cancer of the lung. One lung was removed, but six weeks later, on December 15, he died in his room at St. Joseph's Hospital in Burbank, directly across the street from the Studio. He was sixty-five years old. *The Jungle Book* was not quite finished, and the Disney artists were left with the painful task of completing it without him. Happily, *The Jungle Book* is a film that he would have been proud of. It takes great liberties with Kipling's original, but these are justified by the end result.

In developing characters for the great shorts of the thirties, Disney had relied heavily on voice talent. The vocal tricks of Clarence Nash and Pinto Colvig were absolutely essential to the emergence of Donald and Goofy as major personalities, and Disney's own falsetto was every bit as much a part of Mickey as the Mouse's big ears and bulbous shoes. Voices for the feature movies had always been chosen with great care, but with one or two exceptions they had not had quite the same strong impact on character development (it would be easy enough, for instance, to imagine Snow White or Bambi with slightly different voices, but try the same thing with Mickey or Donald and all is lost). The features were planned so carefully that a little leeway was possible in voice selection, whereas a cartoon starring Goofy relied to a considerable extent on the spark that Colvig's voice mannerisms provided.

The Jungle Book was the first feature film of which it can be said that the voice talents were more than just appropriate. Phil Harris, George Sanders, Sterling Holloway, Louis Prima, Verna Felton, Pat O'Malley, and Sebastian Cabot were chosen to speak for the animals of Kipling's jungle—all of them actors whose voices had distinct personalities that would to a large extent dictate the approach the animators would have to take. We have remarked more than once that animators think of themselves as actors, and now they took on the challenging task of matching their own skills to the performances of the live actors.

The two greatest successes of the film are Baloo the bear,

whose voice is that of Phil Harris, and Shere Khan the tiger, played by George Sanders. Harris knew how to dominate a recording session, improvising on the "script" supplied by the story boards and building the character into something that felt real and alive. The animators then had the challenge of entering this character and making him perform on screen.

The ideal Disney villain is menacing and comic at the same time. We must sense that he is a real threat, but unless we can laugh at him too, he could destroy the whole mood of the film. Shere Khan is a tiger stalking an innocent boy—not the usual stuff of humor—but Sanders's delivery, threatening and pompous at the same time, has just the right edge to it, and it is impossible to imagine in retrospect that he could have been replaced by any other actor.

Several other characters—Sterling Holloway's snake, for example, and an ironically inclined vulture with a Liverpool accent—are excellent. Louis Prima's Dixieland ape also has some good moments. Mowgli, the boy brought up in the jungle, is less distinctive as far as voice is concerned, but this is made up for by the quality of the animation, which captures admirably the mixture of agility and awkwardness which seems just right for his young body.

Before he died, Walt Disney had—on the strength of a board of drawings by Ken Anderson—given the go-ahead for the next feature project, which appeared in 1970 as *The Aristocats*. This film blends the vernacular style of *One Hundred and One Dalmatians* with *The Jungle Book*'s developments in voice characterization, and the result is a delightful comedy that has enjoyed great popularity.

An aristocratic cat named Duchess (Eva Gabor) and her three kittens become the objects of the evil designs of their mistress's butler. Stranded in the French countryside, they are befriended by an alley cat called O'Malley (Phil Harris again). The film follows their adventures as they make their way back to Paris, only to be confronted once more by the black-hearted butler. This time the villain gets his just desserts and Duchess and O'Malley live happily ever after (the story line is reminiscent of *Lady and the Tramp*).

The plot is full of amusing incidents and is enlivened by some well-established secondary characters who include the country dogs, Napoleon and Lafayette (Pat Buttram and George Lindsey), and a pair of English geese (played by Carole Shelley and Monica Evans).

Winnie the Pooh and the Honey Tree (1966) and *Winnie the Pooh and the Blustery Day* (1968) are a pair of admirable

Scenes from *The Aristocats*, ▶
which was released in 1970

The Aristocats

Some of Ken Anderson's
sketches for *The Aristocats*.
Overleaf: a moonlit night in Paris,
from the finished production

Winnie the Pooh and the Blustery Day

Featuring Tigger, Eeyore, and, of course, Pooh Bear,
Winnie the Pooh and the Blustery Day, 1968,
is a charming adaptation of an A.A. Milne story

featurettes made during this same period. Apart from American-izing some of A.A. Milne's characters, the Disney artists dealt very capably with the difficult task of translating the atmosphere of the original to the screen. The second film is especially good, with imaginative animation of the book itself (wind and rain threaten to blow or wash the words from the pages). Most of the characters are well conceived, with Tigger perhaps the out-standing success.

Important animated sequences were included in two recent live-action films—*Mary Poppins* (1964) and *Bedknobs and Broomsticks* (1971). These owed a great deal to a new matte sys-tem developed by Ub Iwerks, which enabled live action and ani-mation to be combined far more effectively than ever before (this system involved filming actors against a "sodium screen," then printing this image along with the animation in such a way as to eliminate all evidence of a "seam" between figure and ground).

Iwerks, whose contribution to the Studio had been so significant, died in 1971.

If we look back over the animated features of the postwar period, we do not, it must be admitted, find any classics to compare with *Snow White, Pinocchio,* or *Fantasia.* Those films profited from the energy that was generated in the breakthrough to fea-ture production and from the fact that Walt Disney gave them his undivided attention. During the postwar period he was often preoccupied with other projects, and while he stayed closely in touch, he never again involved himself quite so intensely with animation. By way of compensation, his artists had become very experienced and could take on more responsibility without this being reflected in a serious loss of quality.

At least five of the postwar features—*Cinderella, Lady and the Tramp, One Hundred and One Dalmatians, The Jungle Book,* and *The Aristocats*—are excellent, each of them moving toward a more informal kind of entertainment. If we put these together with the first five features and the best shorts of the thirties and forties, we have an extraordinary body of work. Walt Disney's achievement can hardly be overstated. He took a mar-ginal branch of the entertainment industry, transformed it into an art form, and then went on to make a major contribution to the history of the cinema.

What makes this all the more remarkable is the fact that it represents only one aspect of his career.

11 The Making of Robin Hood

There is a degree of overlap in the production of Disney animated features. Before one is finished, the next is already in a fairly advanced stage of planning. Several possible stories will be investigated and one selected as the most likely candidate. Almost everyone will be involved in this process, with the director, Woolie Reitherman, and his top animators very much to the fore. But the man who has the greatest responsibility at this stage is Ken Anderson, whose wide experience in layout, story, character design, and art direction makes him an excellent choice for the task of developing new projects. While *The Aristocats* was still on the boards, Anderson was exploring possibilities for the next film. Studio executives favored a "classic" as the subject of the next movie. Ken Anderson suggested a new treatment of the Robin Hood legends, and everyone was enthusiastic.

Once an overall approach and the broad outlines of the story had been decided on, the Studio began to look around for voice talent to fit the characters, and a notable array of acting ability was assembled. Peter Ustinov was signed to play Prince John, a vain and insecure lion who is the pathetic villain of the piece. Terry-Thomas was cast as the snake Sir Hiss, Prince John's constant and obsequious companion. Robin Hood, portrayed as a fox, is played by Brian Bedford, and Phil Harris is

320

featured once again, this time as the voice of Little John. Other talents concerned include those of Andy Devine, Pat Buttram, and country and western singer Roger Miller.

Except for a few technical improvements, such as the introduction of the Xerox camera, the process of producing an animated feature has not changed much since *Snow White*. It is still essentially a team effort (more so than ever now that Disney is no longer there to give direction). The movie develops in a piecemeal way, with some sequences fully animated while others are just reaching the story-board phase. Production is a slow business (three to four years separate the first tentative sketches from the completed project) with ideas being fed in from many different sources. Apart from the imaginative work, there are many practical matters to be taken into consideration. Model sheets must be made so that each character will be drawn consistently, and a close liaison must be maintained between the director and the inking and painting department to make sure that such things as color configurations are completely understood and do not become too cumbersome. (Should the yoke of Alan-a-Dale's tunic be a different color? Would that make the character easier to read against certain backgrounds?) Exposure sheets must be prepared and camera schedules planned. The musical director (George Bruns in this case) begins to think about the score. Specific songs must be written for some sequences before they can be animated. A hundred activities, all seemingly independent of one another, are carried out at the same time, eventually coming together as ninety minutes or so of motion picture entertainment. Everything seems casual and unplanned. What makes it all pull together is the fact that the key figures in the production team have worked as a team for decades and know what to expect from each other.

The first animator to work in earnest on *Robin Hood* was Ollie Johnston. While the remainder of the staff was still engaged on another project, Johnston began to develop the character of Prince John, building on Ustinov's voice track and Ken Anderson's character sketches. (Anderson had turned, for inspiration, to the cartoon segments of *Song of the South*—recalling that everyone had enjoyed working on that picture and theorizing that it represented "the kind of thing we do best.") In delineating the personality of the decadent lion, Johnston was very much guided by Ustinov's interpretation of the character—so much so, in fact, that it is impossible to watch Prince John's scenes without seeing a strong hint of the actor's features under the animal's shaggy mane. Johnston added touches of his own, rounding the character out; then the other animators joined him,

Terry-Thomas, the voice of the snake ▶ Sir Hiss, acts out a scene at the recording studio. Below, he studies a story board with Ollie Johnston, Woolie Reitherman, and Larry Clemmons (kneeling)

324

Ken Anderson, left, seen here with
two assistants, was art director and character
designer for *Robin Hood*

A *Robin Hood* story board,
illustrating the theft of
Prince John's gold

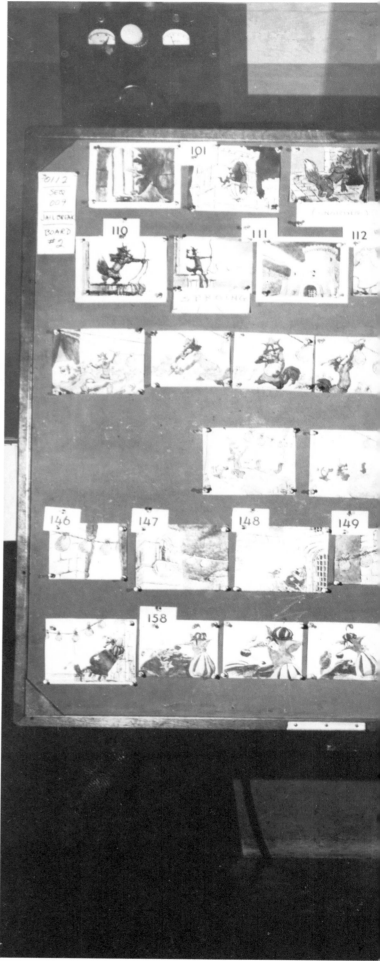

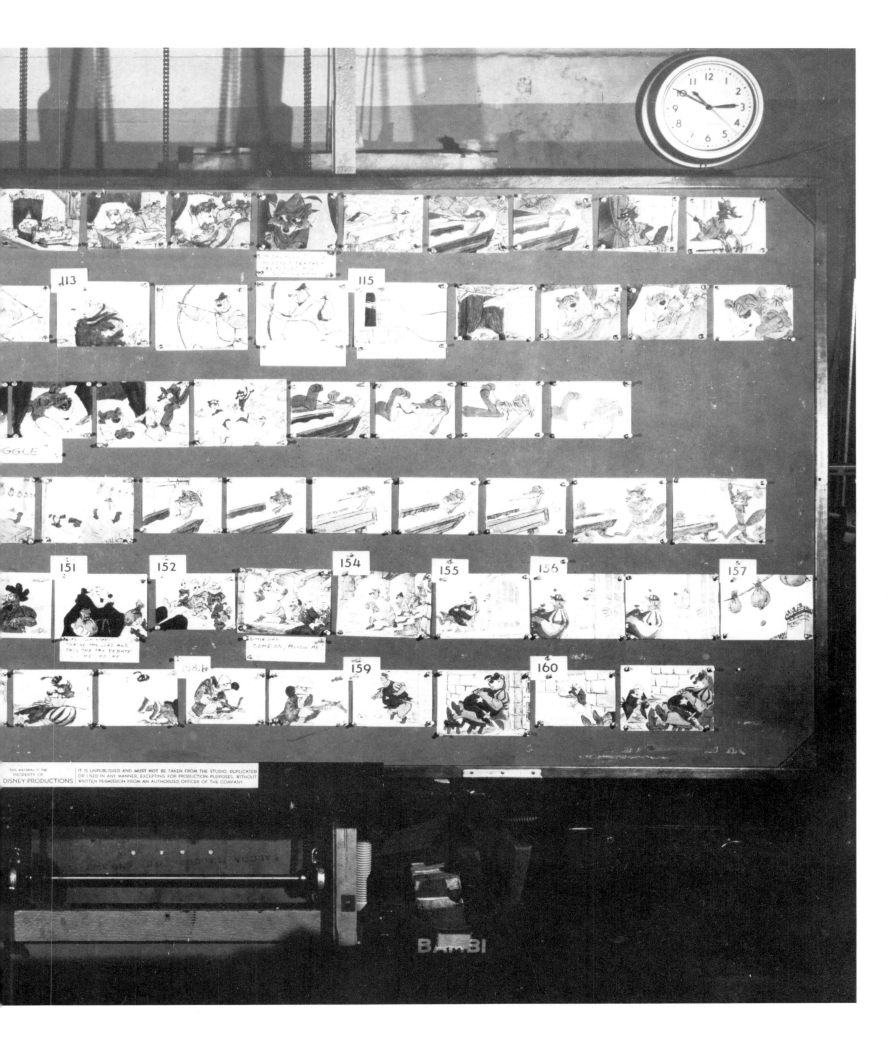

Robin Hood and Little John in Sherwood Forest

making their own contributions. No one person is totally responsible for the overall concept of Prince John. His character is blended from the contributions of a dozen different people.

Further projects are already being planned. In one important respect, then, this discussion of Disney animation must remain incomplete, since we are talking about a going concern. Just how much of a future there is for animated features depends on the extent to which younger artists can be attracted to a craft which demands a long and exacting apprenticeship. The present

Like many other Disney films, *Robin Hood* uses animals to caricature human types

The Making of One Frame

This image is just one of more than a hundred thousand that must be photographed for an animated feature such as *Robin Hood,* and each camera set-up is itself the end product of a complex sequence of diversified activities. The following pages illustrate some of the key phases in this sequence

is head of the team of back‹
rs who translate layout draw‹
iled full-color renderings. The
e careful to provide just the
setting. Usually it will be low-
the animated characters can be
against it. At the same time,
kground painter can contribute
atmosphere of a film, provid‹
and richness of detail that
nation convincing

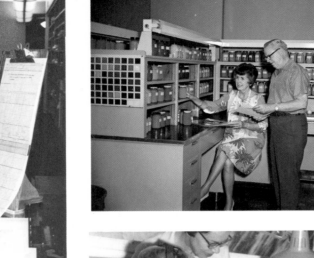

When drawings are sent to the ink and paint department, they are checked to ensure that no technical errors have crept in. Here, Mimi Thornton works at a mechanical table which is an exact duplicate of those used in the camera department. It can be used to ascertain the correctness of trucking shots, pans, zoom effects, or any other kind of camera movement that might have been called for. Details of these are codified in the exposure sheet

When an animation drawing has been checked, a Xerox camera is used to transfer it to the cel—a sheet of transparent celluloid

The Disney ink and paint department includes a color laboratory where colors are prepared and checked for consistency. Grace Turner, then head of the department, is seen here with Steve McAvoy selecting pigments for use in *Robin Hood*

Once an animation drawing has been Xeroxed onto a cel, it is passed to a specialist who fills in the character with opaque color—a delicate task demanding great care. A single air bubble or speck of dust would seem gigantic when magnified on the theater screen

Before any cels are allowed to leave ink and paint, Katherine Kerwin subjects them to a final check similar to the one that has already been run on the drawings

Eventually, each set-up—cel and background —is delivered to the camera department and photographed individually

Far left: a *Robin Hood* story conference with, left to right, writer Larry Clemmons, director Woolie Reitherman, art director Ken Anderson, and animator Frank Thomas. Left: Milt Kahl, one of the Studio's top artists, at his animation desk

dynasty of animators can carry the weight of production for a time, but there is an urgent need for reinforcements.

For the time being, however, the organization that Walt Disney built continues to occupy its unique position in the motion picture industry.

III
LIVE-ACTION
FILMS

12 Actors and Animals

Walt Disney's greatest contribution to the motion picture industry was the genius he brought to the art of animation. Since World War II, however, his Studio has become equally well known for its live-action movies and its television shows. Many of the live-action features have been relatively modest productions, but others—such as *20,000 Leagues Under the Sea* and *Mary Poppins*—have been lavish productions in the grand Hollywood tradition. The one thing that they all have in common is that they are carefully designed for family audiences (in recent years, Disney movies have found themselves in almost sole possession of this lucrative market).

Disney had had limited experience in live-action production stretching back to his Kansas City days (the Alice Comedies had, of course, involved the filming of a number of juvenile performers), but the release in 1941 of *The Reluctant Dragon* can be seen as a significant departure from the mainstream of the Studio's productions. At one level this film is a documentary about Disney animation, but it becomes more than that as the result of a linking narrative device which has Robert Benchley visiting the Burbank premises with the intention of selling a movie idea (he performs this chore under duress, prompted by his domineering wife). When Benchley arrives at the main gate, he is given a pass and a uniformed escort who is to conduct him into the presence of Mr. Disney. Managing to elude his guide, he finds himself involved in all kinds of Studio activities—story conferences, art classes, recording sessions, and the like. Friendly animators show him the secrets of their craft while a charming young lady introduces him to the magic of the paint laboratory and the multiplane camera, also demonstrating to him how sound effects are produced. Eventually Benchley does reach Disney, only to discover that the idea he is trying to sell has already been made into a movie. These incidents are punctuated by short cartoon inserts, including one called "The Reluctant Dragon," and all kinds of tricks are introduced to help the narrative along (at one point the movie changes from black-and-white to Technicolor). *The Reluctant Dragon* is something of a curiosity. Unpretentious and charming, it gives us an interesting if somewhat fictionalized account of the Disney Studio during its golden age.

This venture did not mark an immediate shift to live-action production, but it did serve to underscore the fact that live-action filming costs a good deal less than animation. As we know, the forties were a difficult time for the Studio, and economic considerations could not be ignored.

Segments of live-action footage began to find their way into package films such as *The Three Caballeros* and *Fun and Fancy Free,* but the real breakthrough came with *Song of the South,* released in 1946, the first Disney film that used a full complement of professional actors to tell an entirely fictional story. It also capitalized on the reputation of Disney animation by including three cartoon episodes, but from the point of view of future developments it was more significant that the live-action sequences were well conceived and executed. *Song of the South* displays the confident professionalism one expects from Hollywood movies of that period. As well as good performances from almost all the actors, the film benefited by the photography of Gregg Toland—best known for his work on Orson Welles's *Citizen Kane*—who was perhaps the greatest cameraman of his generation. Disney must have been well satisfied with this venture. It showed him that the principles which the Studio had been refining for almost two decades could be successfully adapted to this more conventional kind of film-making.

A little more than two years later, in January, 1949, Disney released *So Dear to My Heart,* which, like *Song of the South,* starred Bobby Driscoll and Luana Patten as children in nineteenth-century rural America. A minimal amount of animation was used in this film; for all practical purposes it is a live-

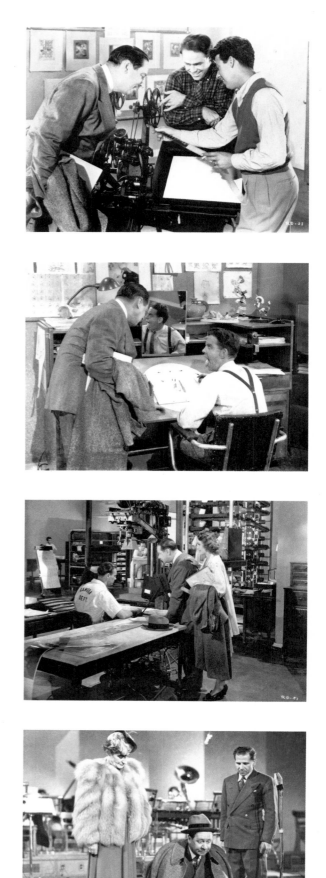

action production telling the story of a boy and his pet sheep. Lacking a central figure as strong as James Baskett's Uncle Remus, the film is less memorable than *Song of the South,* but it is another well-made movie with a good deal to recommend it.

The next phase in the development of Disney live-action production came about largely as the result of a historical accident. Because of postwar monetary restrictions, a sizable amount of Disney capital, the product of accrued royalties, was frozen in the United Kingdom. This meant that funds which were not available to the company in the United States could be used in the British Isles. On the advice of his brother Roy, Walt Disney decided to use these funds to make live-action films in England. The fruits of this venture were four costume dramas—*Treasure Island, The Story of Robin Hood and His Merrie Men, The Sword and the Rose,* and *Rob Roy, the Highland Rogue*—which were released between 1950 and 1954.

All four of these films can be described as unpretentious, well-told, satisfying adventure stories. *Treasure Island,* the first and probably the best of the series, is based on Robert Louis Stevenson's classic novel and is highlighted by Robert Newton's mesmerizing performance as Long John Silver. Long John, with his eye patch, wooden leg, and almost mechanical mannerisms, is half menacing and half funny, an archetypal Disney villain who could have fitted without much difficulty into any of the animated features. Newton, squeezing every last drop of melodrama from the character, steals scenes with apparent ease and provides the spark that lifts *Treasure Island* above the ordinary—although even without Newton the movie would have had enough good qualities to ensure its success. The screenplay is simple but effective, Byron Haskin's direction is clean and straightforward, the acting is good throughout, and the action sequences are handled with vigor and style.

The same general virtues are to be found in the other British adventure stories. These films, which featured performers such as Richard Todd, Jack Hawkins, James Robertson Justice, and Glynis Johns, introduced Disney to the reservoir of acting talent that was available in London, one he would draw upon often in future projects.

Beyond that, these movies make imaginative use of the natural beauties of the English and Scottish landscape. Well photographed, they capture the softness of damp summers and are full of mysterious glimpses of castles half hidden by lush vegetation or standing starkly on windswept moors. Disney involved himself closely in all aspects of the production of these films, and spent a good part of his summers in England.

◀ In *The Reluctant Dragon,* 1941, Robert Benchley finds himself on the loose in the Disney Studio. In the bottom picture, Benchley is seen with Clarence Nash and Florence Gill, the voices of Donald Duck and Clara Cluck

Walt Disney relaxes in Uncle Remus's rocking chair

Song of the South

Although it includes segments
of animation, *Song of the South,*
released in 1946, is primarily
a live-action costume drama.
Set in the Deep South, the
film stars James Baskett as
Uncle Remus

So Dear to My Heart

Song of the South was followed, in 1949, ▶
by *So Dear to My Heart,* another nostalgic
look at America's rural past.
The film reaches its climax in
the picturesque setting of a county fair.
Bottom left: on location for
So Dear to My Heart. Surrounded by
equipment and crew, Luana Patten
waits on the bank of a creek while
her double poses in the water
so that the director can set up
his shot. Bottom right: creating an
artificial rainstorm for a dramatic
sequence in the movie

Treasure Island

Starring Robert Newton and Bobby Driscoll,
Treasure Island, 1949, was the first in a series of costume
dramas made in the British Isles

Modest as these movies were, they did a great deal to restore the fortunes of the Studio and must have made Disney increasingly aware of the part that live action would have to play in his future plans. By the early 1950s he was fully committed. Animation would continue, but the Studio facilities would have to be modified to accommodate other kinds of production.

The Disney Studio had one great advantage over its competitors. Because of its background in animation, it was geared to deal with unconventional ideas. If Disney wanted to make a costume drama, that presented no problem—Hollywood was full of skilled technicians who could supply the know-how—but thirty years had taught him that this was not the only way to make movies. He had, of necessity, become unusually resourceful. He was, by inclination and habit, a pioneer.

At some point soon after the war, he seems to have conceived the idea of making a film about the pioneer spirit. He realized that the last frontier within the political orbit of the United States was Alaska. The conventional Hollywood approach to a subject such as the last frontier would have involved a couple of major stars, a director with a reputation for handling epic subjects, and a big budget, but Disney was not bound by convention and his approach was quite different. He got in touch with a man by the name of Al Milotte, who owned a camera store in Alaska. Milotte and his wife, Elma, had experience with 16mm filming, and Disney asked them to shoot some footage for him, without being very specific about what it should be. He asked merely for glimpses of Alaskan life that might suggest some possible line of development. The Milottes traveled around the Territory, shooting anything that seemed interesting. Periodically the film would arrive at the Studio and Disney would screen it. One month it might be salmon fishing, the next panning for gold or the mechanics of copper mining. For a while, nothing emerged that inspired any particular treatment or narrative line.

Al Milotte had for some time wanted to visit the Pribilof Islands—bleak rocks in the Bering Sea—to film the thousands of fur seals that migrate there annually to mate and raise their pups. He asked Disney if this would be of interest. Disney wired him to go ahead, and soon footage of seals began to arrive at the Studio. According to James Algar, who was one of those entrusted with the task of structuring this footage, it was difficult at first to make much sense of the material they were screening, but Disney saw something that held his interest. The seals were acting out a primitive rite that had been repeated for thousands

On location in Scotland during
the filming of *Rob Roy, the Highland Rogue*

of years. The problem was to present this rite in dramatic terms that would be readily understood by a theater audience. The Disney staff began to research the subject and to put together the story of the seals' life cycle; eventually they developed a clear pattern of events which could provide a usable framework for a movie. The film sent by the Milottes was tailored to this story, and the result was a twenty-seven-minute picture titled *Seal Island,* released in 1949.

Seal Island was not an easy movie to sell. Distributors could not envision what market there would be for it, but eventually a Pasadena theater gave the film a short run. Audience response was good, and *Seal Island* was nominated for an Academy Award as the best short subject of the year. The film won the Oscar and Disney's True Life Adventure Series was successfully launched. In searching for the last frontier, Disney had discovered a new frontier—nature. The commercial cinema had never dealt with nature as a primary subject. The potential was, of course, enormous.

Between 1950 and 1960, more than a dozen True Life Adventures were produced by the Studio. The two-reel format introduced by *Seal Island* was used for most subjects—titles include *Beaver Valley, Nature's Half Acre, The Olympic Elk, Bear Country, Prowlers of the Everglades,* and *Water Birds.* Six feature-length films were also made—*The Living Desert, The Vanishing Prairie, The African Lion, White Wilderness, Secrets of Life,* and *Jungle Cat.*

The Milottes were involved in several of these productions, but many other cameramen also contributed to the True Life Adventures—most of them trained naturalists. The same basic formula was used for all the films. A subject was chosen and crews dispatched to the appropriate locations to gather footage (films such as *Secrets of Life* demanded laboratory filming rather than outdoor work). The raw material was sent back to Hollywood and edited into usable form by a team headed by James Algar, Winston Hibler, and Ben Sharpsteen. These men, like Disney, had been trained in the animation side of the business, and this to some extent influenced the final product. They understood a certain way of telling a story and stuck to it—a fact which gives these films a character rather different from that of many of the nature films seen on television today. Recent nature movies have generally attempted an objective approach to their subject matter, but the Disney films were quite openly subjective. The producers relied on the audience's tendency to identify with the animals at an emotional level, so animal behavior was interpreted in human terms. The structure of each movie and

Seal Island

Filmed by Al and Elma Milotte, *Seal Island* was the first of Disney's True Life Adventures. It was made, almost by accident, as an offshoot of a projected film about Alaska. Though somewhat marred by a rather coy sound track, it created at one stroke a completely new genre—the general-interest nature film

The Living Desert

One of the most successful
of the True Life Adventures,
The Living Desert, 1953, is a
feature-length production marked by
spectacular nature photography

The Vanishing Prairie

During the production of
The Vanishing Prairie, 1954, one cameraman, above,
disguised himself as a buffalo so that
he could mingle with the herd

350

The African Lion

A specially constructed camera truck allowed Al and Elma Milotte to shoot
extraordinary wildlife footage for *The African Lion,* released in 1955
(see also overleaf)

356

A swarm of locusts, filmed for *The African Lion*

The True Life Adventures took film-makers into all kinds of terrain
and led to the development of many kinds of special equipment, including such bizarre
items as the propeller-driven snowmobiles used in the production of *White Wilderness*, 1958

the commentary that accompanies it were conceived with this end in mind.

The True Life Adventures have sometimes been criticized for this subjectivity, and to some extent this criticism is justified. Certainly the material is presented in such a way that we are not given much chance to interpret it for ourselves. At the same time, we must take into consideration the fact that these films were not intended to be scientific documents—they were designed for the enjoyment of a mass audience that was not yet prepared to accept this kind of material without a measure of sweetening.

No one can question the quality of the photography. Disney gave the naturalists time and equipment, and they repaid him with some of the finest nature footage that had ever been shot. Good lightweight cameras were available, but unfortunately the equivalent in sound-recording equipment did not yet exist, so whole sections of the sound track had to be produced at the Studio. The ingenuity of sound-effects man Jim MacDonald was tested over and over again.

Spin-offs from the True Life Adventures include the People and Places series and, more significantly, the many later Disney films which blend animal footage with conventional live-action dramas. *Perri,* released in 1957, was the story of a squirrel; its material was similar to that used in the True Life Adventures, but was organized in such a way that it corresponded with the fictional narrative on which the film was based.

In later films, clever editing has been used to combine semidocumentary footage with scenes involving human performers in such a way that animals appear to respond intelligently to fictional situations. Other studios had used this technique for series such as *Lassie* and *Rin-Tin-Tin,* but Disney producers often used nondomestic animals such as bears, coyotes, even wolverines in this way. Since many of these creatures could not be trained in the conventional sense, movies of this kind demand great patience on the part of both animal handlers and cameramen. Producers such as James Algar, Winston Hibler, Harry Tytle, Ken Peterson, and Roy E. Disney (Roy's son and Walt's nephew) have developed tremendous expertise in this field.

Nevertheless, these films raise the same kind of problems that were posed by *Bambi.* The dual necessity of making the animals' behavior seem naturalistic and making them seem to respond to fictional situations tends to become an impossible burden, and the results are apt to be unsatisfactory.

Walt Disney with Luana Patten,
Charlie McCarthy, Edgar Bergen,
and Mortimer Snerd

13 Davy Crockett and Other Heroes

As early as the 1930s, Walt Disney had been aware of the potential importance of television—perhaps because Mickey Mouse cartoons were used in early tests of transmitting equipment—and he was careful to retain television rights to all his films. By the late 1940s, the other major studios were seriously worried about the impact the new medium was having on theater attendance, and tried to recoup some of their losses by selling the home-screen rights to their backlog of productions. Disney was almost alone in holding out against the short-term advantages of this course of action.

In view of his foresight in this respect, one might have expected Disney immediately to involve the Studio in television production, but he did not. When the networks approached him with invitations to launch a television series, he declined their

offers (perhaps because of his bad experience with an earlier radio show). He did, however, agree to put together a single sixty-minute special for the Coca-Cola Company, to be broadcast by NBC on Christmas Day, 1950. The task of writing and producing the show was allocated to Bill Walsh, whose first job for the Studio had been devising gags for the Mickey Mouse newspaper strip. He recalls telling Walt, "But I don't know how to produce a TV show." Disney's reply was, "Who does?"

Walsh describes this first television venture as being stuck together with glue and chicken wire. "It used Edgar Bergen with Charlie McCarthy and Mortimer Snerd and we got the voice in the mirror from *Snow White* which conjured up the old films, and we slipped in a lot of footage promoting films that were going to come out pretty soon." This show, titled *One Hour in Wonderland,* got excellent ratings and was followed the next year by *The Walt Disney Christmas Show,* sponsored this time by the Johnson and Johnson Company and broadcast by CBS.

Davy Crockett

Starring Fess Parker and Buddy Ebsen, *Davy Crockett* was the great success of Disney's first television season, inspiring millions of youngsters to acquire coonskin caps

The Mickey Mouse Club featured the
Mouseketeers, a group of youngsters with
no previous show-business experience.
The star of the series, bottom,
was Annette Funicello

When, a little later, the American Broadcasting Company once again asked Disney to consider the possibility of a series, he revised his position. He was still not entirely enthusiastic about television for the sake of television, but he did see the value of regular programing as a promotional vehicle for his theatrical productions and other ventures. Besides, he was anxious to go ahead with his plans for building Disneyland, and in order to raise the necessary funds he needed a financially secure partner. In return for the prestige of a Disney series, ABC agreed to make a major investment in the park. The new series was, quite appropriately, titled *Disneyland*.

Having retained television rights to all his films, Disney had a great reservoir of past productions to draw on, but a good deal of fresh material was prepared for the initial season. Bill Walsh, series producer, recalls how almost at once they came up with a hit of quite stunning magnitude: "We were planning to do a series on American folk heroes—like Johnny Appleseed, Daniel Boone, and Big Foot Wallace—and the first one we picked out, by dumb luck, was Davy Crockett. At that time he was considered just one more frontiersman. We shot it down in Tennessee and when we got the film back to the Studio, we found we didn't have quite enough footage for three sixty-minute shows. So Walt said, 'Why don't you take some drawings and stick them all together and give an idea of what the show's going to be about.' So we put the drawings together, sketches of Davy's life, and Walt said, 'Well, that looks kind of dull. Maybe we can get a song to go with them.' We got Tom Blackburn, who wrote the script, and he said, 'But I never wrote a song before in my life.' We told him to try it. He and George Bruns, who composed the score, went down the hall. They came back in about twenty minutes and said, 'Well, this isn't much.' And they began, 'Born on a mountaintop in Tennessee. . . .' I thought it sounded pretty awful, but we didn't have time for anything else."

The song was, of course, "The Ballad of Davy Crockett," which—like the television episodes themselves—enjoyed enormous success. There was only one snag: everyone knew that Davy Crockett died at the Alamo, which meant that the three original episodes could not be extended in any straightforward chronological way (some time later two more stories were filmed for television).

The initial production was shown in three parts: "Davy Crockett, Indian Fighter," "Davy Crockett Goes to Congress," and "Davy Crockett at the Alamo." Although they were transmitted in black-and-white, they were filmed in color, which meant that the footage could advantageously be re-edited for theater release. Seeing this slightly shorter version today, one must observe that it stands up remarkably well, having the same kind of basic strengths as Disney's British costume dramas. The story is told with crispness and a minimum of fuss. Acting and action sequences are excellent. The landscape is used to create atmosphere and the result is a well-constructed, fast-moving adventure story. As biography the plot may be a bit oversimplified, but it remains essentially faithful to the spirit of the legend. Although Crockett made his name in the Indian wars, he is shown to have been sympathetic to the Indians, defending their civil rights in Congress. Fess Parker plays the hero with a rugged dignity which seems completely appropriate, and he receives excellent support, especially from Buddy Ebsen.

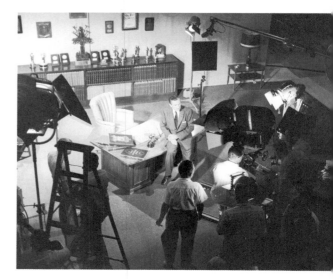

The original *Disneyland* series was broadcast on Wednesday nights and continued in that time slot for four years. For the 1958–59 season the name was changed to *Walt Disney Presents* and the program was moved to Friday evenings. During the 1960–61 season *Walt Disney Presents* was shown on Sunday evenings; in the fall of 1961, the program made a major switch, moving to the NBC television network, where it has kept its Sunday evening time slot. After the move to NBC, all Disney television shows were transmitted in color and the name was changed once again—to *Walt Disney's Wonderful World of Color.* The title was later altered to *Wonderful World of Disney,* but these changes are irrelevant to the central point, which is that the sixty-minute weekly format which Disney developed in 1954 has remained immensely popular—adding up to one of television's all-time success stories.

Another hugely popular Disney show was *The Mickey Mouse Club,* which was launched on October 3, 1955, and televised each weekday afternoon until 1959. Once again, Bill Walsh was entrusted with the task of getting the new series off the ground.

"Walt told me he was taking me off the weekly show. I said, 'Thank God—I'm exhausted.' He said, 'There's a new show I want you to do called *The Mickey Mouse Club.* This one will be an hour every day.' "

Finding children for the show was a problem in itself.

"All we knew," explains Walsh, "was that we had to go on the air in a couple of months with a show that would be broadcast five times a week, and we had to find the kids who could do it. I remember Walt saying, 'Don't get me those kinds with the tightly curled hairdos—tap dancers—get me children who look like they're having fun. Then later we can teach them

◄ Another Disney television series featured
the adventures of *Zorro*

◄ A camera crew films Disney as he introduces
one of his television shows

to tap dance or sing or whatever.' He suggested that if we went to ordinary schools and watched the kids at recess, pretty soon we'd find there would be one we would watch—whether he was doing anything or not—because that would be the one we'd be interested in. And that would be the kid we'd want for the show. So we used this technique and we found Annette and Darlene and Cubby and the bunch—and for some reason or another they all became popular."

The show developed a pleasant, informal format with which children could identify. The talents of the Mouseketeers were combined with old Disney cartoons and many other kinds of material. Dramatic serials, such as "Spin and Marty," became a popular feature of the program. In Walsh's words, "We developed various techniques by simple force of being there. Everything the kids could do, they did—and the key was Annette Funicello. For some reason or other, from the very first week of the show Annette got all the fan mail. Nobody understood what the heck was going on. There were many other kids on the show—very good, some of them—but for some reason Annette got all the mail, so everything was more or less keyed to her." The show was still getting excellent ratings when it ended, but Annette had outgrown her role.

Other series such as *Zorro* and *The Mouse Factory* enabled the Disney Studio to retain an important share of the television market. Over the years, it has continued to aim its programing at the most stable area of the market—the family audience—allowing for gradual shifts of taste rather than attempting to make radical changes.

In 1954, the year in which the *Disneyland* television series was launched, the Studio released *20,000 Leagues Under the Sea,* easily its most ambitious live-action picture up to that point. Far removed from its modest predecessors, *20,000 Leagues* was planned as a big-budget movie using major Hollywood stars (Kirk Douglas, James Mason, Paul Lukas, and Peter Lorre) and spectacular special effects.

Oddly enough, *20,000 Leagues* came into being as a by-product of the True Life Adventures. Bill Walsh and Card Walker had discussed the possibility of making an undersea film for the nature series, and this triggered the notion of adapting Jules Verne's classic for the screen. Disney was not enthusiastic at first, but Walsh and Walker eventually convinced him that the subject matter was ideal for a Disney audience. There was, of course, no doubt that this was a good title—one that was internationally known. Disney decided to buy the property from

20,000 Leagues
Under the Sea

Released in 1954, *20,000 Leagues Under the Sea*
was the Studio's most lavish live-action film
up to that point. It featured elaborate sets, exotic locations,
and spectacular scenes shot in a special water tank

Blending exciting action with a drama of ideas,
20,000 Leagues Under the Sea centers on the exploits
of the submarine *Nautilus*, right, commanded by James Mason,
below, in the guise of Captain Nemo.
His unwilling guests are Kirk Douglas, Peter Lorre,
and Paul Lukas. A highlight of the story,
opposite, is a battle with a giant squid

MGM, which owned the rights. To write and direct the film, he called in Earl Feldman and Dick Fleischer, two young men who had collaborated on some interesting B movies for RKO. Soon *20,000 Leagues* was in production.

The project demanded elaborate sets and a great deal of trick photography. Much of the action was shot in a large water tank on one of the Disney sound stages; other scenes were filmed in an outdoor tank at the Fox lot, and location work was done in Jamaica and off San Diego. One high spot of the action is a violent fight between the crew of the submarine *Nautilus* and a giant squid—a sequence that called for all the ingenuity the Studio could muster. The first version, shot at tremendous expense, did not satisfy Disney. The squid did not look real enough and the action was filmed against a pink sky which provided quite the wrong atmosphere. A new squid was prepared and the sequence reshot, this time during a simulated storm.

The Jules Verne original provided a marvelous basis for a film combining fantasy and adventure. Script and direction were excellent and production values outstanding. James Mason was cast as Captain Nemo—half villain, half hero—bringing a sense of icy rage to the sinister commander of the *Nautilus*. Paul Lukas played an eminent scientist who, along with his apprentice, Peter Lorre, is captured by Nemo. All three characters, in the best Jules Verne tradition, are a little out of the ordinary. Their eccentricity is balanced by the down-to-earth figure of the

Swiss Family Robinson

Adapted from Johann Wyss's classic novel,
Swiss Family Robinson, 1960, starred John Mills
and featured a spectacular tree house which
later formed the basis for a popular attraction
at both Disneyland and Walt Disney World

whaler, played by Kirk Douglas. The whaler is of course brave and strong and handy with a harpoon. More important, his viewpoint is uncomplicated by intellectual aspirations, making him the character with whom most of the potential audience would identify. So far as the protagonists are concerned, *20,000 Leagues Under the Sea* deals in terms of simplifications, but it grips our imagination because it is convincing as a battle of ideas and emotions.

Swiss Family Robinson is another major production that is taken from a classic adventure story. Released in 1960, with John Mills in the starring role, this is the story of an emigrant family shipwrecked on a tropical island. We see how they learn to cope with their unfamiliar environment and how they deal with a band of Oriental pirates. Despite some spectacular scenic photography, this film never manages to sustain the dramatic tension of the better Disney adventure films. Much of the blame for this seems to lie with the screenplay, which puts foolish demands on the actors both in terms of dialogue and of emotional response.

The Shaggy Dog, released in 1959, was the first of the Studio's zany comedies. It starred Fred MacMurray, giving a great boost to his flagging career. He had starred in many light-hearted comedies in the thirties and early forties, and *The Shaggy Dog* was to some extent conceived as an updated version of that kind of film, the main difference being that it was geared chiefly to the juvenile market. It was followed by other similar vehicles for MacMurray's talents, notably *The Absent Minded Professor,* 1961, and *Son of Flubber,* 1963. The British actress Hayley Mills was featured in several Disney films during this period, including costume pieces such as *Pollyanna* and contemporary comedies like *The Parent Trap.*

The Studio was now enjoying success with a wide variety of live-action productions, and animation was also thriving. The outlook for Disney was very bright, a fact made all the more remarkable because at this time other major studios were experiencing a sharp decline in their fortunes.

◀ Starring Fred MacMurray as the inventor of an antigravity substance, *The Absent Minded Professor,* 1961, is a zany comedy notable for remarkable special effects

◀ Hayley Mills, second from left, starred in several Disney films, including *Pollyanna*

14 Mary Poppins

In 1964 Disney released *Mary Poppins,* a film which became one of the greatest hits in the history of the motion picture industry. Adapted from P.L. Travers's children's stories, the movie provided Julie Andrews with a spectacular screen debut and smashed box-office records at home and abroad.

Disney had been aware of Mrs. Travers's remarkable nanny for many years before the film went into production. The Poppins books had been favorites of his own two daughters, and he had made several attempts to obtain the screen rights to them. It seems likely that he initially thought of them as providing a suitable basis for an animated feature based on the Poppins character. Mrs. Travers was not anxious to part with the rights, fearing that Hollywood's vision of her heroine might result in travesty, but by the early sixties her position was softening a little. While visiting London, Disney called on Mrs. Travers and finally persuaded her that the time was ripe for a screen version and that he was the man to produce it (several other studios had been bidding for the property and Rodgers and Hammerstein were interested in the possibility of turning the stories into a musical). Back in Burbank, Bill Walsh, who was slated to co-produce the movie, and Don DaGradi began to work on the script, taking fragments from the original stories and weaving

Julie Andrews and Dick Van Dyke on the set

Mary Poppins, released in 1964,
used all the resources of the Disney Studio,
combining live action with animation
and featuring startling special effects

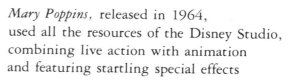

Shooting the "laughing" sequence ▶

them into a continuous narrative. Richard M. and Robert B. Sherman were called in to write music and lyrics.

Next there came the vital decision of casting an actress to play Mary Poppins herself. Julie Andrews had enjoyed great success on Broadway, first in Sandy Wilson's nostalgic gem *The Boy Friend,* then in *My Fair Lady* and *Camelot.* "Walt saw Julie in *Camelot,*" Bill Walsh recalls, "and he liked her in that. I think he was trying to get Mary Martin, who was interested in the part at one time, or Bette Davis. It was fluctuating quite a bit as to who would finally be Mary Poppins, but he kind of liked Julie. He liked the way she whistled. She's a great whistler and he thought that was amusing."

The part of Bert—street musician, pavement artist, chimney sweep, and friend to Mary Poppins—went to Dick Van Dyke, whose television show was at the peak of its popularity. David Tomlinson, a talented British character actor, was chosen for the part of Mr. Banks. His screen wife—modified into a moderately militant suffragette—was played by Glynis Johns, who had acted in earlier Disney films. The two children, Matthew Garber and Karen Dotrice, had also had previous experience at the Disney Studio—in a movie called *The Three Lives*

One of the most spectacular
sequences in *Mary Poppins* is the
chimney sweeps' dance,
set on the rooftops of London

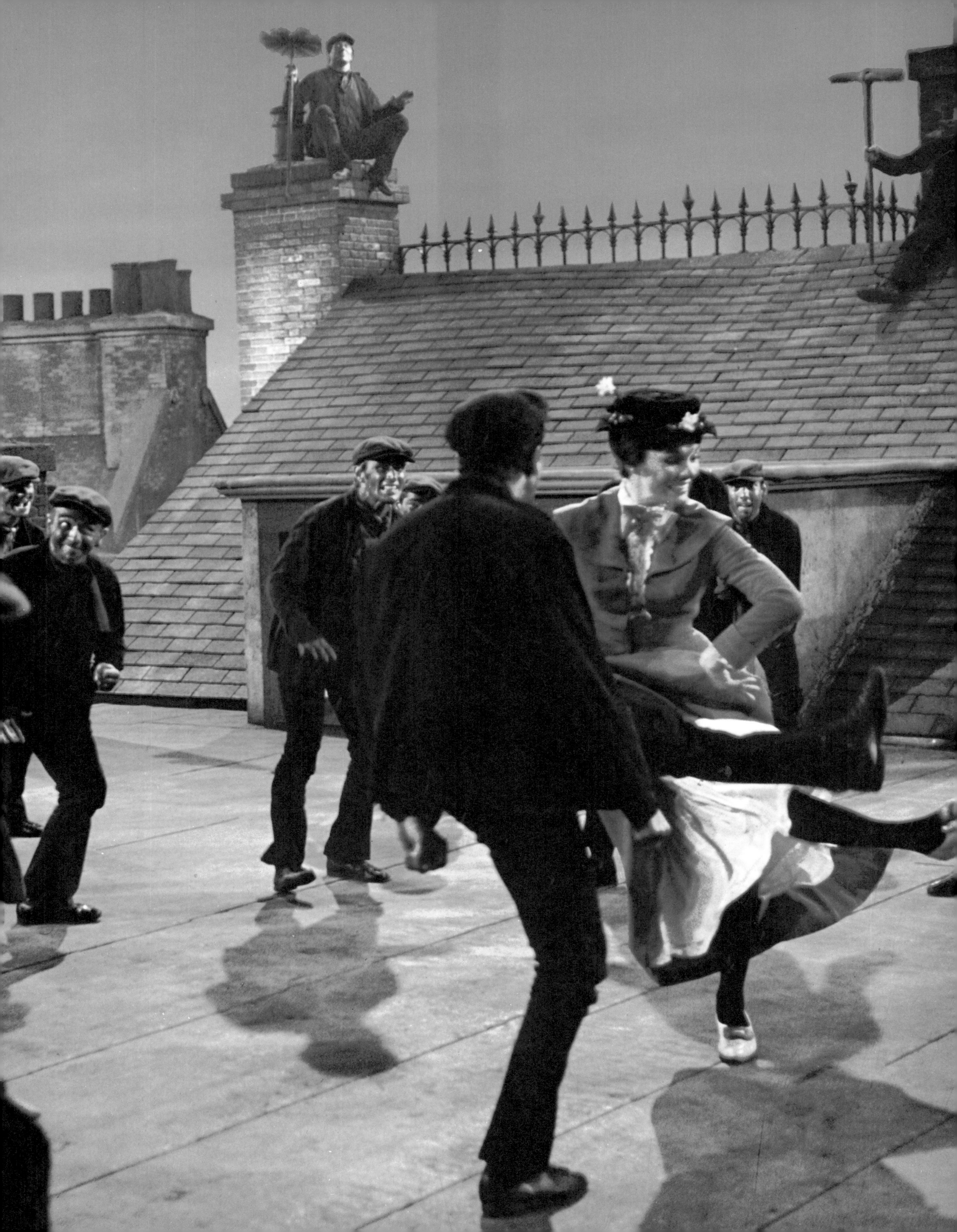

Glynis Johns finds herself
caught up in the dance

Dance routines required hours
of exhausting rehearsal

of Thomasina. Most of the cast was British, and another Briton,
Robert Stevenson, was assigned to direct the picture.

Mary Poppins is a unique movie, imaginative and entertaining. Those who expected a direct adaptation of Mrs. Travers's stories may have been a little disappointed, but it could
not have been otherwise. Her delicate fantasies work beautifully
in words, but literary artifice does not translate into film without undergoing a considerable change. Walsh and DaGradi had
to provide the movie with a structure, and they could only do
this by altering the raw material to some extent.

Julie Andrews is certainly a more glamorous and youthful
version of Mary Poppins than the one we meet in Mrs. Travers's
stories. She brings to the character a charm and spark of her
own. Her singing voice and dancing ability are great assets, but
the key to her performance is her ability to seem prim and
proper yet perpetually on the verge of some kind of marvelous
insanity. Primness is Mary Poppins's solitary link with everyday
reality—a fragile self-discipline that manages, just barely, to im-
pose a modicum of form on the tides of fantasy that flow just
below the surface.

The Happiest Millionaire, 1967, features Fred MacMurray as an eccentric patrician

The Love Bug, 1969, is built around a Volkswagen with a mind of its own

Bedknobs and Broomsticks, 1971, stars David Tomlinson and Angela Lansbury

David Tomlinson is outstanding as the bank-executive father, secure in the knowledge that London is at the center of an empire on which the sun never sets. Glynis Johns brings a nice sense of humor to the character of his wife, who is herself somewhat out of touch with reality and constantly shifting roles, so that at one moment she is militant and at the next acquiescent. The part demands a deftness of touch which Miss Johns provides in full measure. The children are excellent, as are many of the supporting actors (Ed Wynn, for example, and Hermione Baddeley). Dick Van Dyke brings a great deal of energy to the film, but his version of a cockney accent leaves something to be desired, and this has a jarring effect at times.

Edwardian London is reconstructed with a good feeling for atmosphere, clever use being made both of remarkable special effects and of simple sets that would not seem out of place on the stage of a Broadway theater. Throughout the film, the real and the imaginary are combined in inventive and believable ways, notably, of course, in the scenes that combine live action with animation. In the production of *Mary Poppins,* all of the Studio's resources were pooled to produce a motion picture that probably could not have been made anywhere else.

The sound track is dotted with memorable songs, in particular, "Chim Chim Cher-ee," "Jolly Holiday," "The Life I Lead," "A Spoonful of Sugar," and "Supercalifragilisticexpialidocious." There is at least one dance routine in the best tradition of the Hollywood musical. *Mary Poppins* is, in fact, an extravaganza of the sort that had been fairly plentiful in the thirties and forties, but which seemed to be a lost art in the sixties.

Since *Mary Poppins,* Disney has released a number of interesting live-action films, good examples being *The Happiest Millionaire,* 1967, *The Love Bug,* 1969, and *Bedknobs and Broomsticks,* 1971. One cannot pretend that these films, not to mention the lesser productions that have emerged from the Studio, have made a vital contribution to the history of the cinema, but they do deserve to be treated with more respect than is generally accorded them.

Walt Disney's position in the pantheon of movie greats results almost entirely from the imagination and vitality he brought to the art of animation. But he was also a very practical man, who knew that the kind of operation he ran required a sound financial base. Live-action production has been vital to the fiscal health of the organization. Without these films there might have been no later animated features—perhaps no Disneyland and no Walt Disney World.

Julie Andrews with Walt Disney

Bill Walsh, center, co-producer of *Mary Poppins*

IV
THE MAGIC KINGDOMS

15 Beyond Film

We can say that Walt Disney was a man with a knack for doing the right thing at the right time, but we must recognize that words like "knack" and "intuition" tend to be used to identify gifts we do not quite understand. It is essential to realize that Disney's decisions generally had their basis in preparation and good timing—that is to say, in hard work and patience. In no instance is this more true than in the most important of his postwar acts—the decision to build Disneyland.

Disneyland grew from an idea that had been maturing in Disney's head for fifteen or twenty years before it became a physical reality. When his daughters were young, he would take them to local amusement parks and playgrounds, and he said later that those often unsatisfying visits triggered the notion that a park could be devised which would be as entertaining for adults as for their children. There is some evidence to suggest that he was thinking about specific rides as early as the late thirties, but the heavy investments he had made in the Burbank Studio and the major feature films of the period precluded any possibility of seriously developing the park idea then. The idea remained in the back of his mind, however, and a few years later, almost by accident, he acquired a new hobby which was greatly to influence the eventual character of Disneyland.

At Walt Disney World, in Florida, Cinderella's Castle is the centerpiece of the Magic Kingdom

Disney's passionate interest in
miniature railroads had
an important influence on his
plans for Disneyland

Shortly after the war, Disney's doctor suggested that he find some leisure activity that would give him a chance to escape the pressures of running the Studio, if only for an hour or two a day. Disney had always loved railroads, and this interest was now fanned by the discovery that two of his top animators were already serious railway buffs. One of these was Ollie Johnston, who remembers the beginnings of Disney's enthusiasm:

"Ward Kimball had his steam engine back in '40 or '41. He got this big steam engine from the Nevada Central Railroad, I think. Walt was always interested and then, along in 1946, I started building a miniature engine—I got a guy to help me build it—and, I think it was the next Christmas, Kimball came into the room and said, 'Hey, let's go up to Walt's office. He's got a Lionel train up there that he set up for his nephew.' So we went up to his office and while we were looking at the model, Walt turned to me and said, 'I didn't know you were interested in trains.' I told him I was building a steam engine. He said, 'You are? I always wanted a backyard railroad myself.' So he came out to where we were building mine, in Santa Monica. He came out two or three times and he started to get ideas on how he was going to build his. They started building it here in the shop, several months later. He had this keen setup around his yard with about half a mile of track. He had a real nice thing with a tunnel—it went under his wife's flower garden and he made her sign a contract that said he could put the track there. He had all kinds of bridges and things for it too.

"We'd work at it here at the Studio sometimes. I'd be working on one of my cars, out there in the carpenter's shop, and he'd say, 'Hey, I think I found out where they keep the hardwood.' So he'd show me where I could find some nice scraps of lumber. He built a beautiful, old-fashioned headlight for his engine, and he built all the cars—cattle cars and boxcars. Walt

Disneyland under construction.
At bottom, Walt watches as the
final touches are put on
Main Street

was good with his hands. Roger Brodie was head of the shop then and he kind of guided Walt along.

"The next thing you know, Walt was thinking about putting a railroad around here, at the Studio. There was a guy in Los Gatos who had some engines that were used in the 1915 Pan American Fair in San Francisco, and Walt was thinking of buying those. Then he got to thinking there wasn't enough room here and before long there was a Disneyland."

In 1952, Disney set up an organization called WED (the initials of his own name) to begin planning the park in earnest. WED consisted, at first, of a handful of designers, mostly co-opted from the Disney animation department. They were men who understood how Disney worked and they were well equipped to interpret his ideas. Plans and models were made for an as yet unchosen site, and part of the impact of Disneyland may well derive from the fact that it was planned this way—with Walt's dream interpreted by his own artists and no attention paid to potential topographical limitations. As the park began to take shape on paper, the Stanford Research Institute was called in to find a site within the greater Los Angeles area. They settled on 160 acres of orange groves in Anaheim, to the south of Los Angeles, which seemed suitable for a number of reasons.

One vital consideration was, as always in southern California, the matter of accessibility for automobiles. The Santa Ana Freeway, which links Orange County with the main urban centers, was already partially built, and its proposed route would take it right past the suggested property. Once the freeway was completed, Disneyland would be half-an-hour's drive from downtown Los Angeles. The land was relatively inexpensive, and Anaheim enjoys a particularly moderate climate—even for southern California—that would permit the park to operate year round. The property was flat and would present no physical hindrance to the execution of the scheme.

The ownership of the land was at that time divided among a number of people, and the practicality of the site would, of course, depend on their willingness to come to terms. That, however, was the least of Disney's problems. First he had to sell his idea to his brother Roy and to the other officers of the company, not all of whom saw an amusement park as a solid investment at just that moment. Disney was a persuasive salesman, but he did not have an easy task. He had been able to stir the imaginations of his creative staffers by presenting them with the overall concept. His financial advisors, however, seem to have been treated to a more gradual revelation of the full extent of the scheme. Tidbits of information were let out, one at a time, each delivered with the infectious enthusiasm that Disney could generate, and resistance was gradually worn down.

Disney sent out a team to seek the views of the men who operated the nation's leading amusement parks. With hardly an exception, their advice consisted of earnest suggestions that he forget the whole thing. These warnings represented generations of experience, but they did not take into account Disney's flair for innovation, the backlog of characters and situations he could take from his own movies, his understanding of promotion and publicity, or his sheer energy and determination. He went right ahead with his plans as if he had received a universal vote of confidence, quite sure as usual of his ability to make the project work. It was probably this self-confidence that eventually persuaded his own advisors that the scheme was feasible (he had been right often enough for them to take his enthusiasms seriously), but their approval was not the same as having the money necessary to proceed. The idea now had to be sold to the bankers who would be needed to capitalize it, and they—despite Disney's track record—were not at all impressed. Fortunately, a number of industrialists were more favorably disposed toward the Disneyland idea, and more than thirty companies agreed to buy concessions in the proposed park. Each took a five-year lease, paying the first and fifth year in advance. This money enabled the project to stay alive, but far larger sums would be needed if the dream was to be realized.

As we have seen, ABC television was anxious to add the prestige of Disney's name to its roster of program regulars, and he now agreed to sign with the network for a period of seven years if American Broadcasting Company—Paramount Theaters, Inc., would purchase slightly more than one-third of the shares in a company called Disneyland, Inc., which had been set up in 1952. This gave the project an enormous boost. Meanwhile the Studio's fortunes were looking up again, so that Walt Disney Productions was able to buy a number of shares equal to those owned by ABC-Paramount. The remainder were divided between the Western Printing and Lithographing Company, which had a long association with the Studio, and Disney himself. Years later, Walt Disney Productions was able to buy out the holdings of both Western and ABC-Paramount.

This new situation offered the banks more than adequate security, and the necessary funds were advanced, setting the stage for construction to begin. Meanwhile, Disney was planning the television series in such a way as to afford Disneyland maximum publicity.

From the top:
The Mousketeers at Disneyland;
a balloon ascent near the Disneyland
Matterhorn; Disneyland characters, c. 1955;
Tricia and Julie Nixon inaugurate the
Disneyland Monorail

When Disneyland opened in 1955, it was surrounded by
orange groves, but the park's success and the Santa Ana Freeway
soon transformed this part of Anaheim into a heavily
developed suburb of Los Angeles

Disney's overall concept for the park has its own kind of logic, which has proved extremely effective. His plan called for a railroad defining the perimeter of the park, with its main station situated right at the entrance. Once past the station, the visitor would have to pass down Main Street—a reproduction of the heart of a small Midwestern town such as Disney himself might have known as a boy. Entered from a small square on which a town hall and a fire station were situated, Main Street was calculated to correspond with one of the archetypes of the American imagination. It was to provide an operating base for many of the concessions, but, more than that, it would establish the right ambiance, so that visitors would be put in a receptive state of mind. Its scale would be slightly less than life-size, to enhance the sense of friendliness and intimacy. Transportation would be available—trams and horse-drawn streetcars—but people on foot would be drawn down Main Street by the imposing edifice at its far end—Sleeping Beauty's Castle—the likes of which has seldom been seen in any Midwestern town.

It would be important to keep people moving in the park, and Disney had an expression which voiced his philosophy in this regard: "You've got to have a wienie at the end of every street." Translated into practical terms, this meant that his planners had to provide a sequence of visual magnets that would

It's a Small World: ►
one of the most popular attractions
at both Disneyland
and Walt Disney World

Walt Disney at Disneyland

keep drawing visitors on to the next attraction. Situated at the hub of the park, the castle would be the biggest of these magnets, and all paths would converge on the traffic circle immediately in front of it.

A visitor who followed a clockwise route from this central feature would find himself, first of all, in Adventureland, next in Frontierland, then in Fantasyland, and finally in Tomorrowland (other possibilities, such as Holiday Land and Lilliputian Land, were considered, then abandoned). Each of these areas would have a specific atmosphere appropriate to its name. Disney characters and references to Disney movies would be found throughout the park.

It was a good plan. It had a sense of structure and continuity which was new to this kind of enterprise, and it capitalized fully on the established Disney image. Everything had been thoughtfully considered and imaginatively developed.

Disneyland was opened on July 17, 1955. Television crews were on hand to record the opening ceremonies, and thirty thousand guests thronged Main Street and explored the farthest reaches of the complex. Millions more saw the opening on their home screens. No entertainment facility had ever enjoyed this kind of publicity, and Disneyland became a national phenomenon overnight. Crowds came flocking through the gates—more than a million between July 18 and September 30, and almost four million during the first complete fiscal year.

Disneyland soon became a regular stopping-off place for all kinds of foreign dignitaries. Walt Disney had built the Versailles of the twentieth century—but it was a Versailles designed for the pleasure of the people. At the time of its inauguration it was not, of course, quite the dense complex that we find today. As yet, no Monorail had been installed, no New Orleans Square divided Adventureland from Frontierland, and many of the most popular rides were not even in the planning stage. What existed was an unusual and agreeable environment suitable for further expansion but already providing novel entertainments for both children and adults. The park could be enjoyed by those who were anxious to participate as well as by those who preferred to stroll and observe. An ample choice of inexpensive dining and refreshment areas was provided. It was a place for families, a place to visit for the whole day, an environment that seemed inexhaustible. Hours could be spent just shopping in the stores along Main Street.

Apart from the originality of its plan, what makes Disneyland radically different from other amusement parks is the fact that it is designed like a movie lot. The skills that go into building film sets are the same skills that went into Main Street and Frontierland. The difference is that a set may consist of facades that open onto nothing, whereas Disneyland's streets are punctuated by doors that give access to rides, entertainments, stores, and restaurants.

Film-makers are trained to think in terms of a sequence of events. One situation must lead into another in such a way as to tell a story. These narrative skills were employed in planning the layout of the park. As the visitor is drawn from one place to another, calculated scenic changes give him the impression of a definite and satisfying sequence of events. The difference is that a movie narrative moves in a straight line, from beginning to end, with the viewer being carried along by the camera, whereas a visitor to the park is free to choose among many options. He can, in effect, write his own story, although its basic elements have been carefully preplanned by the designers.

A plaque in Disneyland's town square reads as follows:

TO ALL WHO COME TO THIS HAPPY PLACE:
WELCOME.
DISNEYLAND IS YOUR LAND. HERE AGE
RELIVES FOND MEMORIES OF THE PAST . . .
AND HERE YOUTH MAY SAVOR THE CHALLENGE
AND PROMISE OF THE FUTURE.
DISNEYLAND IS DEDICATED
TO THE IDEALS, THE DREAMS, AND THE HARD
FACTS THAT HAVE CREATED AMERICA . . .
WITH THE HOPE THAT IT WILL BE A SOURCE OF
JOY AND INSPIRATION TO ALL THE WORLD
JULY 17, 1955

This probably represents an accurate record of Walt Disney's sentiments, and the fact that the park now attracts almost ten million visitors a year indicates that his sentiments have been successfully translated into reality. Visitors are not all that the park has attracted, however. When it opened, it was an island of fantasy set in an ocean of orange trees. That is no longer the case. Urban sprawl would have reached this part of Orange County sooner or later, but the sweet smell of Disney's success speeded the process considerably. As the crowds poured in, the land around the park was snatched up by eager speculators, lending a slightly sinister note to the plaque's homage to "the hard facts that have created America." Disneyland is now hemmed in by ugly motels and counter-attractions hoping to catch some of the park's overspill.

Once inside Disneyland, all this becomes irrelevant as the

Many of the windows on the Main Streets of both Disneyland and Walt Disney World bear the names of members of Disney's family or of people within the Disney organization. Examples here include the names of Walt's father, Elias, his grandson, Christopher D. Miller, and art director Ken Anderson

The parks are full of signs, each one designed and executed with great care and attention to detail. No one style prevails. The right idiom and the right materials are found for each location

Like the signs, posters within the parks are always appropriate to their location and to the attraction they advertise

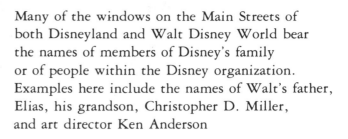

Everything, down to the most humble artifact, is carefully considered. Waste bins, for example, are designed to be highly visible without clashing with the mood of their surroundings

outside world vanishes and the planners' values prevail—but Disney watched these haphazard developments with displeasure, regretting the fact that he had been unable to afford enough land to provide his dream with an insulating belt of greenery. He also regretted that he had built no hotels at Disneyland—a natural source of income which he had neglected because it lay outside the experience of his staff. He vowed that the same thing would not happen again—and this was no idle threat. The success of Disneyland had persuaded him that a second park was desirable.

Disney wanted his new park to serve the Eastern states, and Florida offered the best environment. Its climate—like that of southern California—would permit year-round operation, and the state attracts over twenty million tourists annually. More than three-quarters of these visitors travel by automobile, and as many pass through central Florida. And, because the vast majority of Florida vacationers are from east of the Rockies, the two parks would not be in direct competition.

Disney was not the kind of man who could be satisfied with merely repeating himself, and he conceived his new project as far more than just another Disneyland. It would be a complete vacationland, cushioned from the outside world, providing hotel accommodations and camp sites as well as all kinds of recreational activities, from boating to birdwatching to golf. The project would also include an industrial park designed to showcase American business, and a small community—Lake Buena Vista—which would include both vacation homes and permanent residences. More ambitiously, EPCOT—an experimental prototype community of tomorrow—became part of the plan. Speaking of EPCOT Disney said, "It will take its cue from the new ideas and new technologies emerging from the creative centers of American industry. It will always be introducing and testing and demonstrating new materials and systems." It would be, he said, a place where "people actually live a life they can't find anywhere else in the world today."

The amusement park, then, would be just one small part of an enormous complex. Conventional transportation would be banned from the entire area in order to control pollution, and every effort would be made to preserve as much as possible of the existing topography and to maintain an ecological balance.

The success of Disneyland made financing for Walt Disney World (as the project was christened) relatively easy, but a very large site would have to be found. Locating the right property was the first order of business. A Disney publication tells the story in the following words:

Walt Disney (in the cap) and Card Walker inspect the site of Walt Disney World

An aerial view of Walt Disney World's ▶ Main Street, with a parade in progress and Cinderella's Castle in the background

"Sheathed in necessary obscurity, Disney representatives set out early in 1964 to obtain control of a large area straddling the line separating Orange and Osceola counties in central Florida. Located between the cities of Orlando and Kissimmee, the site is at the crossing point of several heavily traveled highways.

"By October, 1965, they had put together 27,443 acres —almost 43 square miles—at a cost of just over $5,000,000. This size would permit for plenty of future expansion and would assure control of its perimeter. For comparison: Walt Disney World covers about the same land area as the city of San Francisco; it is about twice the size of the island of Manhattan."

On November 15, 1965, Walt and Roy Disney, accompanied by Governor Haydon Burns, spoke to the press and officially launched the Walt Disney World project.

Surveying his property from the air, Disney decided that the shores of Bay Lake—its largest natural body of water—was the spot to begin Phase One of the development, and the practicality of this choice was borne out by detailed studies. He died six months before the earth-moving equipment arrived at the site, but he had already supervised the planning of Phase One down to the last detail and laid down general principles for the development of the whole property.

As scheduled, Walt Disney World was opened by Roy Disney in October, 1971.

In the process of developing Walt Disney World, the Disney organization found novel solutions to problems which have long plagued city planners and ecologists. A special section by Peter Blake, himself a practicing architect and editor of *Architecture Plus,* details Walt Disney World's many innovations and their impact on architecture and urban design. It begins on page 425.

16 Animation in the Round

As a visitor moves about the Disney theme parks, he encounters many kinds of live entertainment—street musicians, dancers, rock groups, parades, and firework displays are integral parts of Disneyland and Walt Disney World. What makes them so special, however, are the fixed elements—the rides and the architecture—which provide a setting for everything else. Behind all this are two vital organizations, WED and its manufacturing division, MAPO (named for *Mary Poppins,* profits from the movie having helped establish it).

All new attractions begin life on the drawing boards of WED's Glendale headquarters, just a short drive from the Disney Studio. Many of the men who work there were formerly employed in animation, and their thinking is always conditioned by this background. A number of the rides for both parks have been designed by Marc Davis, formerly one of the Studio's top animators. He begins each of them as if he were planning a cartoon. His first task is to establish the atmosphere and chief features of the ride, including all the characters who will contribute to it. Then he prepares a story board which gives the project a structure and a sequence. When everyone concerned is happy with the story board, a model is built—carefully lit and large enough to walk through—so that a truer sense of the intended experience can be obtained.

Disney tries out dance steps
with Buddy Ebsen. Ebsen's dance routine
was filmed and used as a basis for
the first of Disney's mechanical figures

Once everything has been approved, construction can begin. Much of it must necessarily be done on site, but a number of the key elements will be manufactured at the Glendale plant. These include the most spectacular features of the rides, the audio-animatronic figures (robot characters) which give the main attractions in the Disney theme parks a technical sophistication that has never been matched by any of their competitors.

Long before he began to build Disneyland, Walt Disney had been a collector of mechanical toys, and these suggested to him the possibility of finding a three-dimensional equivalent for the art of screen animation. In the mid-forties he began to experiment with mechanical puppets, and Ken Anderson worked secretly with him to devise some theatrical settings. Then films were made of Buddy Ebsen dance routines, and Disney engineers (whom he later rebaptized "Imagineers") made a small model of Ebsen which reproduced his movements with reasonable faithfulness. The figure was mounted beneath a proscenium arch above a large console, giving the whole the appearance of a sinister Punch and Judy show, the kind of thing Boris Karloff might have toyed with in some epic of the macabre. At this time, the electronics industry was still in its infancy, and the console had to house cumbersome vacuum tubes as well as many purely mechanical elements—fly wheels and escape mechanisms—with which a clockmaker would be quite familiar. The console was programed by something closely resembling a piano roll—a long strip of paper, punched with patterns of holes, which looped through it and triggered the required responses. The Ebsen puppet worked, but the machinery was too clumsy to suggest any immediate application; for many years it lay neglected, but it has now been restored for an exhibit at Walt Disney World.

Lowering mechanical animals ▶
into place on the banks of Disneyland's
Jungle Boat Ride

The building of Disneyland prompted a new round of experiments. At first the WED engineers worked with models that had simple cam-and-lever joints, but before long they began to try out more flexible systems which employed pneumatic and hydraulic power transmission controlled by electrical inputs. This was sufficient to supply the kind of crude movements needed for such things as the animals dotted around the jungle ride. Then someone came up with the idea of using sound, recorded on magnetic tape, to activate the pneumatic and hydraulic valves, and the full possibilities of audio-animatronics were finally realized. Sound impulses—sometimes more than four hundred per second—were recorded on a thirty-two-channel tape. These released mechanisms, buried within lifelike plastic figures, which could control movements down to the flicker of an eyelid. The tape system also permitted these movements to be synchronized with prerecorded dialogue or music, as well as with lighting effects and whatever else might contribute to the atmosphere of a ride.

The first audio-animatronic models made were some exotic birds which eventually formed the basis of Disneyland's Tiki Room. The birds, perched among tropical vegetation, put on a little show for visitors, singing and cracking jokes. It was not until 1964, at the New York World's Fair, that the full potential of audio-animatronics was revealed to the public. Disney contributed a number of attractions, including the Ford Motor Company's "Magic Skyway," General Electric's "Progressland," and Pepsi-Cola's "It's a Small World" (the last adapted for both Anaheim and Orlando). The most impressive exhibit, however, was "Great Moments with Mr. Lincoln," which Disney prepared for the Illinois pavilion.

Visitors were confronted with a startlingly lifelike facsimile of the nation's sixteenth president, who rose from his chair and addressed his latter-day countrymen. Lincoln not only talked, he emphasized his thoughts with naturalistic gestures and his eyes raked the audience as though challenging opponents to debate. He shifted his weight from one foot to the other and his expression changed with the sense of his words. He almost seemed to breathe. The impact was extraordinary.

This success was not easily won. Indeed, only a few months before the opening of the pavilion it had seemed that Lincoln would never be ready in time. The sheer energy locked up in the hydraulic and pneumatic systems of any audio-animatronic figure is considerable, and unless this energy can be precisely controlled, the figure can become quite violent. The Lincoln figure was very complex and posed serious control problems. The

The Hall of Presidents

From a technological point of view, the Hall of Presidents, in Walt Disney World, is probably the most sophisticated attraction Disney engineers have yet built. Featuring lifelike full-scale figures of every American president, its highlight is a speech given by Abraham Lincoln

The computer center situated in the service basement beneath Main Street controls many of the attractions and services throughout Walt Disney World

President smashed his chair and threw mechanical fits that threatened the safety of the men working on him. But Disney was determined that the figure be ready in time, and eventually the power was harnessed.

Equally sophisticated audio-animatronic figures are now featured in many attractions at both Disneyland and Walt Disney World. Pirates of the Caribbean, the Mickey Mouse Review, and both Haunted Mansions offer good examples, but perhaps the most successful ones are to be found in Walt Disney World's Hall of Presidents and at the Country Bear Jamboree, versions of which have been installed in both parks.

The Hall of Presidents once again features the words of Abraham Lincoln, but this time the familiar figure is surrounded by all his peers, from George Washington to the present incumbent. The presidents are introduced in chronological order, a spotlight falling on each in turn. Each acknowledges the announcement of his name with a modest bow or some other appropriate gesture. As Lincoln speaks, the other figures nod their approval and seem to study the impact his phrases are having on the audience. The effect is quite uncanny.

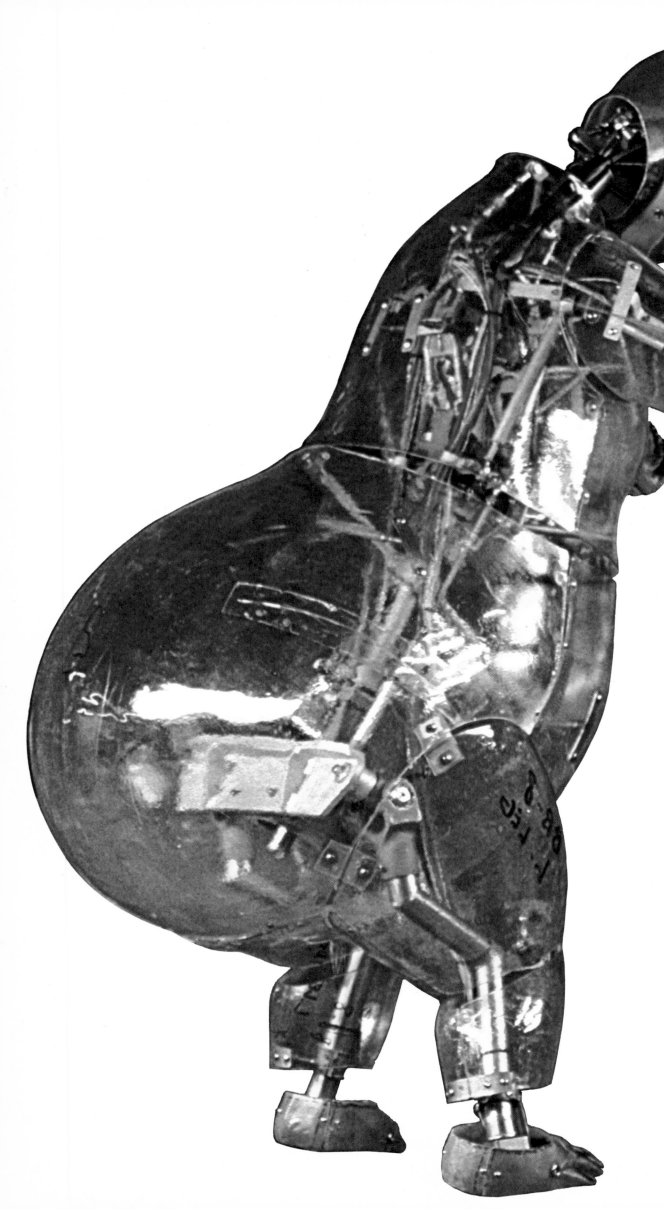

Country Bear Band

The complexity of the
audio-animatronic figures can
be judged from these
photographs taken at WED
during the preparation of
characters for the Country
Bear Jamboree

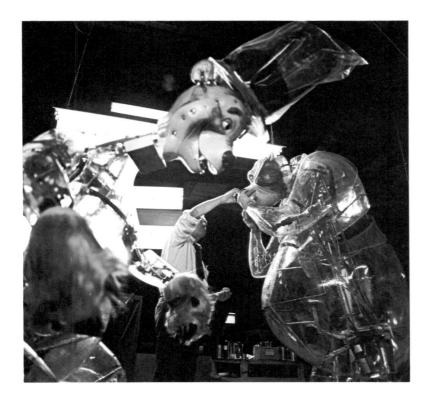

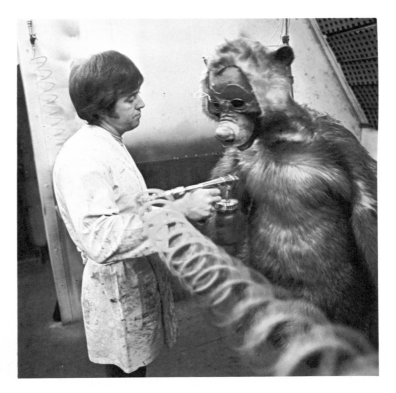

The Country Bear Jamboree is a more lighthearted affair. A dozen audio-animatronic bears put on a performance straight out of the Grand Ol' Opry. The greatest success of the characters in the Bear Band (and this holds true of all audio-animatronic figures) is the skill with which their eyes have been programed. The audience's attention is instinctively drawn to the eyes; if they were not convincingly naturalistic, the entire illusion would break down.

Years of experience in the field of screen animation have taught the Disney artists how to use movement with economy. A sense of reality is often best transmitted by suppressing movement—for example, a character may express surprise more effectively by raising an eyebrow than by throwing up his hands. It is such knowledge that has made audio-animatronics so valuable an asset to the parks, for without it, all the engineering skill that goes into these figures would be wasted.

17 Inside the Magic Kingdoms

The sibling theme parks of Disneyland and Walt Disney World offer a kind of experience that has not been successfully duplicated elsewhere. Disney had a unique vision and developed an organization capable of implementing his ideas. John Hench, a key figure in that organization and vice-president of WED, has responsibility for all design decisions affecting the parks. He has given extensive thought to the reasons for Disney's success:

"Part of it, I suppose, was Walt's exploitation of very old survival patterns. He had an instinct for this. I think that if anyone really wanted to take the time to examine it, he would see that these survival patterns are the basis of our aesthetics, our sense of pleasure. We've carried these things around for 20,000,000 years, in our DNA chains or whatever it is. We are the successful survivors, so we must still carry these mechanisms with us. The things that please us are obviously the ones that boost our survival potential—and the ones that we don't like are those that threaten us."

Hench illustrates Disney's instinct by referring back to the early cartoons:

"Mickey was so-called Lollipop Art—because he was made from circles. I'm oversimplifying it, but circles have never hurt anybody—they are women's breasts and clouds and other soft

forms. Felix the Cat, on the other hand, was full of angles and sharp points, and I really think this was the main difference between the two. It explains the success of Mickey, who just won't quit. Walt was a highly intuitive person and he sensed these things, and, as a result of this, the Studio has probably developed more awareness than any other design group in this field.

"A lot of designers allow contradictions into their work because they're careless or because they don't really understand what they are doing. These contradictions will cancel what they're trying to say. If someone wants to make an automobile that will look slick and powerful and he designs something that triggers a very old image of a dead whale on the beach, the customer won't buy it. Look at the Hudson. It was a perfectly good car, but nobody would believe it. I haven't really analyzed the Edsel, but again it gives you an example of a company which was perfectly skilled at engineering and did a wonderful job of preselling the car—but nobody would touch it."

Hench, whose training was in animation (he was, at different times, in background, effects, layout, and art direction), recognizes that Disney's unique knowledge of the field was a great influence on the design concepts that give the parks their special character:

"Walt had a high sensitivity, I think, for timing and the way ideas relate to each other—and this of course came from the film work. This is what film is all about, connecting ideas so that they relate to each other. A motion picture is an act of communication. It consists of ideas—sometimes very complex ones—that you want other people to understand, and you want them to understand them the way you intended them to, without wandering off on their own. So you want to keep the structure clean and simple. Live-action filming has to count on a lot of accidents, but in a cartoon we could gradually eliminate the things that contradicted what we were trying to say. With the background we had, this was a very easy thing to apply to the third dimension."

In other words, animation is the most completely controlled form of film-making imaginable. As we have seen in earlier chapters, everything is preplanned. Nothing is left to the temperament of stars, to the day-to-day inspirations of director and cameraman, or to the vagaries of light and weather. Disneyland and Walt Disney World are controlled environments engineered to conform to the principles Disney had developed in making his animated films. All the elements of a movie must be made to complement each other—and this criterion was adapted in designing the parks.

The Haunted Mansions

◀ Disneyland's Haunted Mansion, with its delicate wrought-ironwork, is designed to blend with the architecture of adjacent New Orleans Square. By contrast, Walt Disney World's Haunted Mansion is built in the style of a Tudor manor house

The interiors of the Haunted Mansions—like all the other attractions—
are developed from a series of continuity drawings which are used in exactly the way
they would be in the development of an animated film

Inside the Haunted Mansion
a pair of hands tries to force
open the lid of a coffin

"It's a concept of relating things in a noncompetitive way," Hench explains. "One of the worst things about, for instance, a World's Fair is that every facility is trying to outshout the others. People are subject to pressure from the Russian pavilion, as opposed to the French, as against the Italian—and it does make for a curious kind of mental fatigue. Also, you have to pick up ideas and then drop them completely as you go on to another exhibit—it's like overrecording on a tape, I guess. Eventually you get very confused. Most people have this experience when they go to a World's Fair. They walk out absolutely exhausted and then can't remember very much of what they've seen—most of the attractions have canceled each other out, as they were probably designed to do.

"Disneyland is a much more pleasant experience—and Disney World too—because at least there's an attempt to relate one idea to the next. You don't have to drop one before you pick up another—they carry through. This again comes from the motion picture background. The division into related themes gives a sense of continuity. Then, of course, there are other things which I think may count on another level—the way, for example, colors are harmonized very carefully. It may not have an impact at a logical level, but I'm sure people respond to it, whether they're trained in this or not."

The movie influence is most obvious within the context of individual attractions. The Haunted Mansion, for example, presents us with an example of a ride that unfolds in time in exactly the same way a motion picture does. We have said that a movie transports an audience from point A to point Z by means of a carefully structured sequence of visual devices—the camera following the action and the audience traveling with the camera. The camera is, in other words, a moving vehicle which carries the viewer through the plot. In the Haunted Mansion, as in many other attractions at the parks, another kind of vehicle—a car that runs on rails—is substituted for the camera. The visitor is first ushered into a gothic lobby where he finds himself, along with a hundred other people, surrounded by sinister portraits. A disembodied voice issues a few words of warning, then the lights are extinguished and the show begins with a teaser—a device planned to set the atmosphere and to draw the viewer into the unfolding situation. The floor begins to drop and a body suddenly appears, hanging from the ceiling high above. The sinking floor immediately establishes a sense of insecurity, but it has the added practical purpose of bringing visitors down to a basement level where they board the cars that take them through the rest of the show. These cars carry the guests through a sequence of spooky environments, each of which exposes them to a new kind of "supernatural" phenomenon (to describe these would be unfair to future riders). The cars, each wired for stereo sound, are built in such a way that the rider can see only what is directly in front of him. Each car is on a swivel so that it can be turned, by electronic signals, to face just what the designer wants it to face at any particular moment. In this sense, then, it is used exactly like a movie camera. The rider is traveling through a programed show which unfolds in time. The choice of where to look is not his to make—it has already been made by the designer, who determines what will be seen, just as a director determines what the movie patron will see.

We have said that the general layout of the parks allows for freedom of choice, but even here there are a number of controlled routes—namely those which are served by the various forms of transportation.

Just as the theme parks deal in everything from nostalgia to space technology, so their transportation systems represent a wide variety of types and eras. Main Street is served by tram cars and horse-drawn vehicles, yet a short walk will take you to a streamlined Monorail. The engines and rolling stock on the railroad circling the park conjure up the golden age of steam, but the People Mover that runs through Tomorrowland is a silent, electrically powered product that belongs entirely to the second half of the twentieth century. Other kinds of transport—from cable cars to river boats—abound, meshed into a complex network made all the more satisfying by the fact that it is so

New Orleans Square

The wrought iron and engraved glass of Disneyland's New Orleans Square
illustrates the great care taken in reproducing architectural styles for the parks

The Crystal Palace

Walt Disney World's
Crystal Palace is a spectacular
glass-and-steel structure
which recalls the engineering
feats of the nineteenth century

Liberty Square

Liberty Square, in Walt Disney World,
reproduces the quiet elegance of an
American colonial town

far removed from the mass-transit systems we are accustomed to
in the "real" world.

The Disney transit systems are designed to afford maximum
pleasure. Their courses are plotted not as the shortest route between A and B, but rather to afford the rider the greatest visual
satisfaction. The Florida Monorail, for example, offers its passengers marvelous panoramas of the lakes and the surrounding
countryside as it runs between the theme park and the hotels.
Disney seems to have learned a great deal from his first backyard
railway layout.

The theme parks exploit all kinds of technical novelties—from
the audio-animatronic figures to a 360-degree wraparound
cinema screen—but what they offer is essentially a theatrical
experience. The Disney organization's primary area of expertise
is show business. Disneyland and Walt Disney World are
shows—a kind of total theater which exceeds the wildest dreams
of avant-garde dramatists. In their ability to cope with sheer
volume of visitors they are quite unparalleled.

Disney had the uncanny ability of providing people with
the kinds of things which set them at ease. "Walt never wanted
to change anybody," says John Hench. "He always figured that
people were great just the way they were. We were always attempting things that would force people to move around somewhere or other, and he would say, 'Look, if they have to walk

through there, you pay them for it somehow.' He never developed that kind of contempt you sometimes find in people in the advertising and publicity business."

The concept of giving people what they want is often held up to ridicule, but the truth of the matter is that we rarely get an opportunity to see this kind of philosophy in action. More often we are confronted with the notion of giving the people what someone *thinks* they want. Disney never consciously played down to the public, treating it, instead, as deserving of lavish attention. The people repaid him by crowding through the gates of Disneyland and Walt Disney World.

The investment made in each of the major attractions at the parks exceeds the budget of any Broadway show. This is made possible by the fact that one ride alone may be enjoyed by as many as forty thousand people in a single day. The necessity of appealing to so many people—of all ages and from every imaginable background—clearly determines the character of the attractions. Most films or stage performances are aimed at a specific segment of the population which has its own well-defined needs and interests. Disney designers do not have the luxury of trying to satisfy the tastes of only one group—their entertainments must appeal to everyone, and this means that they must work with universal concepts.

Several attractions—Main Street, Frontierland, New Orleans Square, and Liberty Square—capitalize on nostalgia, a sentiment to which everyone responds to some degree. Its opposite, the concept of progress, is embodied in Tomorrowland. The Jungle Ride, the Swiss Family Robinson's Tree House, and Pirates of the Caribbean all exploit a yearning for the exotic, while the Haunted Mansion and 20,000 Leagues Under the Sea attempt to satisfy our urge to confront the unknown. One could take every feature of the parks and explain its appeal in terms of some instinctive or emotional response common to almost all of us.

This emphasis on the "common factor" does not encourage the designers to indulge in intellectual subtleties, but it does make for a fascinating series of archetypal experiences. A great film or play may broaden the horizons of thousands of people, introducing them to fresh ideas or deepening their understanding of the human condition. The Disney parks have a very different goal. They are designed to satisfy the *existing* imaginative appetites of tens of millions of men, women, and children.

PETER BLAKE

18 The Lessons of the Parks

This chapter is based on an article published in the
June 1972 issue of ARCHITECTURAL FORUM; magazine article
copyright © 1972 Whitney Publications, Inc.

At Walt Disney World, the streamlined Monorail glides past Cinderella's Castle, which towers almost 200 feet high—much higher than its predecessor in Disneyland

There was a time, not very long ago, when the word "Disneyland" was considered, by architects and urban designers, to be one of the vilest pejoratives that could be applied to any cityscape. "Disneyland," to them, meant honky-tonk, crassness, phoniness. It was everything that the Art of Architecture was against. "Disneyland," especially to those who had never seen the place (present company included), was the very personification of lower-midcult America—a kind of national monument to vulgarity.

The first honest-to-goodness modernist to discover that there was a great deal more to Disneyland than met the eye— and a great deal that would, indeed, meet your eye if you only took the trouble to look—was Charles Eames, the architect, furniture designer, film-maker, and certified avant-gardist. Eames, who lives in Venice, California, went to see Disneyland in the 1950s and came back completely enthralled. Since he is not especially articulate in any language other than that of the film, Eames was not very good at communicating to his many admirers what it was that he saw in that 230-acre enclave in Anaheim. He just rolled his eyes, raised his arms heavenward, and said, "OK, go see for yourself!"

It was fifteen years before I took his advice. And when I

did, the first place I went to see was Walt Disney World, near Orlando, Florida—that enormous offshoot from the comparatively tiny Disneyland on the West Coast. I still do not know what Charles Eames was trying to say about Disneyland when he threw up his expressive arms in the 1950s, but I do know that I, a trained and practicing architect, saw things both in Orlando and, later, in Anaheim that are not taught in any schools of architecture I have ever attended or visited. At best, some of the things that are a reality in these two incredible "New Towns" are discussed vaguely and abstractly in courses on urban design and then dismissed as simply unattainable, given today's economic and political climate.

Walt Disney did not know that such things as vast urban infrastructures, multilevel mass-transit systems, People Movers, nonpolluting vehicles, pedestrian malls, and so forth were unattainable, and so he just went ahead and built them. In doing it he drew on all kinds of resources that no other city planner had ever before considered seriously, if at all: he drew on the experience of film-makers to chart the progression of pedestrians through a sequence of urban spaces; on the expertise of set designers to create a variety of streetscapes, and on the knowledge of cartoonists to "color-code" the buildings along those streets; above all, he drew on his own ability to please people, creating an urban environment (of sorts) that endlessly fascinates and endlessly attracts—and this at a time when people were leaving most of our *real* urban environments in droves.

What Disney really accomplished in Orlando and, to a lesser degree, in Anaheim was to build the only truly interesting New Towns constructed in the United States since World War II. While most of us who visit Walt Disney World or Disneyland primarily see and enjoy the frosting on the cake, there is much more to these "fun cities" than that. These two places—Walt Disney World in particular—are very serious, very creative experiments in urban design. Now that they have finally been recognized as such, it seems unlikely that any American school of architecture will ever again graduate a student without first requiring him or her to take a field trip to Orlando.

Walt Disney World—or WDW—is located in central Florida, a twenty-minute ride from the Orlando airport on Interstate Route 4. Its vital statistics are awesome: it covers 27,443 acres, which makes it twice as big as Manhattan Island and twice as big as the much-touted New Town of Columbia, Maryland. It represents an initial investment of $400 million, four times that for Columbia and five times that for another urbanistically certified New Town—Reston, Virginia. And it was visited in its first year by 10.7 million people, about the number that visit Washington, D.C., annually—a city which has been around for quite a bit longer.

But size, financing, and tourism are not the most significant aspects of WDW. One of the things that makes this vast experiment so significant to the future of architecture and city building is the kind of technology that went into it, continues to go into it, and will go into it during the next few years.

For example, the Magic Kingdom—the principal tourist attraction—is a small city constructed entirely on top of a service-and-utility basement made up of tunnels traversed by electric carts, storage areas, repair shops, and a complete network of readily accessible pipes, sewers, ducts, cables, and even of vacuum tubes that dispatch garbage collected above ground to an off-site compacting plant developed in Sweden and never before used in the United States. Such a vast infrastructure has not existed anywhere else before, except possibly at Rockefeller Center in New York City.

The Magic Kingdom, plus the extensive recreational areas to the south of it, represent the first new urban complex built since World War II to be fully equipped, from the very start, with a fast, efficient, and quiet mass-transit system—a Monorail perfected by WED (Walt E. Disney) Enterprises from the original German Alweg patent (which was used in Disneyland in the 1950s, and still creaks along a bit haltingly in that first-generation New Town). In addition to the impressive Monorail, this urban complex is served by two hundred watercraft—allegedly the ninth-largest navy in the world, in numbers if not, perhaps, in tonnage; it is also served by a railroad, by electric carts and trains, and by aerial tramways of the sort used in ski resorts and in European cities like Zurich.

WDW is remarkable also in that it is the first New Town in the United States (and probably in the world) to have set aside almost one-third of its total acreage for a really spectacular conservation project—7,500 acres of cypress-and-hardwood swamp dotted with pine islands, inhabited by alligators, birds, snakes, bears, and fish—protected from vandals by a team of dedicated professional conservationists. And WDW is full of other quite remarkable innovations: it was the first New Town in the United States to build its own STOL (short take-off and landing) airport, for example. It was probably the first New Town in the United States to start out by building a complete prefabrication plant which manufactures fully equipped, steel-framed hotel-room units. And WDW must be the first New Town anywhere,

MAIN STREET ➡
⬅ FANTASYLAND
ADVENTURELAND ➡
FRONTIERLAND ➡

The huge service basement that serves the Magic Kingdom is a modern network of tunnels and service areas. Sewers, pipes, and cables are easily accessible to repair crews

surely, which comes equipped with its own fleet of submarines—a fleet said to be the fifth largest in the world, exceeded in tonnage only by those of the United States, the Soviet Union, Britain, and France!

But that is not all: WDW contains an extremely well-planned satellite community called Lake Buena Vista, and will soon contain something to be called EPCOT, or Experimental Prototype Community of Tomorrow. And WDW's two-hundred-acre artificial lake may become the first in any New *or* Old Town to be animated by its own surfmaking machines.

The temptation to poke fun at WDW is there, of course, and it is true, also, that WDW is not a city in the ordinary sense of the word. It evades a good many problems—housing, schools, employment, politics, and so on. Understandably, Walt Disney Productions are trying their best to avoid such problems. They are in the fun business, and they know that business to perfection. Why should they push their luck?

Still, and apparently without realizing it, the people who run WDW so efficiently have built something much more significant than the nicest Fun City in the world. They do not seem to realize that they are conducting a truly remarkable ex-

Walt Disney World's submarine fleet is claimed to be the fifth largest in the world. These nonlethal cousins of Captain Nemo's *Nautilus* give visitors a glimpse of an underwater world complete with mermaids

periment in urban technology and urban psychology; in the next few pages, we shall attempt to look behind the obvious fun and games that beguile every visitor to Mickey Mouse Land and identify what architects and urban designers can learn from the leading Pop artist of our time.

Walt Disney himself did realize what he was going to be doing down there in that huge swamp southwest of Orlando. When you get right down to it, everything that is truly visionary about this New Town was dreamed up by him. "I don't believe there's a challenge anywhere in the world today that's more important to people everywhere than finding solutions to the problems of our cities. But where do we begin? Well, we're convinced we must start with the public need. And the need is not just for curing the old ills of old cities. We think the need is for starting from scratch on virgin land and building a community that will become a prototype for the future." That is the way Walt Disney put it when he introduced the concept of WDW to the people of Florida. Few professional advocates of urban resurrection ever made a more articulate plea for their cause. But because Disney was supposed to be America's Number One Funster, none of the professional urbanists paid very much attention to the nicely filmed and neatly illustrated presentation. "I did a lousy job in that footage, didn't I?" Disney asked one of his associates after the WDW presentation was filmed. Possibly so. It was one of his last public efforts, and technically it may not have been his very best. But it carried an unexpected depth of conviction, an impressive sincerity—and, very possibly, the most serious message he had ever been able to communicate. And that, it seems, was exactly what he meant it to be.

The heart of WDW, the reason for its existence, is the so-called Magic Kingdom, the hundred-acre extravaganza that dazzles the eye. It is a marvelous and absolutely stupefying piece of giant confectionery, a kind of Candy Kremlin, made up of six smaller pieces of candied surrealism: Adventureland, Fantasyland, Frontierland, Main Street, Liberty Square, and Tomorrowland.

Tomorrowland may be the only disappointing piece of the giant cake, for it is just another one of those futuristic projections that have been proven false ever since the New York World's Fair of 1939. Apparently, the designers of the Magic Kingdom were quite unaware of the fact that the Future they created is, actually, everywhere—though it does not always show. In WDW's candy extravaganza, the *real* Tomorrowland is the vast infrastructure that no paying customer ever sees. That infrastructure—a term used by urban planners to describe the basement required by any rationally designed city to contain all the mechanical and other facilities that make a city function properly—contains all the utilities and all the equipment needed to serve the Magic Kingdom from below. The *real* Tomorrow-land is also above grade: the grid of trains and other earthbound vehicles, and of skybucket aerial vehicles (none of which pollute the atmosphere). These mass-transit facilities are the sort of thing that urban designers like Manhattan's Jaquelin Robertson have long tried to introduce into our center cities. And the *real* Tomorrowland is also an electronic communications network that was designed by RCA to look out for mechanical and physical trouble throughout WDW; a jet-engined power plant that supplies all the needed juice; and much, much more.

Some visionary aspects of the Magic Kingdom, in terms of urban design, *do* meet the eye. The scale of the streets and of the buildings that form them is a case in point. The buildings, with their silly and charming little fake-facades, are only about seven-eighths of the size found in what we laughingly refer to as the Real World. They are that reduced height at pedestrian level, and they become even smaller in scale as they rise, creating an illusion of greater height by creating a distorted perspective. And the spaces created between these buildings—the streets and plazas formed between them—are even smaller than that when compared to those vast "pedestrian plazas" created by urban designers in the Real World whenever they run out of ideas. These are comfortable spaces, quite different in scale from those of the Automobile World but entirely in keeping with the scale and the pace of the Pedestrian World. Mel Kaufman, the highly unconventional builder of a number of seemingly daffy Manhattan office buildings, thinks that every architect, landscape architect, city planner, developer, and designer should study WDW with care. "What is Main Street?" he asks. "It is an ordinary shopping center where they sell souvenirs, film, rent baby strollers and wheel chairs, sell ice cream and other food, have a movie house—all functioning as would any ordinary shopping center. Except for one thing. It's a stage set of Main Street circa 1900. Now that's not architecture, is it?"

Probably not, but Kaufman and many others think that it works better than conventional architecture would. "The Disney policy, simply stated, is to transmit pleasure and well-being to the public," Kaufman says. "Why not put up a shopping center with a bunch of false and fun fronts? Why bother to create 'architectural validity' in a silly thing like a shopping center?" Kaufman, who was quite rightly carried away by the experience of WDW, might on second thought wish to backtrack just a bit. After all, not every shopping center need necessarily be turned into a Fantasyland. Only most.

The Main Streets at WDW and in Disneyland are superlatively good musical-comedy stage sets designed by some of the best set designers of their time. Like other stage sets, they are covered with a kind of Pop sauce made of plastics, glass fiber, paint, and anything else that happened to be handy. Such playful, romanticized architecture has been tried by bona fide architects as well: the late Eero Saarinen made a stab in that direction at Yale's Stiles and Morse residences. And, in a sense, this sort of thing has been sanctified by Jane Jacobs, for it is the scale that really matters, and the thoughtful little amenities that make Main Street a pedestrian's pleasure. "You can walk around the main thoroughfares all day and never end up having aching legs," Kaufman points out. "The walks are paved with a resilient asphalt product—and the black asphalt is then painted over with red or blue or green stripes." Architects have long abandoned "purist" notions about leaving materials in their natural state, and Dayglo Architecture is the latest mannerism, accepted by all and sundry. But Main Street's amenities are not skin deep; in addition to resilient sidewalks there are places to sit and rest and contemplate—even while lining up to watch those far-out life-size ghosts in the Haunted Mansion, or to converse with the thirty-six computerized, vinyl-clad presidents of the United States in the Hall of Presidents. And there are innumerable facilities for keeping Main Street as clean as the most compulsive sanitation man might want to see it.

Main Street is, in short, an object lesson in pedestrianism. It is Disney's answer to Detroit, and it is so effective because the answer is given not in the dry prescriptions of a city planner, but in the funny squeaks of Mickey Mouse.

How Main Street—both in the original Disneyland and in Walt Disney World—was designed is quite fascinating. John Hench, perhaps the most design-conscious spirit in the top echelons of the Disney organization, has a highly original explanation. "If you look carefully at Main Street, and at all the rest in the Magic Kingdom, you will find that the visitor is taken, step by step, through a sequence of related experiences. We never jar him—we just lead him along, making the trip as interesting as we know how." Hench does not think that conventional architects and urban designers understand this sort of sequential development, and he feels that many of the architects and planners with whom the Disney organization has worked have little concept of how people respond to visual sensations—

or, for that matter, to colors and spaces. He does not feel that these related, sequential experiences along Main Street and elsewhere have to be soothing. Quite the contrary: it was Hench who insisted that the architects of the A-frame Contemporary Hotel let the Monorail run right through the hotel's main concourse—an idea first considered in story sessions with Dick Irvine, who was then guiding the WED creative group through the master plan of Walt Disney World. The architects were appalled by the idea but finally gave in; today that incredible lobby, with its rather corny futuristic trappings and its silent, porcelain-enameled snakes gliding through the ten-story-high space, is, quite simply, the most stunning experience along your way through WDW.

Whenever and wherever possible, Disney and his successors used their own designers and engineers to create the buildings and spaces and systems at Disneyland and at WDW. The reason was quite simple: their designers knew how to create happy environments, and their engineers knew how to make these environments work. The designers needed no outside help anyway—they had been pleasing people for several decades. And the Disney engineers, who usually started with an established system that worked reasonably well, found ways of refining those systems so that they became capable of much higher levels of performance: the Monorails and other People Movers are cases in point.

The creators of the Magic Kingdom had to solve some basic problems. The large property that they had purchased had to be restructured if it was to support anything more than alligators. The Magic Kingdom would have to be built on top of some kind of elevated platform, if only to keep those alligators out of the streets. Their solution was to excavate a 200-acre lake; use some of the resulting fill, chemically stabilized, to create a more contoured landscape (which would, incidentally, conceal the few motorways in sunken cuts—as it does, for example, in Le Corbusier's masterpiece of urban design, the center of Chandigarh, in India); and use the rest of the fill to raise the level of the Magic Kingdom. Excavating the service basement out of the fill instead of going underground avoided the problem of water seepage and produced an efficient infrastructure to support the amusement area above it.

Such an infrastructure was useful not only to house and make accessible all the pipes and wires that serve the amusement area above, but also to get actors and supplies to the proper buildings and spaces in the Magic Kingdom. It would hardly

◀ The A-frame Contemporary Hotel is built around a ten-story-high lobby that matches some of the best twentieth-century spaces in drama and in scale. It doubles as a Monorail station

look right to have an "American Indian" stalk through Tomorrowland on his way to a pow-wow a quarter of a mile away. The infrastructure enables him to surface in Frontierland and drop out of sight there when his tour of duty is over.

The service basement also contains tailoring workshops to service the 100,000 costumes presently on the racks; it contains employee cafeterias, laundries, dry-cleaning establishments, offices, and innumerable utility stations. (The power plant is off to the north, away from the Magic Kingdom, as are warehouses and garbage-compacting and Monorail-servicing facilities.) The tunnels or streets within the infrastructure are wide enough to accommodate electric carts that carry supplies from the warehouses to the service basement. There is no nonsense about the basement—it is just raw concrete, fluorescent lights, cinder block, and paint—and all the mechanical and electrical service lines are readily accessible in case repairs are needed. That sort of accessibility is, of course, completely unknown in "real" cities, which explains why our streets are regularly torn up. City planners all over the world have for decades dreamed of urban basements like the one at WDW.

Disneyland, in Anaheim, was built without such a service basement. Here the amusement area proper measures only about seventy acres in size, most of it elevated above the flat surrounding countryside. It would have been possible to create the kind of service area that was built at WDW, and the people who manage Disneyland (and are fiercely proud of their "first generation" New Town) regret this. In Anaheim the amusement area had to be surrounded with, rather than underpinned by, repair shops, storage facilities, and so forth, all of which have to serve the Fun City facilities from its perimeter. The creation of a true infrastructure at WDW was a major step forward in terms of urban technology.

In some respects, however, Disneyland is more successful than WDW. The High Establishment architect Philip Johnson, who has seen and enjoyed both, thinks that the rather tight, rather small scale of Disneyland is more successful than the wider streets and taller buildings at WDW. "The really dense crowding at Disneyland creates an awful lot of excitement that sometimes gets lost in the looser scale of Disney World," he said recently. There are other things at Disneyland worth noting: it was and continues to be *the* urban laboratory of the Disney organization, and it is the proving ground, the test range, for much hardware before that hardware is wheeled out in Orlando. The submarine fleet and the Monorail system were tried out first in Anaheim, and so were the sky rides and the different carts

Here the Monorail emerges from the vast lobby of the Contemporary Hotel. The steel-framed hotel rooms were prefabricated and then inserted into the A-frame structure

and trains. Finally, a really first-rate People Mover system was developed at Disneyland—a system so obvious and so simple, mechanically, that it should have been invented decades ago.

The Disney People Mover, unlike most other recent systems of this sort, is not wedded to complicated mechanical gadgetry. It depends, in fact, on only one simple principle of physics: friction. The right-of-way of the Disney People Mover is a continuous row of little wheels that spin, and these wheels have rough edges. The compact, four-passenger capsules that move on this right-of-way have equally rough bottoms, and when the rough wheels rotate against those rough bottoms, the capsules move. That is fundamentally all there is to the Disney People Mover, though it has been somewhat improved from the original Disneyland prototype, to the point where it can now carry Contemporary Hotel guests at WDW from the A-frame to a nearby shopping center. (The principal improvement was to make the wheels and the bottoms nonslippery on rainy days.)

Once you enter Disney World, you leave your car in one of several tremendous parking lots which are strategically located on the perimeter of the property. (There is bus service as well.) The principal lot, designed to accommodate 12,000 cars, is adjacent to the Main Gate, where you buy your ticket. From there you can proceed by any number of comfortable transportation systems to your first destination.

The most impressive of these systems is the Monorail, which runs in a wide loop that links hotels and parking lots to the Magic Kingdom. A vast improvement over the rather sluggish Monorail at Disneyland, the one at WDW is sleek, quiet, and swift; it whizzes past the Polynesian Village Hotel and right through the huge concourse of the A-frame Contemporary Hotel. The Monorail's loop was designed for future expansion as additional hotels are built, and one spur takes off northward toward a service garage. The train is a delight straight out of *The Shape of Things to Come,* and its public-address system is possibly the only intelligible one ever designed for any transportation facility anywhere. Its doors open out automatically and with precision, the way the Radio City Music Hall Rockettes kick their legs. The touch of the dramatic artist is evident in every little detail—and it is a much more interesting touch than that of the conventional city planner.

In addition to the Monorail system, WDW has a steam-powered railroad, electric carts, boats and buses and submarines. Its fleet of 200-odd ships is serviced by docks of impressive size and equipment. The submarine fleet is of the Jules Verne variety, and fish-tailed.

While the Magic Kingdom was designed primarily for pedestrians, the many land-, water-, and air-borne transportation systems available make it easy for the visitor to take off in any one of several directions whenever the spirit moves. Most of these mass-transit systems are included in the price of admission to the park, and they are infinitely more comfortable, colorful, and quiet than any to be found in American cities.

There are some roads that traverse and circumvent WDW and are used by service vehicles and by management cars. But these roads are out of sight, secreted among the artificial hills and behind the artificial buildings. Indeed, some of them tunnel under the waterways, in cheerful disregard for the laws of nature.

Some of the sophisticated transportation technology—like much of the sophisticated urban technology to be found at WDW and Disneyland—is masked by the fun-sauce that covers everything. But it is there. The skyride aerial buckets, which work much better than most of their ski-resort ancestors, suggest methods of transportation for our cities that are, in fact, now being somewhat timidly explored by city planners in the United States. And the electric trains that service the Magic Kingdom from a large supply depot hidden away somewhere are an imaginative adaptation of available conveyor-technology to urban problems. The Disney organization, in its uninhibited way, has picked whatever was available and suitable in *any* technology and in *any* discipline—and adapted and refined it to solve the problems at hand.

The "People Mover" in Disneyland consists of a chain of identical capsules propelled on a bed of rollers. Each unit holds four passengers

At this writing, only two hotels have been completed at WDW, both designed by the architectural firm of Welton Becket & Associates. The first is the A-frame "Contemporary," the other the vaguely Californian "Polynesian Village." Three or four others are in the planning stage—among them a "Venetian," a "Persian-style," and one described as "strongly Thai in motif." Like most other buildings at WDW, these hotels might not qualify for conventional architectural awards. But they are much better than one had a right to expect. The Contemporary Hotel contains the fantastic ten-story space that is crossed by the Monorail. The Monorail platform is carpeted, and doubles as a stage from which hotel guests are entertained by bands of musicians. This vast lobby is, unhappily, decorated in a style once described as Italian Easy-Payment Provincial, but even those absurdities are easily overlooked in a space as impressive as that of the great railroad stations of the nineteenth century. The Polynesian Village Hotel, with its roof of self-oxidizing steel, is

Constructing the Contemporary Hotel

All the hotel rooms built at Walt Disney World were prefabricated in a plant erected on the site by U.S. Steel. The completed modules were moved to the hotels on flat-bed trucks and hoisted into position

in some respects an even better piece of architecture. The buildings are residential in scale and casually grouped to form landscaped courts and gardens. The gardens contain a swimming pool equipped with an artificial waterfall and underwater Muzak.

The significance of these first two hotels is not architectural but technological, for in both of these structures all hotel rooms and baths were completely prefabricated. The U.S. Steel Corporation built a plant on the northeast edge of the park, which then proceeded to turn out completely prefabricated steel-framed modules that were fully wired, equipped with all necessary piping (including a sprinkler system), and further endowed with lighting fixtures, carpeting, and even some built-in furniture. The modules are 14½ feet wide, 8 feet tall, and 39 feet long.

The plant was capable of producing these modules at a rate of about a dozen a day, and the total output required by the first two hotels was 1,500 units (each complete with a very fancy bathroom). Since the plant can manufacture similar units in any number of sizes, it has been prefabricating motel rooms (with baths) for customers outside the WDW complex as well.

Because nothing *really* serious was supposed to be happening at Walt Disney World or at Disneyland, nobody in city planning paid very much attention to this particular experiment until *Architectural Forum* published a twenty-page article on the subject in June of 1972. Meanwhile, magazines all over the world had paid considerable attention to such box-building projects as Habitat, at Montreal's Expo '67—a slightly primitive exercise in industrialization that succeeded in escalating building costs over conventional construction by 300 to 400 percent! The U.S. Steel experiment at WDW, by comparison, while not initially reducing construction costs, speeded up the building process and achieved a precision of finish that has not been reached by any similar prefabrication system to date.

As of this writing, no major governmental or other private effort at prefabrication in the United States has produced so many beautifully and precisely engineered modules so fast and so efficiently. (Certainly, no modules manufactured by a housing agency, for example, include artificial moonlight on dimmers, as WDW's do.) But, then, U.S. Steel, at WDW, had certain very important advantages over prefabricators in the Real World. For example, the Disney people were able to write the road regulations that govern the transportation of prefabricated modules. In the Real World, the maximum permissible width is usually 12 feet; in WDW this was stretched to 14½ feet, which can make a great deal of difference in the planning of such units. Moreover, WDW wrote its own building codes, which permitted the prefabbers in some instances to use much more advanced techniques and materials. However, there was no lowering of safety standards when these codes were written; if anything, the WDW modules conform to fire-safety standards that are much more rigid than those set up in the Real World.

The prefabricated hotel rooms are the most obvious example of technological innovation at WDW. There are other, less obvious examples that may be even more significant. Among these are systems designed to avoid or minimize pollution in all its forms. One of these systems is the underground pneumatic tube network that instantly devours litter. Others are a modern incinerator which was designed to purify its own emissions; a sewage-treatment plant that removes virtually all suspended solids; a so-called Living Farm of trees and plants that filters waste water after it leaves the sewage-treatment area; and an energy plant whose gas-turbine generators supply half the power for WDW and whose waste heat is converted into chilled water which, in turn, is used to cool many of the buildings at WDW. This particular piece of equipment is a major technological innovation.

The Swedish-designed pneumatic garbage system (called AVAC) has fifteen stations throughout the Magic Kingdom, and also services the Contemporary Hotel. There are conventional trash cans scattered throughout the area, and clean-up crews collect plastic trash bags from the cans and drop them into the nearest AVAC receptacle, whence the bags are inhaled through the underground network to a compaction station at 60 miles per hour. At present, the system consists of 12,000 feet of 20-inch-diameter tubing, all leading to a very small compacting plant at the edge of the Magic Kingdom. The system is automated, and operates in carefully timed cycles. There are various safety features, among them some to assure that the system will not inhale small children who might wander into the vicinity of an intake.

After compaction, the garbage is incinerated in a plant equipped with the best filters and wet scrubbers available. They capture the fly ash, so that only clean steam is emitted from the plant's smoke stack. The scrubbers use waste water from the nearby tertiary sewage-treatment plant, and this water is then recycled back to the plant. There, any residual fly ash can be used to help clean the waste water.

The tertiary sewage plant operates on the so-called "activated sludge" process, which removes 97 percent of all suspended solids. The effluent is chlorinated and fed into the swamp waters of the WDW nature conservatory. Some of the waste water is eventually channeled into the irrigation grid of the Living Farm.

This farm was developed by the University of Florida's Institute of Food and Agriculture Sciences (IFAS) in collaboration with WDW scientists. It is an advanced waste water recycling system that depends on the natural filtration capabilities of trees and plants.

The Living Farm now consists of about a hundred acres, which are fed by the waste-treatment plant. It processes about a million gallons of waste water a day, but its capacity will increase as WDW is further developed. Eventually, roads will wind through the Living Farm so that visitors may tour it.

All these systems are electronically supervised by a "total network" information-communications network that ties all of WDW together by means of computers, closed-circuit TV, and telephones. It is a truly astonishing urban monitor, unequaled anywhere in the world.

The nearest thing in WDW to a *real* town is the community of Lake Buena Vista, a complex of high- and low-rise structures that may eventually cover 4,000 acres and house 16,500 full- or part-time residents and employ 4,000 workers. It is not nearly as adventurous as Walt Disney's dream of an Experimental Prototype Community of Tomorrow (EPCOT), which is described below; but unlike EPCOT, the community of Lake Buena Vista is practical in today's terms. It is, in fact, well under construction.

Lake Buena Vista has four high-rise hotel/motel buildings. The architecture is considerably above Miami Beach standards, and WDW has ruled out all garish signs. Lake Buena Vista also has an eight-bed hospital, linked to a major hospital in Orlando by closed-circuit TV, which will enable Orlando's doctors to diagnose a patient's problems by remote control, and a 10,000-square-foot steel-and-glass administration building. An initial development called the Golf Course Community started construction with a cluster of twenty-seven neatly planned and neatly designed row-houses, some of which may be operated, experimentally, by fuel cells which develop six kilowatts of electricity and carry the total energy, cooling, and heating load for three town-houses each. These are a byproduct of the Space Program at Cape Kennedy, a hundred miles to the east. Eventually, there will be 2,500 housing units.

The pattern of other development may include homes in "jungle clearings," along fairways, and in clusters on the waterfront. Some may be detached houses. At least one high-rise condominium is planned for the harborfront. The clusters will generally have at least five units, which is the minimum number that the planners feel can provide a sense of community in an isolated location. Neighbors will not, however, have to face each other. While the backs of the houses will be close, they will look out toward the natural surroundings of the Buena Vista park—waterway, lake, jungle, or fairway.

The community of Lake Buena Vista is surprisingly innovative in much of its planning. The governing idea, as elsewhere in WDW, is that visitors (or residents) arrive from the Real World in cars which they leave in a parking lot. From there, they can proceed by electric cart or similar nonpolluting vehicle, by bicycle, or on horseback to destinations within Lake Buena Vista. The New York architecture and planning firm of Hart, Krivatsky & Stubee, who were consultants to WDW on this and other areas, have laid out a complete system of waterways. All the basic roads, waterways, trails, and utilities were completed in 1972, as was the eighteen-hole golf course.

Waterways are useful drainage devices, but at Buena Vista, as elsewhere in WDW, they double as charming transportation arteries, sometimes winding through untouched woods, in other places passing row-house clusters, restaurants, shops, beaches, the golf course, and other recreational facilities. Various kinds of water-borne craft have been investigated, and there has even been talk of building a floating shopping center on barges.

In many ways Buena Vista, like other portions of WDW, avoids or bypasses the issues of most modern towns and cities.

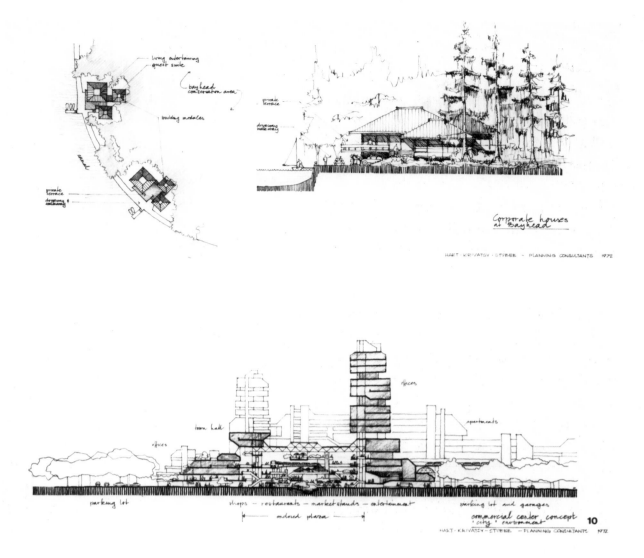

Early sketches of the Lake Buena Vista community show, above, waterfront houses planned for second-home owners, and a cross-section, below, of a multilevel urban center. The latter may be realized when the experimental city EPCOT is built

Buena Vista was designed as a recreational community, its houses owned cooperatively by individuals or by corporations looking for a way to take their executives out of the Real World now and then to let them relax. There may be no full-term schools, but there will be commercial areas and office buildings if demand materializes for them.

Such commercial development may include two kinds of retail areas. The first would face the water and consist of small-scale souvenir and convenience shops to suggest the atmosphere of a lively bazaar. The second center is intended to be a regional shopping district, and it may become the ultimate in multilevel enclosed-mall extravaganzas. But basically, this will be America's first "Second Town"—an alternative life style that may prove attractive enough to become the preferred one.

Despite the obvious unreality of Buena Vista in many social respects, its components do carry some meaning applicable to the Real World. It is, like much of WDW, anti-Detroit and "people-oriented"; and the planning, on the smallest scale (as in the residential clusters) as well as the broadest, is easily as good as that found in more highly touted New Towns across the nation.

One purpose of WDW is to make money, and in this it is succeeding beyond expectations. But Walt Disney had much more important things in mind: he wanted to use the tried and tested amusement park formula to finance some revolutionary experiments in urban and suburban planning and conservation.

If all that Disney had really wanted was to build another amusement park in Florida, he could have done it on 250 acres. Instead, he bought more than a hundred times that much, for $5.5 million, and proceeded to use it to change a portion of the surface of the globe qualitatively as well as physically.

For Disney to carry out a scheme of this sort with any degree of efficiency, he needed almost total control of the operation. To this end, the company petitioned the Florida state legislature for authorities to permit its needs to be approved. As a result, a government agency called the Reedy Creek Improvement District (RCID) was established. This body operates as the government on the property; it levies its own taxes, funds those utilities under its control, enforces the building code which permits acceptance of new ideas, systems, and materials, and sets its own zoning criteria. (The standards that RCID has set are higher than those found in most American communities.)

Planning for WDW followed ecological considerations. The 27,443-acre area was defined by two primary natural-drainage channels with a ridge between them. These channels immediately identified the most buildable parts of WDW: the Magic Kingdom had to be located on one naturally high ground and the town of Lake Buena Vista on another.

Central Florida's main ecological problem is water. In the summer, three-fourths of the WDW properties were submerged; in the dry season, one-fourth. The objective was to make most of the dry-season areas dry all year round. To achieve this, a sophisticated drainage system was built to keep three-fourths of WDW dry year-round without unduly lowering the water table, which could have adversely affected the total ecology of the area.

The water reclamation plan drawn up by the Disney organization involves forty miles of canals and an expenditure of $7 million. The canals wind so as to jibe with natural stream threads—instead of cutting through the swamps in a rectangular pattern, as is the common practice in Florida. When the canals are properly grassed and mulched, they will look and function like natural rivers.

While this water-control system was being constructed (using some highly sophisticated, French-patented, double-ballasted automatic gates), a 450-acre natural lake was cleansed and the 200-acre artificial lake was dug.

The 7,500-acre wilderness area, a semitropical jungle, contains some 150 species of birds, 41 species of trees, and 13 species of ferns—and there will soon be more. Many of Florida's wildlife species are seriously endangered, and Walt Disney decided to create a refuge for them. Fred Harden, one of the nation's most dedicated and highly qualified conservationists, was put in charge. He began by adopting a spectacular collection of red-cockaded woodpeckers, Florida black bears, deer, a Florida panther, dozens of alligators (some measuring twenty feet in length), and he is busy planting and replanting to support this wildlife. Eventually, some of the wilderness may be opened to some visitors, but Disney's idea was to set aside this area for serious ecological studies. These will include work with new and changing ecological cycles, and interrelationships of carefully chosen plants, animals, and water conditions.

To Walt Disney, conservation of the natural environment was only one objective. The other was the creation of a man-made environment that would involve people just as much as the sight of a baby egret learning how to fly.

And so he proposed the creation of the Experimental Prototype Community of Tomorrow. EPCOT will not be started until about 1978, and it will never be finished.

◄ The Seven Seas Lagoon at sunset, seen from a restaurant atop the Contemporary Hotel

For the truly adventurous idea behind EPCOT is that it will be a community in a constant state of flux, always at least twenty-five years ahead of its time, in which new systems and concepts can be tested in practice a generation or so before they are likely to become generally accepted. EPCOT, in short, will be a huge laboratory for the testing of cities of the future, a functioning community inhabited by perhaps 20,000 people, operating in the tomorrow today.

The initial designs are diagrammatic: a vertical core built on a multilevel platform containing transportation nodes, shops, and services; from this central core, streets or other transportation lines radiating like the spokes of a wheel, the pie-shaped areas between them to be filled in with residential communities.

In October, 1966, when Disney was talking to some of his closest associates about a film they were then making to explain the EPCOT idea to the people of Florida, he began to formulate what he had in mind for this experimental community. "It will be a 'think project'—not a 'think factory.' And not only 'think'—here these things will actually *work*. . . . EPCOT is going to be a community that becomes one module in a city complex. We'll be able to show what could be done with proper city planning." Somebody mentioned that James Rouse, the idealistic developer of Columbia, Maryland, had recently told a city-planning conference at Harvard that seeing Disneyland was one of the most important experiences in his professional life. "Well, we won't let it go to our heads," Disney said. He added, more seriously: "EPCOT will be a living, breathing community, not a retirement village. It will be a working community. It will worry about pre-school education, home environment, employment. The family unit will be the key. EPCOT will be no architectural monument; but it will be a showcase of what American ingenuity and enterprise can do." He ticked off additional problems and possible solutions, indicating that he was really quite familiar with some of the most avant-garde theories developed from Le Corbusier to the present. Admittedly, some of his ideas were a bit simplistic, but that would obviously be straightened out in the realization of EPCOT. He knew exactly how to go about enlisting the support of American industry for such a project: industry had a need to exhibit its wares, but almost no expertise in ways of attracting visitors to those exhibits. Disney knew better than anyone else in the twentieth century how to draw a crowd, and so he would supply the audience if industry supplied the products. It had worked beautifully for both Monsanto and Walt Disney in Disneyland, where Monsanto constructed an extraordinary reinforced-plastics prefab house (designed at the Massachusetts Institute of Technology) and Walt Disney supplied the visitors. That prefab is in all the history books of modern architecture, but, more important, it is also in the minds of countless millions who were drawn to it by Disney's delightful cunning. EPCOT, he felt sure, would be similarly supported by American industry.

Much of the initial planning for EPCOT is tentative. By the time EPCOT gets under way, so-called "megastructures" may have lost some of their present charm. And the term "Architectural Monument"—currently a pejorative—may have regained some respect. (Disney must surely have been impressed by Rockefeller Center—a monument as well as a crowd-pleaser!)

Still, what a wonderfully imaginative idea to propose a vast, living, ever-changing laboratory of urban design! Not even Le Corbusier ever proposed anything so radical. Certainly, if EPCOT were to become the plaything of hucksters, it would be little more than an architectural fashion show. But if it evolves out of that same remarkable mix of pragmatism, idealism, and business acumen that has characterized all of WDW to date, it could be one of the most productive research tools yet devised for a rapidly urbanizing world. Walt Disney's successors, conscious of the fact that EPCOT and the wilderness area are what he *really* had in mind all along, seem determined to make it come true.

What a wonderfully ironic notion it is that, in this turbulent century, urban man might, just possibly, be saved by a mouse.

At dusk, Mickey Mouse approaches Cinderella's Castle. Mickey is the official host of the Magic Kingdoms

Academy Awards

1. Short Subjects. 1931/32. "Flowers and Trees"
2. Honorary. 1931/32. To Walt Disney for the creation of Mickey Mouse
3. Short Subjects. 1932/33. "The Three Little Pigs"
4. Short Subjects. 1934. "The Tortoise and the Hare"
5. Short Subjects. 1935. "Three Orphan Kittens"
6. Short Subjects. 1936. "Country Cousin"
7. Short Subjects. 1937. "The Old Mill"
8. Scientific or Technical. 1937. Walt Disney Productions for the design and application to production of the multiplane camera
9. Short Subjects. 1938. "Ferdinand the Bull"
10. Honorary. 1938. Walt Disney for "Snow White and the Seven Dwarfs," with the following citation: "Recognized as a significant screen innovation which has charmed millions and provided a great new entertainment field for the motion picture industry"
11. Short Subjects. 1939. "The Ugly Duckling"
12. Songs. 1940. "When You Wish Upon a Star." Music by Leigh Harline, lyrics by Ned Washington
13. Score (original score). 1940. "Pinocchio." Leigh Harline, Paul J. Smith, and Ned Washington
14. Honorary. 1941. Walt Disney, William Garity, John N.A. Hawkins, and the RCA Manufacturing Company for their outstanding contribution to the advancement of the use of sound in motion pictures through the production of "Fantasia" (certificate)
15. Honorary. 1941. Leopold Stokowski and his associates for their unique achievement in the creation of a new form of visualized music in Walt Disney's production "Fantasia," thereby widening the scope of the motion picture as an art form (certificate)
16. Short Subjects. 1941. "Lend a Paw"

17. Score (scoring of a musical picture). 1941. "Dumbo." Frank Churchill, Oliver Wallace
18. Irving Thalberg Memorial Award. 1941. To Walt Disney for consistent high-quality production
19. Short Subjects. 1942. "Der Fuehrer's Face"
20. Scientific or Technical. 1946. Arthur F. Blinn, Robert O. Cook, C. O. Slyfield, and the Walt Disney Studio Sound Department for the design and development of an audio finder and track viewer for checking and locating noise in sound tracks
21. Honorary. 1947. James Baskett for his able and heartwarming characterization of "Uncle Remus," friend and storyteller to the children of the world
22. Songs. 1947. "Zip-a-dee-doo-dah." Music by Allie Wrubel, lyrics by Ray Gilbert
23. Short Subjects (2 reel). 1948. "Seal Island"
24. Honorary. 1949. Bobby Driscoll. Outstanding juvenile
25. Short Subjects (2 reel). 1950. "In Beaver Valley"
26. Short Subjects (2 reel). 1951. "Nature's Half Acre"
27. Short Subjects (2 reel). 1952. "Water Birds"
28. Documentary (short subject). 1953. "The Alaskan Eskimo." Walt Disney, Producer
29. Documentary (features). 1953. "The Living Desert"
30. Short Subjects (2 reel). 1953. "Bear Country"
31. Short Subjects. 1953. "Toot, Whistle, Plunk, and Boom"
32. Documentary (features). 1954. "The Vanishing Prairie." Walt Disney, Producer
33. Art Decoration, Set Decoration (color). 1954. "20,000 Leagues Under the Sea." John Meehan; set decoration, Emile Kuri (plaque)

34. Special Effects. 1954. "20,000 Leagues Under the Sea." Walt Disney, Producer, and Special Effects Department
35. Documentary (short subject). 1955. "Men Against the Arctic." Walt Disney, Producer
36. Short Subjects. 1957. "The Wetback Hound." Larry Lansburgh, Producer
37. Documentary (short subject). 1958. "Ama Girls." Ben Sharpsteen, Producer
38. Documentary (features). 1958. "White Wilderness." Ben Sharpsteen, Producer
39. Short Subjects (live action). 1958. "Grand Canyon"
40. Scientific or Technical. 1959. Ub Iwerks of Walt Disney Productions for the design of an improved optical printer for special effects and matte shots
41. Honorary. 1960. Hayley Mills for "Pollyanna." Outstanding juvenile
42. Documentary (features). 1960. "The Horse with the Flying Tail." Larry Lansburgh, Producer
43. Actress. 1964. Julie Andrews. "Mary Poppins"
44. Film Editing. 1964. "Mary Poppins." Cotton Warburton
45. Songs. 1964. "Chim-Chim-Cheree." Music and lyrics by Richard M. and Robert B. Sherman
46. Score (music score, substantially original). 1964. "Mary Poppins." Richard M. and Robert B. Sherman
47. Visual Effects. 1964. "Mary Poppins." Peter Ellenshaw, Eustace Lycett, Hamilton Luske
48. Scientific or Technical. 1964. Peter Vlahos, Wadsworth E. Pohl, and Ub Iwerks for the conception and perfection of techniques for Color Traveling Matte Composite Cinematography
49. Short Subjects. 1968. "Winnie the Pooh and the Blustery Day"
50. Short Subjects. 1969. "It's Tough to Be a Bird." Ward Kimball, Producer
51. Visual Effects. 1971. "Bedknobs and Broomsticks." Danny Lee, Eustace Lycett, Alan Maley

◄ On the eve of the opening of Disneyland, Walt Disney surveys his kingdom

Bibliography

Compiled by David R. Smith, Archivist, Walt Disney Archives

BOOKS

Alberti, Walter. "Walt Disney," in his *Il cinema di animazione, 1832–1956. Turin:* Edizioni Radio Italiana, 1957.

Arnoldi, Edgar M. *Zshizn i Skazki Walt Disney.* Leningrad: Iskoosstvo, 1968.

Benayoun, Robert. *Le dessin animé après Walt Disney.* Paris: J.-J. Pauvert, 1961.

Bessy, Maurice. *Walt Disney.* Paris: Editions Seghers, 1970.

Comfort, Mildred Houghton. *Walt Disney, Master of Fantasy.* Minneapolis: Denison, 1968.

Disney, Walt. "Mickey Mouse Presents," in Nancy Naumberg, ed., *We Make the Movies.* New York: Norton, 1937.

Feild, Robert Durant. *The Art of Walt Disney.* New York: Macmillan, 1942.

Hammontree, Marie. *Walt Disney, Young Movie Maker.* Indianapolis: Bobbs-Merrill, 1969.

Jacobs, Lewis. "Walt Disney: Virtuoso," in his *The Rise of the American Film: A Critical History.* New York: Harcourt, Brace, 1939.

Jungersen, Frederick G. *Disney.* Copenhagen: Det Danske Filmmuseum, 1968.

Miller, Diane Disney. *The Story of Walt Disney*, as told to Pete Martin. New York: Holt, 1957. (Reprinted in paperback edition by Dell, 1959, and serialized in *Saturday Evening Post* beginning November 17, 1956.)

Montgomery, Elizabeth Rider. *Walt Disney, Master of Make-Believe.* Champaign, Ill.: Garrard, 1971.

Schickel, Richard. *The Disney Version: The Life, Times, Art, and Commerce of Walt Disney.* New York: Simon & Schuster, 1968. (Reprinted in paperback edition by Avon, 1969.)

Taylor, Deems. *Fantasia.* New York: Simon & Schuster, 1940.

Thomas, Bob. *The Art of Animation: The Story of the Disney Studio Contribution to a New Art*, with research by Don Graham. New York: Simon & Schuster, 1958.

Thomas, Bob. *Walt Disney: Magician of the Movies.* New York: Grosset & Dunlap, 1966.

Turney, Harold. *Cartoon Production.* Hollywood: Film Guide, 1940.

ARTICLES

Alexander, Jack. "The Amazing Story of Walt Disney," *Saturday Evening Post*, October 31, 1953; November 7, 1953.

"The Big, Bad Wolf, and Why It May Never Huff nor Puff at Walt Disney's Door," *Fortune*, November 1934.

Birmingham, Stephen. "Greatest One-Man Show on Earth: Walt Disney," *McCall's*, July 1964.

Blake, Peter. "Mickey Mouse for Mayor," *New York*, February 7, 1972.

——. "Walt Disney World," *The Architectural Forum*, June 1972.

Boone, Andrew R. "When Mickey Mouse Speaks," *Scientific American*, March 1933.

Borsock, William. "What Can You Learn from Disney's Work," *SM/Sales Meetings Magazine*, July 1969.

Bradbury, Ray. "The Machine-tooled Happyland," *Holiday*, October 1965.

Bragdon, Claude. "Mickey Mouse and What He Means," *Scribner's Magazine*, July 1934.

Bright, John. "Disney's Fantasy Empire," *Nation*, March 6, 1967.

Bristol, George T. "Snow White: Inanimate Characters Become a New Force in Merchandising," *Dun's Review*, April 1938.

Butwin, David. "Whistle While You Work," *Saturday Review*, February 6, 1971.

Charlot, Jean. "But Is It Art? A Disney Disquisition," *The American Scholar*, Summer 1939.

Collier, Richard. "Wish Upon a Star: The Magical Kingdoms of Walt Disney," *Reader's Digest*, October 1971.

"Color-shooting in Fairyland: Building the Story of Pinocchio," *Popular Mechanics*, January 1940.

Dando, Pat, and Shoen, Judy. "Disney: The People Pros," *Institutions/Volume Feeding*, October 15, 1972.

Davidson, Bill. "The Fantastic Walt Disney," *Saturday Evening Post*, November 7, 1964.

——. "The Latter-Day Aesop," *TV Guide*, May 13, 1961; May 20, 1961; May 27, 1961.

Delehanty, Thornton. "Disney Studio at War," *Theatre Arts*, January 1943.

DeRoos, Robert. "Magic Worlds of Walt Disney," *National Geographic*, August 1963.

Disney, Lillian. "I Live with a Genius," *McCall's*, February 1953.

Disney, Roy. "Unforgettable Walt Disney," *Reader's Digest*, February 1969.

Disney, Walt. "The Lurking Camera," *Atlantic*, August 1954.

——. "Mickey as Professor," *Public Opinion Quarterly*, Summer 1945.

"Disney Dollars," *Forbes*, May 1, 1971.

"Disney Moves East," *Life*, October 15, 1971.

"Disney Planned a City," *SM/Sales Meetings Magazine*, July 1969.

"The Disney Story: From Mickey Mouse to Buena Vista," *Motion Picture Herald*, November 20, 1954.

"Disney Troupe Goes to War," *New York Times Magazine*, November 15, 1942.

"Disney World: Pixie Dust over Florida," *Time*, October 18, 1971.

Eddy, Don. "The Amazing Secret of Walt Disney," *American Magazine*, August 1955.

Ehrlich, Henry. "Florida: Preview of the New Biggest Show on Earth," *Look*, April 6, 1971.

English, Horace B. "'Fantasia' and the Psychology of Music," *Journal of Aesthetics and Art Criticism*, Winter 1942.

"Father Goose," *Time*, December 27, 1954.

Fishwick, Marshall. "Aesop in Hollywood," *Saturday Review*, July 10, 1954.

Foster, Frederick. "Walt Disney's Naturalist Cinematographers," *American Cinematographer*, February 1954.

Garity, William E. "The Production of Animated Cartoons," *Journal of the Society of Motion Picture Engineers*, April 1933.

—— and Ledeen, J.L. "New Walt Disney Studio," *Journal of the Society of Motion Picture Engineers*, January 1941.

Goldberger, Paul. "Mickey Mouse Teaches the Architects," *New York Times Magazine*, October 22, 1972.

Gordon, Arthur. "Walt Disney," *Look*, July 26, 1955.

Greer, Gordon G. "Disney World: The Smart Way to See It," *Better Homes and Gardens*, April 1972.

Holliday, Kate. "Donald Duck Goes to War," *Coronet*, September 1942.

Hollister, Paul. "Walt Disney, Genius at Work," *Atlantic*, December 1940.

"How Disney Combines Living Actors with

His Cartoon Characters," *Popular Science Monthly*, September 1944.

Iwerks, Ub. "Movie Cartoons Come to Life," *Popular Mechanics*, January 1942.

Johnston, Alva. "Mickey Mouse," *Woman's Home Companion*, July 1934.

Knight, Arthur. "Up from Disney," *Theatre Arts*, August 1951.

La Farge, Christopher. "Walt Disney and the Art Form," *Theatre Arts*, September 1941.

Low, David. "Leonardo da Disney," *New Republic*, January 5, 1942. (Reprinted November 22, 1954.)

McDonald, John. "Now the Bankers Come to Disney," *Fortune*, May 1966.

Mann, Arthur. "Mickey Mouse's Financial Career," *Harper's*, May 1934.

Marx, Wesley. "The Disney Imperative," *Nation*, July 28, 1969.

Morgenstern, Joseph. "What Hath Disney Wrought!" *Newsweek*, October 18, 1971.

"Mouse and Man," *Time*, December 27, 1937.

Nugent, Frank S. "Disney Is Now Art—But He Wonders," *New York Times Magazine*, February 26, 1939.

Potter, William E. "Walt Disney World: A Venture in Community Planning and Development," *ASHRAE Journal*, March 1972.

Reddy, John. "The Living Legacy of Walt Disney," *Reader's Digest*, June 1967.

"Riding the Coattails of Mickey Mouse," *Business Week*, September 11, 1971.

"A Silver Anniversary for Walt and Mickey," *Life*, November 2, 1953.

Smith, David R. "It All Started with a Mouse: The Walt Disney Archives," *California Librarian*, January 1972.

"Super Toys," *Esquire*, December 1971.

Theisen, Earl. "Sound Tricks of Mickey Mouse," *Modern Mechanix*, January 1937.

"Tinker Bell, Mary Poppins, Cold Cash," *Newsweek*, July 12, 1965.

Wallace, Irving. "Mickey Mouse and How He Grew." *Collier's*, April 9, 1949.

"Walt Disney Accused," *Horn Book*, December 1965.

"Walt Disney: Great Teacher," *Fortune*, August 1942.

"Walt Disney—Teacher of Tomorrow," *Look*, April 17, 1945.

Whitaker, Frederic. "A Day with Disney," *American Artist*, September 1965.

"Wide World of Walt Disney," *Newsweek*, December 31, 1962.

Zimmerman, Gereon. "Walt Disney: Giant at the Fair," *Look*, February 11, 1964.

Index

(Numbers in *italic* type refer to captions to the illustrations)

Acknowledgments

This book would not have been possible without the full cooperation of Walt Disney Productions. Thus it is only proper to begin these acknowledgments with my thanks to the officers of the company—especially Card Walker, Ron Miller, and Vince Jefferds—for providing encouragement, office space, and unimpeded access to all parts of the Studio and other Disney facilities.

Special thanks are also due Diane Disney Miller, daughter of Walt Disney, who was kind enough to read the manuscript and offer her comments.

Most previous studies of Walt Disney have suffered from an unfortunate degree of factual inaccuracy. If this one escapes that fault, much of the credit belongs to David Smith, Disney archivist, whose patient research into all aspects of the Studio's history has made my task very much easier.

Carol Svendsen, also of the Disney Archives, was a mine of informal information and, along with Jim Stewart, Special Assistant to the President, took care of day-to-day arrangements during my months at the Studio.

I would like to extend my warmest thanks to the many past and present members of the Disney production staff who gave freely of their time in interviews, correspondence, and general discussion of their experiences at the Studio. I am particularly grateful for the assistance of James Algar, Ken Anderson, Art Babbitt, George Bruns, Les Clark, Jack Cutting, Marc Davis, Al Dempster, Floyd Gottfredson, Don Graham, Don Griffith, Joe Hale, John Hench, Dick Huemer, Ollie Johnston, Milt Kahl, Ward Kimball, Eric Larson, Jim MacDonald, Lester Novros, Woolie Reitherman, Frank Thomas, Grace Turner, and Bill Walsh.

Other Disney personnel who dealt patiently with persistent requests and inquiries include Leroy Anderson, Jack Brady, Jan Hedge, Mary Holoboff, Bob King, John Landon, Jim Mathews, Don McLaughlin, Bob Moore, Frank Reilly, Sue Schwendeman, Dave Spencer, and Bob White.

I would also like to thank the Harry N. Abrams staff, especially Margaret L. Kaplan and Nai Y. Chang, for making the whole project run so smoothly.

Special thanks as well to two distinguished Disney connoisseurs—Eduardo Paolozzi, who long ago encouraged my interest in this subject, and John Dowd, who, like Paolozzi, has added a new dimension to Disney scholarship.

Finally, it was my wife Linda who had the major role in making this project such an enjoyable one, since she participated fully in the research, contributed substantially to the choice of the visual material, and worked closely with me on the preparation of the manuscript. For us, creating this book has been a shared and stimulating experience.